CONTRACT LAW IN PERSPECTIVE

John Tillotson, BA, LLM,
Lecturer and Course Director for EC Law
University of Manchester

Cavendish
Publishing
Limited

Published in Great Britain 1995 by Cavendish Publishing Limited, The Glass House, Wharton Street, London WC1X 9PX.

Telephone: 0171-278 8000 Facsimile: 0171-278 8080

First published by Butterworths in Great Britain 1981.

© Tillotson, John 1995
  Third Edition   1995

British Library Cataloguing in Publication Data. A catalogue record for this book is available from the British Library.

Tillotson, John
Contract Law in Perspective – 3Rev.ed
I Title
344.2062

ISBN 1-85941-002-2

Printed and bound in Great Britain

Preface

The introduction to, and aims of, this book are to be found in the opening section of Chapter 1. It is essentially a book for students – students on law courses or on courses which contain law. The book examines not only the law relating to contracts but contracts themselves, the relationship between the law and contract practice, and various 'views' of contract – not only from the legal standpoint but also from the ground occupied by others, particularly business contract-makers and those concerned with the study of law and the society in which it operates.

To the extent that this book seeks to modify and 'round out' the study of contract law, it lends support to the argument that traditional legal treatments of contract are in no real sense 'core' studies either for potential lawyers or for non-legal students.

Professor Treitel has commented that 'trends in the transactions with which this branch of the law is concerned' are reflected in 'the difficulty and interest of the subject'. It is my belief that Contract, since time immemorial a 'lowly' first-year subject, has long failed to get its just deserts as a subject for study. Only through continuing close examination of its functions and its relationship with the transactional world it serves can the law be adequately understood and assessed.

In this third edition, I have sought to take account of all recent, significant developments within the topics covered. I also wish to draw particular attention to the writings of those whose books and articles are listed in the selective bibliographies at the end of each chapter.

The following companies very kindly allowed the inclusion of copyright material: British Steel Corporation, The Institute of Civil Engineers, BL Cars Limited, Leyland Vehicles Limited, the Road Haulage Association Limited, the Motor Agents Association (now the Society of Motor Manufacturers and Traders), Hotpoint-Morphy Richards Limited, and the Textile Services Association Ltd.

I must also express my thanks to Abi Walker and Carole Overall for their invaluable secretarial assistance and to my publishers for their continuing efficient and friendly co-operation.

John Tillotson
July 1995

Contents

PART ONE

Table of Cases

Table of Statutes

Table of Abbreviations

Abbreviations

AC	Appeal Cases
All ER	All England Reports
BLR	Building Law Reports
Ch	Chancery
CLJ	Cambridge Law Journal
CLY	Current Law Yearbook
CMLR	Common Market Law Reports
Com LR	Commercial Law Reports
ECR	European Court Reports
EG	Estates Gazette
HCP	House of Commons Papers
ICR	Industrial Court Reports
IRLR	Industrial Relations Law Reports
JALT	Journal of the Association of Law Teachers ('The Law Teacher')
JBL	Journal of Business Law
KB(D)	King's Bench (Division)
LQR	Law Quarterly Review
LMCLQ	Lloyd's Maritime and Commercial Law Quarterly
MLR	Modern Law Review
NLJ	New Law Journal
OJLS	Oxford Journal of Legal Studies
QB(D)	Queen's Bench (Division)
SLT	Scots Law Times
WLR	Weekly Law Reports

PART ONE

1   Introduction, aims and general principles

Introduction and aims

... the student is, or should be encouraged to study the principles of the law in their context, and to consider critically whether they are apt to meet the needs of society today ... those who are responsible for schools of law have to decide how to find the balance between these three elements, knowledge, analysis and the social context.

Sir Robert Goff

If I am faced with the alternative of forcing commercial circles to fall in with a legal doctrine which has nothing but precedent to commend it or altering the doctrine so as to conform with what commercial experience has worked out, I know where my choice lies. The law should be responsive as well as, at times, enunciatory, and good doctrine can seldom be divorced from sound practice.

Lord Wilberforce

The main aim of this book is to present a broader view of the basic features of contract law than that found in the traditional 'black-letter' treatments of the subject. The idea of putting the law into its social, political or economic context is not new. However, the aim of looking not only at but also beyond legal rules has been pursued more vigorously in some areas than in others. Most expositions of contract law do not venture beyond the rules. They tell us little or nothing of the social or economic significance of those rules, or how they relate to the practices of the business community. At a level suitable for student readers, this books starts to remedy those defects.

Debate and argument regarding the state of the health of contract law continue more energetically than ever before. Atiyah (1989) has said that 'modern contract law probably works well enough in the great mass of circumstances but its theory is in a mess'. In fact, numerous critiques and suggested theories of contract law have been produced over the last 50 years or so. Many of them point to a 'transformation' of contract law, a movement, observable in the case law and statutory interventions within contract particularly over that last half-century, from 'principles to pragmatism', from 'doctrine to discretion' or from 'market-individualism to consumer-welfarism'. Indeed, as will be seen from the cases, the 19th century foundations of contract law, built on the concepts of promise and agreement, have been to some extent shifted and overlaid by an increased emphasis on such open-ended notions such as reliance, reasonableness and fairness.

3

This can lead to situations where it may be said that the 'old' view of the courts would give rise to a certain result but the 'new' approach would produce a different decision. Has the 'new' replaced the 'old' or are there competing approaches?

On a modest scale, discussion of such changes and debate are built in to this examination of contract law today, together with consideration of the likely influences operating on the law which have led to such changes. Here, an essential factor is the changing nature of the relationship between contract itself, the individual and the government.

Part One begins by establishing some 'views' of contract. Legal and business perspectives are introduced, as are some sociological and economic ideas and influences. These 'views' of contract are set within the framework of a shift from what is generally described as a *laissez-faire* to a mixed economy, welfare state form of society – a shift that broadly coincides with the rise and fall of so-called freedom of contract, and hence with a transformation of contract's function and substance. The planning and dispute-solving roles of contract law are examined by reference first to a perceived 'divorce' between large elements of the business community and the law and second to the operation of a widely-used form of business contract itself.

Part Two deals with those areas of the substantive law of contract which are considered to be of most significance today. It is the intention that the approach adopted allows the ideas and influences – the context – discussed in Part One to permeate and inform the rules, which are themselves related to salient features of business contracting practice. Within the traditional boundaries of contract law particular, though not exclusive, attention is paid to agreement; promissory estoppel; terms and breach; exclusion of liability; misrepresentation, mistake and economic duress; restraint of trade; frustration; and the recovery of damages. The major theme followed is the decline of freedom of contract (ie freedom as to the negotiation of terms) in the face of such related phenomena as increased legal – statutory and judicial – recognition of inequalities of bargaining power, the prevalence of business standard form contracting, and wide-ranging governmental involvement in all aspects of contract today.

This theme enables us to relate the changing law to standard form agreements used in both inter-business transactions (eg in engineering, building and export sales) and in consumer transactions. It allows attention to be drawn to the growing distinction between contracts for the supply of goods and those for the provision of services. Also, in the course of crossing traditional legal boundaries, it allows us, albeit briefly, to assess the role of contract law in the fields of government – contracting and competition policy.

Having gone thus far, it becomes necessary to examine more fully than usual the relationship between the law and certain regularly found clauses in business contracts – price variation clauses, indemnity clauses, exclusion and limitation of liability clauses, 'force majeure' clauses, arbitration clauses and liquidated damages clauses. In the same vein, attention is drawn to the 'battle of the forms' and its relationship to the mechanics of agreement.

The vast majority of cases to be found in this book are of modern origin and therefore illustrate contemporary business situations. Discussion of many of them is, however, on a modest scale as is inevitable in a work of this nature. Ultimately there is no substitute for the law reports or a casebook. At the end of each chapter is a bibliography drawn from a wide range of materials and a series of questions designed to test and expand on the subject-matter of preceding pages. It is important that students are encouraged to pursue further reading from these references. The choice of questions aims to keep links between the various topics in the book firmly in the forefront of the student's mind so that a co-ordinated view of contract will eventually emerge. The final chapter offers advice on answering problem questions with an eye to providing not only legal but, wherever possible, business solutions to the matter under review.

General principles: the nature and content of contract law

In a society where the exchange of goods and services is central to its economic order, as in a developing capitalist society based on free enterprise, a means of supporting the process of exchange needs to be found. In this context the foundations of modern contract law were established. As was said at the time: 'Contract is the juristic form for the distribution and utilisation of the goods and personal abilities that are in existence in society.' By the third quarter of the 19th century, accelerating industrialisation in Britain, generated by scientific innovation, economic entrepreneurship and increasing access to both capital and labour, had given rise to an unprecedented boom in trade, both at home and in expanding markets overseas. This boom had been accompanied by a similarly massive development of that area of the law – particularly contract, commercial and company law – which is designed to facilitate and regulate business relationships.

At this time, Disraeli could unblushingly declare that the government had as much control over the economy as it had over the weather. It is unremarkable therefore that the development of the law governing the rights and duties arising, for both individuals and business concerns, out of the ever-increasing volume of market transactions should be almost entirely the work, not of the legislature, but of the courts – operating against a background of *laissez-faire* policy, and functioning, on a case-by-case basis, as dispute solvers for a business community that was generally not averse to utilising the available legal machinery.

Our first requirement is to outline very briefly the nature and content of the general principles that became established during the 19th century, 'classical' period of contract law. Also, we must say something of the relationship of those principles (the 'general part' of contract law) to additional legal rules particular to specific transactions such as those for the sale of goods or for the provision of services.

The distinction between the general part and rules relating merely to particular classes of contracts is by no means clear cut. However, we may broadly state that general principles apply to *all* contracts irrespective of subject-matter or parties and belong to contract law, whereas contractual particularities – such as the legal method of classifying goods (which is quite different from the economist's) or the statutory right of a party to return goods taken on a consumer credit basis – can be said to be the subject matter of some related branch of the law like, in these examples, commercial and consumer protection law. Many contractual problems, however, involve a consideration of both general principles *and* particular rules. Let us consider, for example, the question of breach of contract. In a legal action, it might well be necessary to take account of the general principle that a serious breach gives the injured party a right to terminate the contract. If the breach has been committed by a seller of goods, it may also be necessary to bring into play further *particular* rules applicable only to a breach by such a contracting party – rules which govern sales and which are to be found in specific legislation, the Sale of Goods Act, first passed in 1893.

The general principles of contract law are still, for the most part, of a judge-made character. Some of them are centuries old but many date from the time of the industrial revolution, when ideas regarding the central importance of voluntary social co-operation through what is known as 'freedom of contract' were very popular. However, since the late 19th century, principles and rules, both old and new, have tended to become incorporated into statutes concerning, to a greater extent, particular transactions and, to a lesser extent, some of the more general contractual issues. Statutes of the former kind have for some time marked out most of the ground rules for what is called commercial or consumer law, and they govern, for example, the sale and hire purchase of goods and many aspects of transport and insurance. A similar process has seen the later emergence, by means of acts such as the Restrictive Trade Practices Act 1956 and the Fair Trading Act 1973, of competition law and a correspondingly radical decline in the applicability of judge-made rules in this field. As regards contracts of employment, a mass of modern legislation and voluntary codes and practices has virtually removed the general principles of contract law from the employment arena.

In broad terms, the general principles of contract law may be regarded today in one sense as a *basis*, necessary in some areas (eg commercial law) but now largely irrelevant in others (eg labour law), for understanding any agreement of a business nature, and in another sense they are to be regarded as a *residue* – those rules that remain untouched, or are merely amended by, by statutory interventions into the judge-made law of transactions. It is the element of regulation and control of business activity – brought about through broad changes over many years of government policy away from the concepts of *laissez-faire* and private enterprise to the present-day preference for a welfare state, 'mixed' type of economy (in which both public authorities and private enterprises operate and which privatisation of the former, in contract terms, has done little to change) – that provides the clearest guide to the residual content of contract law at the present time.

Contract law, in yet another sense, is something of *an exercise in abstraction*. Classical 'general theory' was concerned with market transactions in much the same way as classical economic theory; with parties (economic units) assumed to have equal bargaining strength and to be endowed with complete freedom of decision. Indeed, the crucial underpinning of contract law during its 19th century development was the idea of freedom of contract: the purpose of the law was not to control the terms on which parties might contract, nor would it readily give relief if agreed terms turned out to be harsh or unfair to one party. In the best interests of individual enterprise and a free market economy, the courts saw it as their prime purpose to uphold contracts wherever possible:

> If there is one thing more than another which public policy requires, it is that men of full age and competent understanding shall have the utmost liberty in contracting, and that their contracts, when entered into freely and voluntarily, shall be held sacred and shall be enforced by Courts of Justice.

Much of the history of contract law since these words were spoken by Sir George Jessel in 1875 concerns the decline and fall of freedom of contract. Over a 100 years on, it is no longer the individual entrepreneur but the government which is primarily concerned with the allocation of resources in the British economy. The facts of economic life have also revealed the myth of equality of bargaining power, presumed to exist between contracting parties and upon which the idea of freedom of contract rests. There was as little equality of bargaining strength between employer and employee in the 19th century as there is today between a large-scale supplier of goods and an individual consumer.

Out of the growing mass of 19th century precedents emerged the ground rules of contract law, which were classified and arranged to give shape and pattern to the general theory – shape and pattern to enable lawyers to analyse and unravel contractual problems, to enable judges to settle disputes brought to court for authoritative resolution, and to facilitate the drafting, by lawyers and others, of contracts which conformed to the emerging rules.

Over a 100 years on, the 'general' body of contract law is by now immense and usually takes the form, in lawyers' books, of a seemingly timeless catalogue of doctrines, principles, rules, sub-rules and exceptions with little or no indication of either the present economic importance and utility of this law or whether or not it is adhered to in practice by the business community. Nevertheless, moral, political and economic forces certainly exerted their influence on the nature and content of 19th century contract law – the prevailing philosophies of *laissez-faire* and individual utilitarianism, classical economics, Adam Smith's concept of the 'invisible hand' and so on. As we shall see, the social and economic environment within which contract law now operates has changed radically since those days, as have the scope and methods of contract practice. The changing nature of the relationships between contract law, its political and economic environment, and business practice is at the heart of a proper understanding of this field of study. Law does not operate in a vacuum.

At this stage our immediate need is to set down some basic features of contract law. In this way we are able to establish a foundation – some legal 'baselines' – upon which to build in Part Two. However our purpose is not to suggest the existence of a body of static 'black-letter' rules. In the following chapter, we will examine some of the ideas behind, and influences on, the law. This will necessarily involve us looking not only at the work of jurists – legal writers – but also at the part played by others who have examined the nature and function of law in a changing society. First though, some basic issues.

Agreement, promises and bargain

At the heart of contract law lie the related ideas of agreement, promise and bargain. A contract is taken to result from an agreement between the parties to it, and agreement itself is seen as coming about through the interlocking mechanism of an offer from one party duly accepted by the other.

There are two important questions, above all others, about agreement that must be fully understood. In recent years the law has been much concerned with the reality or genuineness of agreement as reached between parties possessing unequal bargaining strength and the marked tendency for economically powerful parties, such as large-scale suppliers of goods or services, to impose their terms and conditions of contract on economically weak parties such as consumers. Where necessity or absence of choice in these circumstances gives the weaker party no real option but to 'agree', the law has moved in several ways to redress the balance of power. This first point can lead us to our second.

Although agreement established the existence of contract it does not necessarily clearly determine its *scope*, ie the full range of rights and obligations created. For example, agreement is reached between S Ltd and B over the sale of a motor car. The contract is in writing and is made up of a number of what are known as *express terms*. These relate to such matters as the price to be paid, the fact that the car is new and the terms of delivery. However, as well as express terms, binding on the parties as a result of their agreement, other *implied terms* may well be added to the express terms by force of law. The Sale of Goods Act lays down that in most instances goods shall be of an acceptable commercial standard. This rule takes the form of an implied term which is just as much an integral part of the contract as the other, express, terms.

If contract is viewed by lawyers from the standpoint of bargain rather than agreement the analysis proceeds on the basis of promises. A promise results from the acceptance of an offer: S Ltd offer to sell the car for £10,000 and when B accepts this offer it becomes a binding promise. At that point S Ltd enter into a legal obligation to sell and deliver the car; their promise must be fulfilled – as must B's promise to pay the price. This leads us to the legal concept of consideration.

Consideration

Consideration, the so-called sign and symbol of bargain, has been described as 'the price for which the promise is bought'. 'Price' really amounts to anything of material value and in our example we can easily identify the car and £10,000 as consideration. However, legal obligations being created at the time of agreement, and agreement normally consisting of the parties' mutual promises, the law of contract therefore regards *promises* as consideration as well. Thus, if S Ltd promise to deliver the car in a month's time and B promises to pay for it on delivery, there is an immediately binding contract from which neither party can withdraw without being in breach, though performance is not due until the agreed date. Mutual promises are known as executory consideration, and the performance of the act embodied in the promise (eg delivery, payment) amounts to executed consideration.

It is important to remember that in legal analysis most contracts are regarded as coming about through an exchange of binding promises, the performance of which may well take place some considerable time in the future. The distinction between executory and executed consideration is, however, of little significance in an over-the-counter transaction.

Like some other contractual concepts, the doctrine of consideration appears at first glance to be perfectly sound, logical and free of complications. However, we will see that the bargain principle can create practical difficulties. It means, for instance, that a simple 'bare' promise – one not supported by consideration from the other party – is not binding. Nevertheless, in some circumstances a party who has *relied* on such a promise may well be able to argue a good case for its enforceability (see Chapter 6).

Intention to create legal relations

It is said that parties must not only reach agreement but *intend* to create a binding relationship. Parties, in fact, rarely consider this question at all and so it is the law itself which has created a presumption that business agreements are binding contracts, while other agreements of a social or domestic nature are not. In a few cases the distinction has been a difficult one for the courts to make, but only rarely is this question of any real legal significance. We will discuss contractual intention again in more detail in Chapter 6.

Terms, breach and other issues

It is often important to establish the *scope* of the obligations resting on the parties to a contract. In the case of a written sales agreement it may be thought that the statements or clauses within the four corners of the document constitute the entire contract between buyer and seller. But we have already seen that other, implied, terms may be incorporated and so place further, in our previous example, statutory-based, obligations on the seller.

Now it is only where a party defectively performs or fails to perform the whole or part of his contractual obligations that an action for breach can be brought. It follows that we may have actions for breach of express terms (written or oral) or for breach of implied terms. Nor are all contractual breaches of the same significance; clearly some are more serious than others (see Chapter 7).

The remedies for breach provided for the injured party by the law of contract reflect this distinction, wider remedies being available in the case of serious breaches. However, the basic common-law remedy for any breach of contract is damages, which are available to compensate the injured party for the loss they have suffered as a result of the breach.

A large and important part of the general law of contract is concerned with the issues outlined above. A number of essential questions are involved. Is there a binding agreement? What is the scope of that agreement? What is the significance of a breach of a binding agreement? What remedies may the law apply? There are, however, other important issues which are not traditionally taken to be the 'proper' subject-matter of a study of contract law. Some of these issues have lately found their way into lawyers' treatments of contract – belatedly reflecting the increasing involvement of government and courts with the points in question. For example: How relevant are the old rules on agreement and promises to modern standard-form contracts prepared by an economically stronger party and presented to a weaker on a 'take-it-or-leave-it' basis?

Does it make a difference if the economically powerful party is a private sector enterprise (eg a motor vehicle manufacturer) or the provider (privatised or not) of a service such as gas, electricity or rail transport? How relevant are the traditional rules of contract law to the contracts entered into by government departments such as the Ministry of Defence or the Department of Health and Social Security? The vast majority of contractual disputes are not decided by the courts – who decides, or settles, them and how? These are important questions to be considered by today's students and tomorrow's practitioners. All these issues are related and it is social, economic and political changes that have thrown them up – mass production, standardisation, imperfect competition, increased governmental regulation and so on – and have created strains upon and the need for a broader view of contract and contract law.

References and further reading

Atiyah (1989), *An Introduction to the Law of Contract*, 4th edn, Part I: The Development of the Modern Law of Contract.

Friedman (1965), *Contract Law in the USA*, Introduction, University of Wisconsin Press.

Parry (1959), *The Sanctity of Contract in English Law*.

Tillotson, 'Anyone for Contract?' (1976) JALT 135.

Questions

(1) In what sense is contract 'self-imposed' liability?

(2) 'In principle it is not easy to see why the law relating to the sale of goods should be different from the law relating to the performance of other contractual obligations, whether charterparties or other types of contract. Sale of goods law is but one branch of the general law of contract. It is desirable that the same legal principle should apply to the law of contract as a whole and that a different legal principle should not apply to different branches of the law': *Roskill LJ in Cehave NV v Bremer Handelsgesellschaft mbH (1976)*. Discuss.

(3) What restrictions or qualifications of freedom of contract are to be found in Sir George Jessel's statement on p 7?

(4) In *Lochner v New York* (1905), a majority of the US Supreme Court declared a New York statute imposing maximum hours for work in bakeries to be unconstitutional: 'No legislature shall pass any law impairing the obligations of contracts.'

Comment on this extract from the dissenting opinion of Justice Holmes:

This case is decided upon an economic theory which a large part of the country does not entertain. If it were a question whether I agreed with that theory, I should desire to study it further and long before making up my mind. But I do not conceive that to be my duty, because I strongly believe that my agreement or disagreement has nothing to do with the right of a majority to embody their opinions in law. It is settled by various decisions of this court that state constitutions and state laws may regulate life in many ways which we as legislators might think as injudicious or if you like as tyrannical as this, and which equally with this interfere with the liberty to contract ... The liberty of the citizen to do as he likes so long as he does not interfere with the liberty of others to do the same, which has been a shibboleth for some well-known writers, is interfered with by school laws, by the Post

Office, by every state or municipal institution which takes his money for purposes thought desirable, whether he likes it or not.

(5)   Explain, in terms of offer, acceptance and consideration, a contract made through the medium of a beverage-vending machine.

2   Contract and contract law

In a lecture given some years ago Lord Scarman expressed the view that the law of contract 'if studied in abstraction ... is no more than a generalised theory about the nature and consequences of agreement coupled with rules ... as to the meaning of words and phrases'. This remark quite clearly carries with it criticism of courses of study in contract law which are in some sense abstract. A study of contract law is dangerously abstract if it concentrates on legal analysis and technicalities at the expense of how contract functions in everyday life – particularly business life.

The lawyer's view of contract tends to focus on the legal implications of contractual breakdown: on rights and obligations and the consequences of litigation. There are other views. The lawyer's preoccupations by no means occupy the forefront of the businessman's mind. For him the contract is primarily a facilitative device within an economic cycle which turns on such processes as the acquisition of materials, the production of finished goods, marketing and sales, finance and payment. Business people and economists are also frequently concerned with the cost of contracting. For example, standard-form contracts are less expensive to produce than 'tailor-made' documents; vertical integration of firms may offer savings on inter-firm transactional costs; insistence on precise contractual performance may be expensive in terms of both money and business relationships.

Lord Scarman's message is quite clear: the person, and that includes the lawyer, who only knows the law of contract, and little or nothing of the rest of contract, has only a small, incomplete, view. Anthropologists, economists, historians, philosophers, sociologists and others have all presented treatments of contract, and, in as much as law is not an end in itself but is a tool of social order, it would appear that contract law can only acquire a full or true meaning if studied and evaluated in the light of findings from other disciplines.

Legal and other views of contract

The early legal history of contract is extensive, complex and not entirely free from controversy. Medieval law, primarily concerned with crime and land, slowly began to recognise claims arising out of informal, oral transactions as opposed to formalised agreements under seal. Of particular significance is the common law's recognition by the 16th century of claims involving the elements of (i) reliance by the plaintiff on an *undertaking* given by the defendant; (ii) faulty performance (later non-performance) of the undertaking by the defendant; (iii) loss to the plaintiff; and (iv) compensation in the form of damages.

Later, the language of the courts began to link the idea of undertaking with that of promise. At that time the moral force of, and duty to keep, promises was very strong. In the view of the American contract lawyer, Professor Corbin, writing in the earlier part of the present century:

> That portion of the field of law that is classified and described as the law of contracts attempts the realisation of reasonable expectations that have been induced by the making of a promise. Doubtless, this is not the only purpose by which men have been motivated in creating the law of contracts; but it is believed to be the main underlying purpose, and it is believed that an understanding of many of the existing rules, and a determination of their effectiveness, require a lively consciousness of their underlying purpose.

Nevertheless, in terms of a person's word being 'as good as his bond', the law stopped short of declaring that all promises were binding. Starting from an inquiry into the reasons why a promise was given, the doctrine of consideration came to set limits to promissory liability. It eventually did so by attempting to contain binding promises within the confines of the related theories of *quid pro quo*, bargain or equivalence. Thus B's counter-promise could be seen as the reason or consideration for A's original promise and the equivalent on which A took up his undertaking. (As already mentioned, we will see later that the 'exclusive bargain' theory, and the doctrine of consideration, have come under severe pressure with the result that seriously made promises, even if *not* forming part of a bargain, may be enforced.)

Thus even before the onset of the industrial and commercial revolutions, contract law had developed considerably, containing basic, interconnecting concepts such as undertaking, promise (and expectations), bargain in the sense of commercial exchange, reliance, loss and compensation. By the 19th century, however, it is no exaggeration to say that an idea of contract in a much more general sense came to the forefront of people's minds – not only lawyers but also philosophers, political scientists, economists, sociologists and others.

Many of the ideas expressed were not new but they were reformulated, brought together and, for a time, given some measure of practical acceptance. Contract came to be seen as the key to wealth and happiness in the emerging market society; hence the 'utmost liberty in contracting' became a prime ethical, political, economic and legal goal. In the words of the American jurist, Roscoe Pound: 'Justice required that each individual be at liberty to make free use of his natural powers in bargains and exchanges and promises except as he interfered with like action on the part of his fellow men, or with some other of their natural rights.' Society itself was regarded as essentially consensual; concerted action and co-operation were the keys to advancement.

The perceived role of the courts in this scheme of things has already been alluded to by reference to Sir George Jessel's words, and he continued: 'Therefore you have this paramount public policy to consider in that you are not lightly to interfere with this freedom of contract.' In a similar vein, Henry Sidgwick in his *Elements of Politics* (1879):

> Suppose contracts freely made and effectively sanctioned, and the most elaborate social organisation becomes possible, at least in a society of such human beings as the individualistic theory contemplates – gifted with mature reason and governed by enlightened self-interest.

Sidgwick's final phase leads us back to the contribution of the economist Adam Smith. In his *Wealth of Nations*, published in 1776, Smith analysed exchange in terms of man's 'natural propensity' to 'truck, barter and exchange'; a propensity which gave rise to contract, trade and the division of labour. His wide-ranging and highly influential exposition sought to show how the individual's self-interested pursuit of optimum gain and happiness was both regulated, and harnessed to the general good, by the economist's law of demand and supply. Equivalence, bargain and reciprocity were easily expressible: 'Give me that which I want, and you shall have this which you want.' The magical ingredient converting individual acquisitiveness into universal good was the 'invisible hand': the individual 'generally, indeed, neither intends to promote the public interest, nor knows how much he is promoting it ... He intends only his own gain, and he is in this, as in other cases, led by an invisible hand to promote an end which was no part of his intention'. We know from a reading of Dickens' *Hard Times* that, although in the 19th century the entrepreneurial contract-makers were happy, and relatively free, to operate according to the dictates of individual enterprise as mystically married to social co-operation and the greatest good, the benefits were not in practice equally distributed – the theory did not apply across the board.

Smith, who advocated minimum regulation of the economy – and therefore of contracts – by the State, did see it as a prime function of the law to uphold and enforce contracts. He stressed that promises were not binding as a consequence of some inherent quality but rather because of the reliance they created in the market and which was not to be disappointed. It is sometimes argued that the main justification for the legal enforcement of agreements or promises is economic. Trade and industry, it is said, would break down if business agreements could be broken with impunity. Legal definitions of contract – a contract is a legally binding agreement, or it is a promise or set of promises which the law will enforce – stress bindingness and enforceability. Professor Hart, in *The Concept of Law* (1961), says that, 'where altruism is not unlimited, a standing procedure providing for such self-binding operations is required in order to create a minimum form of confidence in the future behaviour of others, and to ensure the predictability necessary for cooperation'.

À propos the above remarks, it is significant that in the early part of the 19th century, the legal focal point for contract settled firmly on the binding nature of reciprocal promises, ie on the *executory* contract, as made *by the parties*. The elements of 'confidence' and 'predictability' referred to by Hart clearly tie in with

15

this shift in legal thinking in that the emerging classical model sought to make it plain that contract was concerned with exchanges and in particular *future* exchanges. As Pound put it much later: 'Wealth, in a commercial age, is made up largely of promises ... Thus the individual claims to have performance of advantageous promises secured to him.'

With clear recognition that promises bind future performance, contract showed obvious potential for planning, including risk allocation, and hence for 'confidence'. All that will be said about the planning function of contract at this stage is that, in an important sense, promises can display varying degrees of bindingness. A promise may be absolute, or it may be hedged round with quali- fications and adjustment mechanisms (eg a price variation clause) capable of being brought into play if and when conditions change between the time of making and performing the agreement.

Two further developments in contract law, following fuller recognition of the executory contract, must be mentioned. A party liable on an executory contract is liable not for what he has done but for what he has not done – he has not performed his promise. In Professor Atiyah's views, 'he must be liable because of his intention, his will, his promise. There is nothing else'. At the same time, in the early 19th century, wide acceptance of the idea of liability based on promises allowed a *general theory* of contract law to emerge. Academics and judges began to use the idea of promise and will as the basis of the law, and contract was no longer merely regard- ed as an adjunct of the law of property or a discussion of particular types of transac- tions. Books came to be written about 'the law of contract in its general and abstract form apart from its specific practical applications'.

As well as this generality (or absence of particularity as we have noted in Chapter 1), the 'classical' model was clearly designed to serve a free market economy – to act as a framework within which the free play of competitive forces could operate. In *'laissez-faire* style the law was conceived negatively as a system of hands off while men do things rather than as a system of ordering to prevent friction and waste so that they may do things': Roscoe Pound.

Therefore, bearing in mind what has been said, an important feature for a time was legal adherence to the consensus or will theory of contract, imported in the main from the writings of continental jurists such as Pothier and Savigny. The former defined a contract as an agreement based on the intention of the par- ties, it being their *will* which created the legal obligation. As Atiyah explains: 'The somewhat mystical idea had gained acceptance that an obligation could be created by a communion of will, an act of joint, if purely mental procreation.' Will theory, however, did not last for long in the courts, being more suited to the elaborations of academic writers than to pragmatic decision-makers. We will see that judicial inquiries into intention and agreement *have continued* by way of *objective appraisal* of external signs and manifestations rather than by a search for the 'elusive mental element'. It has, however, taken a long time for

16

the law to move away from passive concentration on the parties and their intentions, wills and promises (party autonomy) and take fuller cognisance of the role and capabilities of the law itself (judicial or legislative) to intervene and so adjust rights and correct imbalances in transactions no longer, if ever, created on a basis of equality and by a process of free choice.

As we proceed to examine substantive elements of contract law in Part Two, we will time and again be reminded of the legacy of 19th century thinking and its continuing effect on the law today. We will therefore close this section by briefly reviewing the key features of the 'classical' model as it emerged from around 1800 onwards – including those contract categories which still appear as chapter headings in the textbooks at the present time:

(1) There was a presumption that contracting parties were possessed of equal bargaining power (cf classical economic theory). This gave rise to the expression 'dealing at arm's length'; each party being self-motivated and self-assertive.

(2) A party was bound not so much because they had made a promise as because they had made a bargain.

(3) Agreement was based on consent and free choice; contractual obligations were therefore self-imposed. Imbalances, whether measured in terms of consideration or unfairness were irrelevant – but not so lack of consent.

(4) Agreement came about through negotiation – through the application of the rules of offer and acceptance.

(5) Pursuit of the parties' intentions carried the courts beyond express statements of intention in the contract itself to presumed intention through the notion of implied terms. (This point has also been touched on in Chapter 1.) Such a trend from a subjective to an objective view of contract is to be seen particularly in:

   (a) a view of agreement based on what the parties say and do rather than what they intended (the two views should of course coincide);

   (b) the use of implied terms to supplement or modify the parties' agreement;

   (c) the development of a new element, considered essential for the creation of a binding contract, known as an 'intention to create legal relations';

   (d) the use of the idea of the implied term to give effect to a presumed intention of the parties not to proceed with their contract in drastically changed circumstances – see the discussion of frustration in Chapter 12.

(6) Although primarily upholders of contracts, absence of consent would, within narrow limits, allow the court to strike down a contract. Among others, fraud, misrepresentation and fundamental mistake were recognised as factors vitiating consent.

(7) The binding nature of contract was 'in principle, a matter of pecuniary calculation. Each party is bound; he must therefore perform, or pay damages for his failure to perform': Atiyah.

Sociology of contract

Towards the end of the 19th century, and developing from a legacy of earlier work by, among others, jurists and moral, social and political philosophers, there emerged a view – or rather a series of views – of law which clearly focused on law as a *social* phenomenon. This development, which is now more than a century old, is best described as the sociological movement in law. It is in large part a reaction against legal formalism – against studying law in a way which tends to isolate it from society, so encouraging the spurious idea that law is in some way autonomous, an end in itself, rather than a means to social order. Sociology of law seeks to put law firmly in its social, political, economic or other context; it looks for relationships between law, legal system and context; and it asks questions about the functions, effects and efficiency of rules. Some lawyers have welcomed the growth of this 'external' view of law. A former Lord Chancellor, Lord Hailsham, said that his 'only abiding concern ... is my fear that the study and practice of law may become too narrowly based and tend to divorce itself from the general culture of which we are all a part, and in which history, language, literature, the physical sciences and philosophy have an equal and distinctive part to play in the framing of our institutions and our system of justice'.

In view of the key role assigned to contract in 19th century thought, it is not surprising that pioneer workers in the field of sociology of law should turn their attention to it. The analysis of contract by the French sociologist Emile Durkheim (1858-1917) attacked not only the prevalent individualist, self-interest view of contract but also the idea that contract seen in those terms (see, for example, Sidgwick's assertions on p 15) could be regarded as a microcosm of society or a model for human relations. He was perhaps the first to see that, within the contractual bond, the element of self-interest inevitably created an inherent contradiction: 'If one gets to the bottom of things, one will see that all harmony of interests conceals a conflict which is latent or simply adjourned.' This is a view of contract – that agreements contain the elements of both harmony and conflict – which applies, in the absence of external regulation, even to negotiated agreements between parties of equal bargaining power: 'Each contracting party, while in need of the other, seeks to obtain what he needs at the lowest price, that is, to acquire the most rights possible in return for the fewest obligations possible.' This question of internal contradiction within individual contracts was, as we will see, developed further by Georges Gurvitch.

Durkheim himself was concerned with refuting the concept of contract as an essentially individualistic and utilitarian act rather than a social one, while taking further a related point that an unregulated self-interest core to contract could in no way enable it to serve as a model for what he termed 'organic solidarity' in society. Apart from the internal contradiction created by 'interest', on a different level Durkheim, contrary to much thinking at the time, would not accept that a society splintered by increasing division of labour could achieve 'solidarity' through the pursuit of economic self-interest within a loose framework of *laissez-faire* control: 'In the fact of economic exchange, the different agents remain outside one another, and with the termination of the operation each one finds himself alone again ... Indeed, interest is the least constant of all things in the world. Today it is in my interest to unite with you. Tomorrow the same reason may make me your enemy.'

It was necessary, in Durkheim's opinion, to place contract in a context wider than that of party autonomy and individual will. An essential third party was society itself: 'A contract is not sufficient unto itself, but is possible only thanks to the regulation of the contract which is originally social.' The true focal point was therefore not individuals but society, which should provide a framework of norms and laws of a more closely regulatory nature from those implied by Sir George Jessel in his famous statement concerning freedom of contract. Durkheim's aim was to see obligatory force granted only to contracts which have 'social value'. In this he took social justice rather than individual utility as his measure of contract. Solidarity in society would not come about through the operation of market forces – demand and supply – and the intervention of the 'invisible hand'. More was required. Social regulation of contract required first of all clear recognition of the social facts of unequal bargaining power as opposed to the economic and legal myth underlying freedom of contract:

> What can the poor worker reduced to his own resources do against a rich and powerful boss, and is there not a palpable and cruel irony in assimilating these two forces which are so manifestly unequal? If they enter into combat, is it not clear that the second will always and without difficulty crush the first? What does such a liberty amount to, and does not the economist who contents himself with it become guilty of taking the word for the thing?

Durkheim insisted that society (and the law) must no longer passively uphold 'unjust contracts which are antisocial by definition' for the reason that the 'agreement of parties cannot render just a clause which in itself is unjust'. He appreciated that not all 'interest' or 'conflict' could be *removed* from either society or contract, but he advanced the view that there must be awareness of the need for an agreed mechanism to find the 'middle term between the rivalry of interests and their solidarity'.

For Durkheim, increasing social regulation of contract in order to arrive at the 'middle term' marked a progress away from freedom of contract towards just 'contracts of equity' – in a general rather than technical sense. In English law such progress can eventually be found in legal recognition of trade unions, in the idea of the 'legislative bargain' (see Gutteridge, p 105) and in consumer-protection measures. It is also reflected in the changing role of the judiciary, once categorised as 'holders of the ring' but now seen to be increasingly paternalistic shapers of 'just' contracts. Nevertheless, English contract law has never bodily shifted from its freedom of contract base; change has been gradual and piecemeal.

A later investigator into the sociology of law, Georges Gurvitch, re-examined the problem of 'the rivalry of interests' in contract and the internal contradiction between individual aims and common purpose. Gurvitch identified the co-operation aspect of contract, the element of common purpose, as 'rapprochement'. This is a view of contract which focuses attention on a convergence of the parties' aims and on the broad harmony that exists between them, in so far as the implementation of the basic obligation of the contract is concerned. However, Gurvitch also saw within the contractual bond what he called 'separation': the divergence of the parties' wills as they sought precisely opposite aims under the blanket of agreement. As Lord Wilberforce has said: 'The words used may, and often do, represent a formula which means different things to each side, yet may be accepted because that is the only way to get "agreement" and in the hope that disputes will not arise': *Prenn v Simmonds* (1971).

For example, although it may be legally admissible in certain circumstances for a *party* to exclude liability for merely defective performance of the contract by insisting on a term to that effect in the 'agreement' itself, in more extreme cases of radical misperformance the courts have often held that it could not have been the intention of *the parties* to 'agree' that an exclusion of liability extended to a failure to implement the basic obligation or core of the contract. This is a judicial presumption put into operation when 'rapprochement' has been eclipsed by Gurvitch's other basic element, 'separation' or conflict.

Where it is recognised that the element of co-operation is adversely outweighed by 'separation' and is only obtained via the shadow, not the substance, of agreement, the legislature or the court should be, and now often is, concerned with the operation of its balancing function which Gurvitch called equilibration, and which Durkheim called finding 'the middle term'. The 'legislative bargain' referred to above was struck by Parliament in order to achieve greater equilibrium between the interests of carriers and cargo owners in contracts for the carriage of goods by sea. The aim was, in Lord Sumner's words, to 'replace a conventional contract, in which it was constantly attempted, often with much success, to relieve the carrier from every kind of liability, by a legislative bargain, under which ... his position is to be one of restricted exemption'. To give one further example: it is within the power of the court under the doctrine of frustration to terminate a contract and discharge the parties from further obligations on the occurrence of an event which is beyond their control and which defeats the commercial purpose of their agreement. The frustration case of *Davis Contractors Ltd v Fareham UDC* (see p 223) throws into sharp relief the 'separation' between parties who, although 'joined' in the provision of housing at an agreed price, find, when things go wrong, that their conflicting interests – to make a business profit and to provide low-cost council housing – are clearly revealed.

Gurvitch concluded that it was impossible to characterise the contractual relationship solely as consensus or conflict: 'the secret of contractual bonds, as well as of exchanges in general ... lies in the intercourse of "rapprochement" and "separation".' The object of certain rules or norms of contract law is to achieve equilibrium between these two opposing features so as to establish acceptable models of contractual behaviour.

It may be argued that the element of co-operation will more readily come to the forefront of contractual relations where the parties are of similar bargaining strength (hence the search for equilibrium where these conditions are not met). Where the possibility of one party exploiting his economic power at the expense of the other is absent, a divergence of interests may well be smoothed away through compromise. This is probably also true where the parties see the need for long-term continuing co-operation, and 'rapprochement' may predominate here at both the negotiation and dispute-solving stages (see Macaulay's study, p 25). The problem of co-operation and divergence of interests also clearly appears in the special case of the relationship between contract law and industrial collective bargaining.

The fundamental changes in society, from the medieval and communal to the industrial and political, which the previous century or so had witnessed, gave rise by the late 19th century to a series of studies of the nature of social groupings and relationships. Economic analysis of change had been couched in terms of innovation, specialisation, the division of labour, mobility of factors of production, markets and profits. Macro-sociology examined change from another angle.

The Austrian sociologist, Ferdinand Tönnies, drawing on a famous and much argued over generalisation by Sir Henry Maine concerning the movement of progressive societies from status to contract, distinguished two theoretical 'ideal' types of society. The first was essentially a pre-industrial 'gemeinschaft' type of society, based on kinship and neighbourhood and engendering close, continuing relationships. The second was 'gesellschaft', in which the individual becomes the central figure and his associations are predominantly motivated by reason and *quid pro quo*. The prototype of 'gemeinschaft' *union* is the family; 'gesellschaft' *association* is typified by the limited company (a legal 'person') and its internal and external networks of contractual relationships.

Tönnies was at pains to show a drift from social *union* to an essential 'separation' of *individuals* in an industrial society, which was merely an 'artificial construction of an aggregate of human beings' in which rationality and calcula-tion were the lynchpins. Nevertheless he looked forward to the development of a society based on unions of 'gesellschaft' where, we might say, Durkheim's 'contracts of equity' would be the norm and in which companies would under-stand and *practice* 'social responsibility'.

The proliferation of the rational, impersonal relationship was also examined by the German lawyer and sociologist, Max Weber (1864–1920), whose analysis of contract – and freedom of contract – was more 'economic' than most of his contemporaries. Influenced by the ideas of Tönnies, Weber drew a distinction between what he called 'status' and 'purposive' contracts. The first 'more primi-tive' type involved the creation of continuing 'total' (social and legal) relation-ships, such as those between husband and wife or landowner and vassal. Such relationships did not 'mean that certain performance of the contract, contribut-ing to the attainment of some specific object, was reciprocally guaranteed or expected. Nor did it mean merely that the making of a promise to another would ... have ushered in a new orientation in the relationship between the par-ties. The contract rather meant that the person would "become" something dif-ferent in quality (or status) from the quality he possessed before'. Weber there-fore identified the status contract with all-inclusive rights and duties and 'spe-cial attitudinal qualities based thereon'.

The archetypal purposive contract was 'the money contract' which was 'spe-cific, quantitatively delimited, qualityless, abstract, and usually economically conditioned'. As a result the purposive contract merely established a 'new ori-entation' in relationships without involving a change in the parties' 'total' posi-tion. It usually achieved some specific, generally economic, performance or result. In this 'purposive' sense, a contract has since been described as 'essential-ly an agreement between two or more individuals to behave in a certain speci-fied way for a certain specified length of time in the future. What distinguishes a contractual relationship from most other relationships is the fact that the reci-procal rights and obligations are limited to those specified in the contract. Thus the relationship between the members of a family can hardly be said to be con-tractual, since there is no detailed listing of the number and duration of the rights and duties': Davis, *Human Society.*

It is also important to appreciate the point that, as Weber clearly saw, while becoming more specific in the sense already indicated, economic exchanges were also, in another sense, becoming more diffused and increasingly less reliant on trust (or, to use Weber's word, 'soul'). Although the term 'credit' sug-gests confidence and faith, such faith rests partly on the law which may, at the request of the business community when expectations are unfulfilled, bring sanctions to bear on exchange defaulters. The purposive market exchange con-tract was, as we have seen, also distinguished from the status contract as creat-ing only a tenuous and temporary association. To the extent that tenuous, impersonal associations are incapable of inspiring high trust, it is necessary to establish legal machinery, which, while not raising low levels of trust, does at least provide a greater required measure of economic certainty.

Viewing contract on a broader economic plane, Weber, writing around the turn of the century, clearly linked the then current significance of contract to 'the high degree to which our economic system is market orientated and the role played by money'. Similarly: 'There exists, of course, an intimate connection between the expansion of the market and the expanding measure of contractual freedom.' However, Weber cut straight through the simplistic abstractions of earlier legal and economic thinking on the subject of freedom of contract. Markets for goods and services (including labour) might be more plentiful, factors of production more mobile, but this did not in itself result in more 'real' freedom. 'The exact extent to which the total amount of "freedom" within a given legal community is actually increased depends entirely on the concrete economic order and especially on the property distribution.'

New developing markets threw up new economic groups with powerful 'market interests' based on capital and entrepreneurship. As was becoming clear to most people, it was the power relations in society, not economic and legal abstractions, which determined the operation of markets and the degree of real freedom in those markets: 'The result of contractual freedom, then, is in the first place the opening of the opportunity to use, by the clever utilisation of property ownership in the market, these resources without legal restraints as a means for the achievement of power over others.' As others had done, Weber illustrated his analysis by means of the contract of employment: 'The more powerful party in the market, ie normally the employer, has the possibility to set the terms, to offer the job "take it or leave it", and, given the normally more pressing economic need of the worker, to impose his terms on him.'

Weber is here not only pointing to the difference between formal and real freedom – the distorting element being inequality of bargaining power – but indicating how formal freedom protects and aggravates inequality: 'The increasing significance of freedom of contract and particularly of enabling laws which leave everything to "free" agreement implies a relative reduction of that kind of coercion which results from the threat of mandatory and prohibitory norms. Formally it represents a decrease of coercion. But it is also obvious how advantageous this state of affairs is to those who are economically in the position to make use of the empowerments.' In short, absence of economic power is a severe limitation on an individual's freedom of contract.

Since Weber's time, new countervailing market interests, representing employees and consumers, have gained legal recognition, so enabling them to bring a greater measure of equilibrium into markets for labour and for goods and services. Above all, the state as welfare-state provider, regulator of, and participator in, markets has removed the worst excesses of free enterprise capitalism. (Are we approaching the era of Durkheim's 'contracts of equity'?) Some observers have analysed 20th century shifts of this nature in terms of a trend away from the individual and back towards 'status' and the group – *collective* bargaining between organised labour and management, the widespread activities of multinational and conglomerate *groups* of companies and *state* trading on an increasingly large scale. (But what of 'privatisation'?)

What is certain is that a law of contract with its roots still set in 19th-century individualism is ill-placed to develop rules or adjudicate on claims concerning, for example, collective-bargaining agreements or restrictive trade practices in a mixed economy. We have already noted in Chapter 1 that where the law of contract has been found radically wanting in the face of business realities, it has been supplanted – either through legislative action or by business 'self-help' mechanisms based on practice and commercial expertise.

Legal and 'living law' of contract

Over 80 years ago, the Austrian jurist Eugen Ehrlich thought there should be more research into brewers' supply of beer than 'on the concept of the juristic person'. Ehrlich's preoccupation was with the rules and practices by which individuals and groups *actually* govern their relations and which consist only partly of the law to be found in statutes and decisions. He called these rules and practices 'living law' in support of his argument that 'the centre of gravity of legal development lies not in legislation, nor in juristic science, nor in judicial decision, but in society itself'. 'Living law' and law as generally understood were therefore, for Ehrlich, different though related phenomena. 'Living law', as the prime mover, was seen as running ahead of the law. Taking another definition of 'living law' – as being 'the legal command reduced to practice, as it obtains in a definite association ... even without any formulation of words' – we can see that practice, say business practice, tends, by running ahead of the law, to grow away from it. (In the 17th century, in order to *remedy weaknesses* in the common law of the time, the judges began to *incorporate* into it what was known as the 'law merchant', a body of relatively sophisticated rules and techniques applicable previously only between merchants, or in particular trades or centres of business.)

What, therefore, is the relationship between contract practice and the law? Do business people make contracts on the basis of the legal rules? Do they enforce contracts in the courts? The answer is: only to varying degrees. Business contract-makers have good relations and profit margins rather than legal rights and duties uppermost in their minds; nevertheless, their contracts have been shaped to a greater or lesser extent by the law – and they can suffer heavy losses through inadvertence to the law. We will also see that enforcement of contracts in the courts has been an expensive operation for at least a century, so contract litigation is often regarded only as a last resort. Profits earned from relationships maintained through goodwill and the compromise of differences will often outweigh damages awarded against a company that now trades elsewhere. An 'association', to use Ehrlich's term, such as the business community is therefore for reasons of perceived convenience and efficiency, and as a simple question of cost, virtually impelled to develop its own 'living law' – customs, practices, techniques and clauses designed to avoid or mitigate business or 'legal' risk and loss:

> The living law is the law which dominates life itself even though it has not been posited in legal propositions. The source of our knowledge of the law is, first, the modern legal document; secondly direct observation of life, of commerce, of customs and usages, and of all associations, not only of those which the law has recognised but also of those it has overlooked and passed by, indeed even of those that it has disapproved.

In 1959 Professor Gower found that 'though contact between law and business has not been lost it seems to be less direct, with a growing aloofness on the part of the businessman and a growing remoteness from commercial realities on the part of the law'. Four years later, in the USA, an important investigation into the 'living law' of contract was made, as we shall see in this next section.

Non-contractual relations in business

Business has to a large extent withdrawn from *contract law* particularly in so far as much greater reliance is placed on amicable negotiation and commercial arbitration, and not the courts, for the resolution of contractual claims. Some observers go much further and suggest that the *contract* is no longer the essential vehicle for economic exchanges. Not that the latter view is by any means unanimous. For example, one commentator states that: 'The contract is of the essence of economic action. Few aspects of business ... are unrelated to contract. Marketing, finance, accounting and many of the other traditional fields of business administration operate within a conceptual framework that is essentially legal in character, and the contract is the most important part of the framework.'

In reply it might first be argued that contract lies more in the tactical field of business operations, merely representing the final step after the strategic policy questions (eg tax considerations, competition and available markets) have been weighed and settled. Contract is hardly of the essence as regards major business decisions, but, of course such decisions often crystallise into a contractual form – the purchase of new plant or materials, the establishment of an overseas investment project or a company takeover bid.

Second, it is essential in this context that we draw attention to Professor Macaulay's article *Non-Contractual Relations in Business* written in America in 1963. The article is concerned with the gains and losses connected with the use of contract to solve exchange problems in the manufacturing industries. It is important to emphasise at the outset that Macaulay does not define contract in the traditional legal way in terms of agreement or promises. His view is different and he uses contract to refer to 'devices for conducting exchanges'. These are: '(a) Rational planning of the transaction with careful provision for as many future contingencies as can be foreseen, and (b) the existence or use of actual or potential legal sanctions to induce performance of the exchange or to compensate for non-performance.'

The parties to an exchange transaction may, jointly or severally, use or resort to these devices to a greater or lesser extent. If, for example, the parties stress the importance of planning in the *creation* of the exchange relationship, and show, or have in the past shown, a propensity to resort to a legal approach to disputes that arise, then the relationship is more contractual, in Macaulay's sense, than would otherwise be the case.

As regards the creation of exchange relationships, planning, if undertaken, tends to centre around four main issues: (i) definition of performances; (ii) the effect of defective performances (in contract law terms – the consequences of breach, dealt with in Chapters 7 and 9); (iii) the effect of contingencies beyond the control of the parties on their future obligations (when will a party be excused from further performance owing to events beyond his control? – in legal terms frustration of contract and 'force majeure', dealt with in Chapter 12); (iv) the legally binding nature, or otherwise, of their agreement. On these points they may exhibit different degrees of planning: (a) explicit and careful; (b) tacit agreement; (c) unilateral assumptions ie 'two inconsistent unexpressed assumptions about an issue'; (d) unawareness of the issue.

This analysis is tested in the next chapter, but it is instructive to compare Macaulay's findings regarding the attitudes of a certain section of the business community towards planning (outlined in more detail below) with the views of Professor Treitel, a leading contract lawyer. It is Treitel's contention 'that contract is pre-eminently concerned with planned relationships; and one of the important functions of contract law is to provide a legal framework within which that planning can take place. To make such planning effective, the high degree of certainty which contract doctrine is intended to create is essential'. Against a background of clear and settled rules regarding, for example, the nature and gravity of breach situations and the rights of injured parties or the legal attitude towards exclusion of liability, contract draftsmen can allocate risks – and therefore settle such questions as pricing and insurance cover. Thus, Treitel concludes, one of the most important objectives of contract law is to *prevent* disputes from arising or from getting to the litigation stage. (It is also interesting to note that the conditions of co-operation that Durkheim sought for his 'contracts of equity' were to be defined 'not only in view of the situation as it presents itself at the moment of contract, but in provision of circumstances which may develop and modify it.')

Macaulay's findings – and other researchers have since come to the same general conclusions – are first that the larger the company, the more likely it is that detailed planning will take place. Such concerns, which probably have legal departments, are, through their economic strength and bargaining position, best placed to impress the planning requirement on their exchange partners. Second, whereas important transactions are 'custom-built' and handled by a detailed contract, routine transactions are, in an age of mass-production, dealt with on the basis of standardised planning, ie by the use of standard-form documents which present the same 'boiler plate' provisions to all customers. Potential problems often arise here through what is called the 'battle of the forms'. This occurs in particular where standard procedures result in a transaction having two 'faces' (a strong element of 'separation') eg a sale to be conducted on, according to the vendor, his standard condition of sale, but according to the buyer on *his* standard conditions of purchase. In legal terms, if this happens there is the possibility that there is therefore no agreement, no contract and no available remedy. In this context, however, Macaulay concludes that 'businessmen are least concerned about planning their transactions so that they are legally enforceable contracts'. (The 'battle of the forms' is discussed in more detail in Chapters on 'Agreement'.)

The article also considers the question of 'adjustment of exchange relationships'. It is necessary to broaden the inquiry a little in order to understand Macaulay's findings. Many contracts, for example purchases of consumer goods over the counter, are on simple fixed terms; other, long-term agreements may *themselves* contain provision for adjustment of terms owing to inflation or other contingencies. The law allows this so long as an agreement does not become so vague as to fall foul of rules on 'certainty'. Macaulay, however, is commenting on a rather different situation where, an agreement *having been made*, one party seeks an adjustment *outside* its original terms and procedures. In law, such unilateral proposals or demands to vary an agreement may require a *new* agreement supported by fresh consideration – the alteration required having to be 'paid' for to be enforceable; the original agreement not controlling the development although, as we will see in Chapter 6, developments in judicial thinking relating to consideration have led to a more realistic approach to adjustments and the renegotiation of contracts. However, Macaulay found that in the business world such adjustments, even withdrawals, were in many instances allowed by the other party 'without dispute'. Cancellation was not cause for an action for breach but, like bad debts, a recognised risk that could be budgeted for. As one lawyer commented: 'There is a widespread attitude (within the business community) that one can back out of any deal within some vague limits.' Similarly, as has already been mentioned, disputes are often compromised on a non-contractual, *ad hoc* basis of what is currently expedient, and the proportion of actions to disputes is very small: 'You don't read legalistic contract clauses at each other if you ever want to do business again': the view of a purchasing agent.

27

Finally, Macaulay asks and answers two questions: first, why does (manufacturing) business use contract – ie detailed planning and use of sanctions – so little? The main reason appears to be that with standardised products there is little room for honest misunderstanding about the seller's goods; testing can quickly show whether they are as specified. (On the other hand, business people may fail to plan because they do not appreciate the risks they are taking and/or they are merely following established patterns of company practice.) In addition, insurance and reserves for bad debts cover up or eliminate many defaults, and there is a widespread use of a variety of effective non-legal sanctions (eg complaints and replacement procedures, the need to maintain business and personal relationships, negotiated settlements, blacklisting) as opposed to recourse to the courts. Macaulay also found evidence of two widely accepted norms of business practice: '(1) Commitments are to be honoured in almost all situations; one does not welsh on a deal; (2) One ought to produce a good product and stand behind it.' Firmly behind these norms is a sure knowledge of the value of trouble-free, continuing relationships with good customers. Distrust of lawyers, the costs and delays which litigation involves and bad publicity are other relevant factors.

In answering the second question, 'Why do relatively contractual practices ever exist?', Macaulay concludes that a planned exchange can serve as a useful communication and accounting aid within the organisation, and planning will also be undertaken if the transaction will involve lengthy and complex performance or if the degree of injury consequent on default is likely to be great, as in, for example, the aircraft industry. Some exchange partners, the government or large corporations, may insist on a contract, and the 'decision whether or not to use contract ... will be made by the person within the business unit with the power to make it, and it tends to make a difference who he is'. (It is unlikely, however, that a government department would need to resort to legal sanctions in the event of a dispute.)

There is no doubt at all as to the importance of Macaulay's article for anyone concerned with the relationship between business transactions, contract and contract law. His study indicates that to some extent business policy and practice operate to exclude contract, as he defines it, from exchange transactions, at least in manufacturing industries. It must be remembered that, as regards exchange transactions, legal experience and expertise may be either *preventive* – operating at the creation or planning end – or in the last resort may operate in a *curative* way, in so far as remedies and awards are regarded as compensatory. To the extent that business transactions operate 'outside' contract, this amounts to a rejection by the business community of one or both these legal functions.

Does this matter? According to Macaulay's evidence, it would seem that it does not, unless you are a lawyer who is therefore losing fees. None of the business people that Macaulay interviewed appeared to be losing sleep over their non-contractual relations. Even if one wished to challenge his findings, one could only do so on the basis of research of equal or greater depth. Nevertheless, as the author himself implies, it would be dangerous to 'write off' contract as a business device on the strength of the article. Whether recognised or not, the basic function of contract and contract law is to facilitate business exchanges. We have already drawn attention to reliance and planning, predictability (or certainty) and co-operation as advantages that may accrue to the business people who use contract in the conduct of their affairs. Conversely, there are few people who would welcome an upsurge in contract litigation, for this would surely mean that the law was, even within the confines placed on it by Macaulay, failing to perform its preventive function.

Macaulay's article and similar subsequent ones are rather narrow in their scope. No account is taken of consumer, as opposed to inter-business, exchange transactions. Is a statute-based consumer credit agreement between a business organisation and a private party a contract? Are mortgage facilities for a home-occupier concluded by way of contract? Does the purchasing of a motor car or the obtaining of insurance coverage amount to a contractual relationship? Are business transactions relating to stocks and shares, bank loans and employment not based on contract? As the picture broadens, so it is possible that the extent of business reliance on contract increases, whether as regards planning or sanctions or both. Are the long-established standard forms widely used in the fields of international trade and finance contracts or not? However, even if it were established that only a small percentage of the business-exchange transactions concluded each year were conducted on a non-contractual basis, then the case for further study of business attitudes to planning and sanctions – and hence to contract law – remains.

Nor must it be forgotten that even on a more traditional view, the law of contract does not normally ripen into Appeal Court decisions but into effective business-exchange relationships. Drafting skills and legal rules function primarily at the request of those individuals, associations, corporations and government departments who are regularly occupied in business and finance. The lawyer's role in this respect is correspondingly that of an expert in planning, framing and applying directive arrangements of goods, services and opportunities. He is speaking to the future, knowing when and how to try and bind it, and when not to try at all. And if formal dispute-solving is required, he is also on hand.

References and further reading

Atiyah (1979), *The Rise and Fall of Freedom of Contract*, particularly chs 14-16.

Beale and Dugdale, 'Contracts between businessmen: planning and the use of contractual remedies' (1975) 2 *British Journal of Law and Society* 45.

Devlin (1965), *The Enforcement of Morals*, ch III, 'Morals and law of contract'.

Durkheim (1964), *The Division of Labour in Society*.

Ehrlich (1936), *Fundamental Principles of the Sociology of Law*.

Fox (1974), *Beyond Contract: Work, Power and Trust Relations*, chs 4 and 5.

Gurvitch (1947), *Sociology of Law*.

Kessler and Sharp (1953), 'Contract as a principle of order', in *Contracts: Cases and Materials* (Prentice-Hall); reprinted in Schwartz and Skolnick, *Society and the Legal Order* (Basic Books).

Macaulay, 'Non-contractual relations in business – a preliminary study' (1963) 28 *American Sociological Review* 55. Also in Friedman and Macaulay (1968), *Law and the Behavioural Sciences* (Bobbs-Merill) and Schwartz and Skolnick, see above.

Macaulay, 'Elegant models, empirical pictures, and the complexities of contract' (1977) 11 *Law and Society Review* 507.

Pound (1972), *An Introduction to the Philosophy of Law*, ch 6 'Contract'.

Simpson, 'Innovation in nineteenth century contract law' (1975) 91 LQR 247.

Tönnies (1957), *Community and Society*, Loomis (ed).

Weber (1978), *Economy and Society*, Roth and Wittich (eds), Vol 2, ch 8 (ii) 'Forms of creation of rights'.

Wheeler and Shaw (1994), *Contract Law: Cases, Materials and Commentary*, ch 2 'Contract theory'.

Questions

(Questions relating to the latter part of this chapter – on non-contractual relations in business – are deferred to the end of Chapter 3.)

(1) 'The economic correlate of common law contract is a free enterprise society.' Discuss.

(2) Comment on the following views of contract:

(a) The contract is 'the juristic form for the distribution and utilisation of the goods and personal abilities that are in existence in society' (Ehrlich, *Sociology*).

(b) 'Suppose contracts freely made and effectively sanctioned, and the most elaborate organisation becomes possible, at least in a society of such humane beings as the individualistic theory contemplates – gifted with mature reason and governed by enlightened self-interest' (Sidgwick, *Elements of Politics*).

(c) 'During the process of production, the owner assumes a mask, increasingly severe, sinister, and in the end almost despotic. Now, as he leaves the intimidating and gloomy factory with his wares, his features unwrinkle, they become bland, modest and agreeable. The man who stands in the market with his goods, though the same person, now wears a disguise that changes his appearance beyond recognition, that of the "guardian of commodities". Every recollection of that lower sphere of production ... of despotism ... has vanished from the thoughts of the man, and the appearance of the commodity reveals no traces of it. The capitalist has now become ... an equal among equals. He has dealings with his own kind only' (Renner, *The Institutions of Private Law and their Social Functions*).

(3) Assess the contribution to a study of contract made by the sociology of law movement.

3 Planning and sanctions

The purpose of this chapter is to examine in practice one of the 'views' of contract discussed in the preceding chapter: in particular, Macaulay's account of contract in terms of planning and sanctions. This is done by reference to a form of export sales contract which is also a good illustration of Gurvitch's elements of 'rapprochement' and 'separation' at work.

The cif (cost, insurance and freight) contract for the international sale of goods is a form of contract which was introduced and developed by mercantile practice and recognised by the English courts in the mid-19th century. The various types of export sale contract (designated by the trade terms cif, fob, ex ship, etc) are indicative of a series of standard frameworks into one of which the parties can fit the particular requirements of their transaction. They represent the long-term outcome of planning and co-operation between sellers, buyers, banks and others with the overall aim of facilitating international trade and safeguarding the parties to it.

The American lawyer, Professor Llewellyn, has written of 'the logical clarity, the singleness, the sharpness of line' – even the beauty – of the cif contract: 'The patterned succession of the seller's proper actions, as he arranges, as he ships, as he sends forward promptly the batch of documents, the neatly matched mortising of the due steps by the buyer, honouring the draft when the documents are presented ... the courtly grace with which the steps and rights of one intervening banker, or two, or three, are laid out as in a minuet ... But the prime test of its legal beauty remains the functional test.' An enormous number of transactions, in value amounting to untold sums, are carried out every year under cif contracts. Here law and practice intermesh; the construct works.

The mechanics of the cif transaction

The duties of the seller and buyer vary according to the trade term adopted and this measure of flexibility naturally allows the parties to select the most convenient model. If the seller has access to first class shipping and insurance facilities, it is likely that cif will be chosen because this is the trade term which clearly makes the seller responsible for arranging the sea carriage of the goods and their marine insurance cover. Also, on this basis the contract price of the goods is settled, being made up of the *cost* of producing the goods, the charges for *insurance* and *freight*, plus the seller's profit.

Although the common aims of the parties – convenience and security – are readily accepted, it is their conflicting aims which create difficulties. They can in many cases best be reconciled, or to use Gurvitch's word, equilibrated, by means of the special legal significance attached to the documents involved in the transaction and by the intervention of the banking system between the parties.

The main aims of the buyer are to become the owner of the goods as soon as possible (or the insurance money if they are lost or damaged) so that he can use or resell them and to obtain the best possible credit terms. The seller's aims are quite different: to transfer ownership only against payment of the price and to obtain such payment as soon as possible. As regards reconciliation of their aims, it is first necessary to identify the main documents which play a crucial role in the cif arrangement. An invoice must be completed in strict agreement with the contract of sale. The seller's obligations also involve him with negotiation of the contract of carriage, evidenced by what is known as a *bill of lading* and which, as a *document of title* (ownership), is regarded as the 'equivalent' of the goods themselves. The seller further arranges the contract of marine insurance with an underwriter who will prepare a policy or certificate covering the agreed risks.

The significance of these documents lies in two directions. A set is airmailed to the buyer and his acceptance of them is taken to constitute the transfer of ownership in the goods to him. This will occur long before the actual goods arrive at the port of unloading but means in a typical case that, by transferring the bill of lading to a sub-buyer, the main buyer can more quickly complete his business with that person. The person holding the bill of lading can obtain the goods from the carrier at the port of unloading; alternatively if the goods are lost or damaged the buyer (or sub-buyer) can claim against the carrier (under the terms of the bill of lading) or against the underwriter (under the policy).

The seller's need for prompt payment and the buyer's wish for credit can be reconciled by the use of the documents in conjunction with the banks. Under the terms of the contract of sale, the seller agrees to accept payment by way of a bill of exchange which performs a function in international trade similar to that of a cheque in domestic transactions. Where a banker's documentary credit system of payment has been agreed, the seller is able to look to his bank in his own country for prompt payment. On his deposit of a set of the shipping documents with the bank as security, the bank will pay the seller against the bill of exchange. His bank will then look for reimbursement from the buyer's bank in his country. The buyer will in turn pay his bank when the term of credit expressed on the bill, eg three months, has expired. It should now be possible to appreciate the judicial statement that a cif contract is 'a contract for the sale of insured goods, lost or not lost, to be implemented by the transfer of the proper documents'. The function of the bill of lading as a document of title is perhaps the most important factor in understanding how, first, the interests of the buyer and seller and, second, the interests of those two parties and the banks can be balanced.

The Ruritanian Bus Contract

The following is an abbreviated and amended form of an actual cif contract used by UK exporters and foreign importers. Finance was arranged through a banker's documentary credit.

CONTRACT OF PURCHASE AND SALE OF OMNIBUSES, GROUPS OF RAILWAY MOTOR ENGINES, SPARE PARTS, CHASSIS, MATERIALS AND TOOLS

Present document witnesseth as follows:

OF THE ONE PART: The entity known as POWELL-GREENE MOTOR CO LTD OF SHEFFIELD England hereinafter called the *Vendor* represented by JOHN SMITH in his capacity of Head of Export Sales and of the other part the entity known as RURITRANS in the City of UTOPAVILLE Republic of Ruritania hereinafter called the *Purchaser* represented by Engineer JOSEF BROD in his capacity of General Manager. Both parties recognising their respective capacities enter into the present contract on the terms and conditions following:

[FIRST]

The Vendor hereby sells and the Purchaser hereby purchases the following:

(1) 125 Omnibuses ... which shall be manufactured by the Vendor in accordance with the technical specifications, plans and characteristics appearing in Schedule I which forms part of this Contract.

(2) Twelve complete groups of railway engines which shall be manufactured by the Vendor in accordance with the technical specifications and characteristics appearing in Schedule 2 which forms part of this Contract.

(3) Two chassis ... which shall be manufactured by the Vendor with a view to building two experimental Omnibuses for urban and intermunicipal use in accordance with the technical plans, specifications and characteristics appearing in Schedule 3 which forms part of this Contract.

(4) Spare parts for the Omnibuses and sets of railway engines to a value of ... subject to the conditions and stipulations mentioned in Schedule 4 which forms part of this Contract.

(5) Materials and tools which shall be used for the repair and reconstruction of Omnibuses parts and pieces up to a value of ... subject to the conditions and stipulations mentioned in Schedule 5 which forms part of this Contract.

[SECOND]

The price of each Omnibus is ... CIF Ruraport this price being deemed to include the price of each Omnibus FOB in the port of England indicated by the Vendor; all risks insurance as provided in paragraph 1 of clause 5 and ocean freight from English Port to the Port of Ruraport. The total price of the 125 Omnibuses ... the subject-matter of this Contract is ... CIF Ruraport.

[THIRD]

The Purchaser undertakes to pay to the Vendor in Pounds Sterling in London the total price of the products mentioned in clause No 2 of this Contract amounting to a total value of ... in the following manner ...

... The Vendor shall use its best endeavours to obtain from the British Government consent to vary the terms of payment in the manner following:

(1)   During the first year the amount shall be twelve per cent (12%)

(2)   During the second year the amount payable shall be thirteen per cent (13%)

(3)   During the third year ...

[FIFTH]

The buyer undertakes to open in favour of the Vendor an irrevocable letter of credit by the National Bank of Ruritania and guaranteed by it at District Bank, Midland Bank, Lloyds Bank, Moscow Narodny Bank, Westminster or any other by common accord ... and three months before that date of shipment which is set out ...

Bank charges originated by this letter of credit shall be for the account of the Purchaser and the Bank shall deliver the documents to the Purchaser against acceptance of the Bills of Exchange mentioned in paragraph (f) of this Clause.

The letter of credit shall be negotiable upon the presentation by the Vendor of the following documents:

(1)   For products received from England:

(a) Set of ocean bills of lading clean on board consigned to Ruritrans-Utopaville-Ruritania and four non-negotiable copies proving shipment with freight paid from port of shipment to Port of Ruraport.

(b) Commercial invoice in sextuplicate.

(c) Packing list in sextuplicate.

(d) Certificate of quality by the Vendor.

(e) Insurance policy issued in negotiable form by underwriters of Lloyds of England or a British Company in Pounds Sterling for one hundred per cent (100%) invoice price plus ten per cent (10%) covering marine risks (Institute cargo clauses – all risks) war risks (Institute war clauses) and strike, riots and civil commotion clauses (FSR and CC clauses of the Institute).

(f)   Ten (10) bills of exchange for acceptance by the Purchaser for ... the value of each shipment.

(g)   Sworn declaration by the Vendor certifying that it has marked the goods in accordance with the directions of the Purchaser and has sent to the latter non-negotiable copies of the documents listed above.

[SIXTH]

The purchaser undertakes to accept bills of exchange to the order of the Vendor for the value of each consignment of products . . .

The said bills of exchange shall be drawn by the Vendor against the Purchaser and accepted by the latter upon presentation accompanied by the relevant documents ...

[EIGHTH]

The spare parts in consignment which are to be supplied and maintained by the Vendor to and for the Purchaser shall be deposited in warehouses under the custody of the latter in the Republic of Ruritania for supply to the users of the omnibuses in Ruritania. These spares shall be the property of the Vendor until payment therefore by the Purchaser.

[NINTH]

The Purchaser undertakes to deliver to the Vendor before the 30th September 1995 a letter from the National Bank of Ruritania guaranteeing unconditionally all the payments which the Purchaser has to make to the Vendor under this contract in Pounds Sterling London ...

[TENTH]

The Vendor undertakes to notify the Purchaser within forty-eight hours (48 hours) following the departure of each vessel of the following: number of omnibuses shipped and/or number of packages of spare parts weight and volume of each of the same.

[ELEVENTH]

The Vendor warrants the Purchaser against any defect which might arise in the omnibuses the subject matter of this contract on the following conditions:

(a) For the term of six months as from the entry into use of the omnibuses.

(b) The alleged defect must be verified by the Vendor in Ruritania within a term of fifteen days subsequent to the date of receipt of the written notice which shall be given by the Purchaser.

(c) The Vendor may take possession of the defective part and send it for its account and expense to England.

(d) The replacement of the defective part may be effected by the Vendor from the warehouse of spare parts in consignment to the Purchaser failing which it shall be sent from the factory within a period of thirty days reckoned as from the date of receipt of claim by the Vendor.

(e) The repairs of defective parts may be effected direct by the Vendor or it may at its option compensate the Purchaser for the expenses which the latter may incur.

(f) This warranty is restrictive to the replacement of parts which become defective during the period established in paragraph (a) above due to defects of manufacture or the use of unsuitable materials but not due to improper use or inadequate maintenance ...

[TWELFTH]

If subsequently to the signature of this contract contingencies should arise such as fire, floods, droughts, disasters, hailstorms, earthquakes, war, military operations of any class, blockade or of any other class outside the control of the parties which totally or partially prevent the performance thereof by the parties, the period of time stipulated for performance of the contractual obligations shall be deemed to be extended for a period of time equivalent to the duration of such contingencies. In the event of these contingencies lasting more than six months each of the contracting parties is entitled to terminate the contract notifying the other party in writing. In this event neither of the parties shall be entitled to be compensated for any loss which might exist ...

The party prevented from performing its contractual obligations on account of any of the contingencies above mentioned shall immediately notify the other party in writing of the existence and duration of same.

The existence of such contingency and its duration in the country of the Vendor or the Purchaser must be proved by a certificate issued by the Chamber of Commerce of the country of the Vendor or the Purchaser respectively.

[THIRTEENTH]

The contracting parties agree to perform this contract in good faith. Any difference which might arise as a result of this contract shall be settled by means of amicable negotiations. If such negotiations should fail and it should not be possible to reach understanding the parties shall submit the matter in dispute to an arbitration tribunal whose decision shall be final. The arbitration tribunal shall be set up in the City of Utopaville and shall consist of a representative of each of the parties and a presiding arbitrator appointed by both parties by mutual agreement ... The award of the arbitration tribunal shall settle the amount of the arbitration expenses and the party which is to pay the same. An award adopted by a majority of votes shall be final and binding on both parties.

In witness of all the foregoing, both parties sign three copies, in Ruritanian, of the same tenor, in the commercial office of the Ruritanian Embassy in London, on the ... day of the month of ... 1995.

References and further reading

Atiyah (1990), *The Sale of Goods*, 8th edn, ch 20 'Export sales' and ch 22 'Bankers' commercial credits'.

Sassoon, 'The origin of FOB and CIF: terms and the factors influencing their choice' (1967) JBL 32.

Schmitthoff (1990), *The Export Trade*, 9th edn, ch 2 'Special trade terms in export sales' and Part 3 'The finance of export'.

Questions

(1) Identify clauses in the Ruritanian Bus Contract which reveal planning by the parties illustrative of Macaulay's first three 'creation of exchange relationship' issues:

(a) definition of performances;

(b) effect of defective performances;

(c) effect of contingencies.

Outline the nature and purpose of the parties' planning in each of these areas.

(2) What evidence is there in the contract as to;

(a) possible adjustments of the exchange relationship during its lifetime;

(b) the settlement of disputes by reference to potential or actual legal sanctions?

(3) Establish and discuss the links between Macaulay's four planning issues and the more traditional legal treatment of related matters.

4   The changing nature of contract

Our introduction to the planning and dispute-solving roles of contract in the last chapter drew us to a detailed examination of a highly significant form of contract much used in present day international business. Nevertheless most of our attention in Part One has so far been centred on the formative years of modern contract, the 19th century 'classical' model, influences on it and views and criticisms of it. Our aim was not merely to give an historical review but to give a clear picture of those basic ideas, doctrines and principles which to a large extent *still* underpin contract law today – and which therefore operate in the very changed circumstances of the modern world.

We have never suggested that the law has not changed during this century. Of course it has, but change has taken the form of adjustments to the 'classical' model and not on the basis of a grand scale reformulation of the law. The main theme of some modern critics of contract law is that a new model is required; the old one – even as amended – is unsatisfactory (and therefore often ignored) either as a guide to planning or as a means of dispute-solving.

What are these 'very changed circumstances of the modern world'? How have they affected the operation or function of contract as a mechanism for conducting exchanges? To what extent has contract law moved away from the 'classical' model? What picture of contract do current legal textbooks present? Will contract law and its 'context' come nearer together – into focus – so that the law can more effectively fulfil its functions? We must look at these questions and attempt some answers before moving on to a more detailed discussion of today's substantive law in Part Two. Statements made about the present state of the law are by no means universally accepted and, in a book of this nature, we must concentrate on the law as it stands rather than speculate or theorise on what it should or might be in the future. Some years ago there were signs that the Law Commission might attempt a reformulation, or at least a codification, of contract but the idea has seemingly lost its appeal.

The decline of freedom of contract

The key to an understanding of the changing nature and circumstances of contract lies in the concept of freedom of contract. As we saw, enthusiasm for freedom of contract went hand-in-hand with support for the operation of a free market. While reminding ourselves of basic flaws in these institutions, let us, through the agency of modern economic and legal analysis, begin to note something of the 'changed circumstances'. First the economists, Hunt and Sherman:

One's view of the desirability of the market system depends on whether one is more impressed with the efficacy and impersonality of this allocation mechanism or with its lop-sided results. Thus one defender of capitalism writes: 'The case for capitalism is at its strongest on the simple thesis that the market knows best how to allocate and use the scarce resource of capital.' A critic of capitalism sees it differently: 'The main reason that freedom of contract has never been as free as advertised – and it is a painfully obvious reason – is that sellers and buyers are not equal in bargaining power. So the terms of sale will simply reflect the power, or lack of it, that each party brings to the market place. So a market is also a financial slaughterhouse, where the strong chop up the weak.'

What is being stressed here is that where there is, as is frequently the case, a significant degree of imbalance between the bargaining strengths of the parties, freedom of contract becomes freedom to exploit or oppress. Equal treatment of unequals by the law results in injustice. Liberty is the myth; power is the reality, as Weber and others argued.

Next the lawyer, Friedrich Kessler:

The individualism of our rules of contract law, of which freedom of contract is the most powerful symbol, is closely tied up with the ethics of free enterprise capitalism and the ideals of justice of a mobile society of small enterprisers, individual merchants and independent craftsmen ... With the decline of the free enterprise system due to the innate trend of competitive capitalism towards monopoly, the meaning of contract has changed radically.

The allocation of resources in the British economy no longer centres on the free market contracts of 'small enterprisers' but on market or non-market operations of massive multinational corporate groups and governmental agencies. The importance of both the individual, and of contract itself, has declined.

In his chapter on 'The changing function of contract', Professor Wolfgang Friedmann in his book *Law in a Changing Society* (1972) examines the factors 'mainly responsible for a transformation in the function and substance of contract'. First he establishes what he considers to have been the four elements which summed up the social function of contract in its 19th century 'classical' era:

(1)   it was the legal key to the freedom of movement of goods, services and the factors of production;

(2)   it provided insurance against calculated economic risks (ie damages as a sanction); and it presupposed

(3)   freedom of will (or choice); and

(4)   equality between parties.

Friedman next identifies his four factors responsible for contract's 'transformation':

(a) The widespread process of concentration in business

The legal result of which is the *mass-produced standard form of contract* presented on 'take-it-or-leave-it' terms. By 'widespread process of concentration in business', Friedmann means much the same as Kessler when he speaks of 'the innate trend of competitive capitalism towards monopoly'. A variety of factors has contributed to this movement in Britain: cartelisation schemes designed, particularly in the inter-war years, to combat the worst effects of economic depression, the nationalisation of basic industries and the creation of the 'public sector' of the economy generally, the growth of trade associations, encouragement of mergers in the private sector; above all the development of mass production and the tendency for 'big fish to eat little fish'. These developments have given rise, as Friedmann states, to the 'same for everyone', 'take it or leave it' contract in many areas of trade and industry. Tickets, model forms, standard conditions: they are now the order of the contractual day.

This is a factor which clearly dilutes or removes the elements of both choice and consent in contract. Where equality has been lost – if it were ever in evidence – the law has, particularly in the last four decades, through, for example, consumer-protection legislation, sought to restore the balance; where near equality remains, as in inter-business dealings, the law tends not to intervene directly but to leave business people *free* to their own devices.

(b) The increasing substitution of collective for individual bargaining in industrial society

The legal result of which is the *collective bargaining agreement* between management and labour. As pointed out in Chapter 1, the contract of employment has, to a large extent, slipped out of the range of contract law over the last 50 years or so. Hence a detailed study of collective bargaining – another form of standard agreement – no longer finds a place in a general account of this kind. None the less it is clear that here we have a transformation which, while diminishing individual 'freedom of will' and consent, moves workers towards equality. Collective agreements are not binding in themselves and if the collective bargain is to be considered a proper study for lawyers, the task is best assigned to the specialist labour lawyer.

(c) The tremendous expansion of the welfare and social service functions of the state

The legal results being the increasing presence of *statutorily imposed terms of contract*, and the spread of *contracts to which government departments and other public authorities are themselves parties*.

The institutionalisation of contract – its use as an instrument of governmental social and economic policy through the medium of public control over terms – can be seen, again, in consumer-protection policy, in landlord-and-tenant legislation, and in measures to be found in statutes concerning sexual discrimination and equal pay at work. Choice and consent are sacrificed for the 'equity' that Durkheim sought. As Atiyah has said: 'The legislation of the past century has carried to great lengths the circumstances in which the individual's freedom of decision is overridden, either in the direct interests of a majority, or to give effect to values which a majority believe to be of overriding importance.' The greater is public control over terms, the less are contractual rights and duties the result of the parties' real agreement. (Inter-business dealings are less affected in this manner, as noted above.)

Also, as Friedmann indicates, the 20th century has seen a dramatic increase in the State's involvement in contract, not as a regulator but as a party. This involvement has primarily taken two forms. First, in its provision of, among other things, health-care, social security, education, motorways and defence, the State is required to buy in construction and engineering works, technical services and hardware and vast quantities of other supplies and materials from independent contractors. In 1984 government-procurement contracts were worth almost £15 million. It is in this area of public sector activity that contract has been the subject of major transformation. It is not merely that where the state is involved (here as purchaser) that we are, again, dealing with massive bargaining strength and standard, 'take it or leave it terms' but that the rules of what is essentially a private sector-based contract law have played and continue to play little or no part. Other extra-contractual mechanisms, in for example the resolution of disputes, have taken over as we will see in Chapter 8.

The second, related development regarding public sector contracting originally involved the taking into state-controlled public ownership such major utilities as gas, electricity and water supply, the coal industry, rail transport and health care in the course of nationalisation programmes introduced shortly after the second World War. Here the State, through public authorities such as the British Gas or the National Health Service is (or was) to be seen as supplier. We will see that in this context contract may play no part at all.

Since Friedmann's 1970s analysis, the pattern of contractual relationships between the State, the private business sector and the individual has changed to some extent but without any significant need to modify his original point. Increasingly, Conservative government privatisation schemes have meant that in recent years public services, both national and local (eg the prison service, refuse collection) are now being provided on a 'contracted-out' basis. Such functions are to that extent no longer carried out directly by public authorities but by private sector organisations under contract to the authority in question. The same 'free market' political philosophy has required that many public utilities be returned to the private sector or, like rail services, become subject to privatisation proposals. However, in contract terms, whether the service is provided by a public sector monopoly or a limited number of large-scale private organisations makes little difference to the consumer.

(d)   The spread of political and economic upheavals

Friedmann's fourth 'transformation of contract' factor is of a somewhat different nature: *the spread throughout the 20th century of such political and economic upheavals as war, revolution and inflation.* The legal result of such phenomena is the *judicial doctrine of frustration*, which allows a party to be excused from performance of his contract. We deal with frustration in Chapter 12 and it will be seen that physical and legal impossibility as legitimate excuses for non-performance of agreed obligations have, due to the political and economic vicissitudes of the 20th century, been augmented by commercial futility brought about by events beyond the parties' control. In such cases, as in other areas, the courts have more and more taken upon themselves a paternalistic role. Operating under principles of reason and justice they have, within limits, released the parties from their obligations. If, however, as in the Ruritanian Bus Contract, the parties have carefully planned for such contingencies by the use of an appropriate term in their agreement, a 'force majeure' clause, they can usually take care of the situation themselves without recourse to the courts.

What has been said so far in this chapter, and throughout Part One of the book, should be sufficient to convince us that changes in political ideology, in social and economic conditions, and, bit by bit, in the law itself have moved the *focus* away from freedom and sanctity of contract, voluntary agreement and the 'classical' model generally. However, it must be stressed that no new 'social welfare mixed economy model' has wholly taken its place. As Friedmann concluded: 'the character of contract as a legal instrument of contemporary society is undergoing profound changes, in which elements of the old mingle with the new'. If we take it that the 19th century contract law supported the free market system, what policy is revealed in present-day contract? To what extent has the law moved away from the 'classical' model?

There is a measure of agreement regarding a shift from clear doctrine, with relationships governed by principles and rules, toward less certain notions of 'fairness', 'reasonableness' and 'judicial discretion'. Contract law has always struggled to serve the conflicting aims of certainty and flexibility. Certainty, it is said, makes for predictability and a legal framework in which planned relationships can proceed with confidence. Advocates of flexibility argue that certainty leads to rigidity and a failure of the law to reflect the needs of a volatile and increasingly complex business world (see Lord Wilberforce's statement on p 3).

Of particular value in understanding these fundamental issues is the current analysis of judicial decision-making put forward by Adams and Brownsword in their book *Understanding Contract*. Their starting point is not what the law ought to be but what it is according to the traditional contract texts; what they call the 'rule-book' with 'an agreed litany of rules, principles and cases'. As their basis for establishing a critical approach to the 'rule-book' – an approach which, while generally absent in traditional presentations, will stimulate inquiry and promote understanding – Adams and Brownsword show how the 'rule-book' materials increasingly display clear signs of the *tensions* created by two *competing* general judicial philosophies. This tension is said to arise from two differing *judicial approaches* to decision-making: a *formalist* (following the 'rule-book') approach and a *realist* (result-orientated) approach. Out of a number of possible stances, a judge may be seen as a strict adherent to the 'paper rules' (a textural formalist) even at the expense of justice or commercial convenience, or he may be a 'strong realist', even an iconoclast (a Denning) for whom precedent is no bar to achieving the right result.

In addition to these *general* judicial ideologies, their analysis also requires account to be taken of the *specific* judicial contract law philosophies of 'market individualism' and 'consumer welfarism', which are *realist* philosophies and which 'dominate contractual thinking in practice'. They are described as follows:

> Market individualism has two limbs, a market philosophy and an individualistic philosophy. The market philosophy sees the function of the law of contract as the facilitation of competitive exchange. This demands clear contractual ground rules, transactional security, and the accommodation of commercial practice. The individualistic side of market individualism enshrines the landmark principle of 'freedom of contract' and 'sanctity of contract', the essential thrust of which is to give the parties the maximum licence in setting their own terms, and to hold parties to their freely made bargains ... judges should offer no succour to parties who are simply trying to escape from a bad bargain ...

> Consumer-welfarism stands for reasonableness and fairness in contracting. More concretely, this is reflected in a policy of consumer protection and a pot-pourri of specific principles. For example, consumer-welfarism holds that contracting parties should not mislead one another, that they should act in good faith, that a strong party should not exploit the weakness of another's bargaining position, that no party should profit from his own wrong or be unjustly enriched, that remedies should be proportionate to the breach, that contracting parties who are at fault should not be able to dodge their responsibilities, and so on. Crucially, consumer-welfarism subscribes to the paternalistic principle that contractors who enter into bad bargains may be relieved from their obligations where justice so requires.

It should be readily apparent that, in line with political and economic developments, 'consumer-welfarism' as described by Adams and Brownsword, has been the main driving force behind contract decision-making over the last 50 years or so, and that its influence has permeated the 'rule-book' to an increasing extent – a 'rule-book' previously dominated, during contract's 'classical' period, by the 'market-individualist' philosophy.

When finally one attempts to put the 20th century's 'transformation' of contract into overall perspective and in so doing provide the necessary insights into, a pathway through, the case law, it is possible to discern three outstanding and related features. First, as regards the institution of contract itself, as Friedmann emphasised, account must be taken of the new widespread use of the standard, non-negotiable form of contract and the vastly increased involvement of the State as both regulator and party. Second, following Macaulay, we must take continuing note of the business community's and the State's – the prime contract-makers-attitude towards and relationship with contract law and its planning and dispute-solving functions. Third, concerning the changing nature of the law itself, the essential point is that what has occurred is not so much a transformation but a bifurcation brought about in large part by the competing ideologies identified by Adams and Brownsword as 'market individualism' and 'consumer welfarism'. Throughout our examination of the case law we will meet shifts of approach by the courts away from traditional, 'classical' analysis to the provision, the availability, of a different approach to the issue in question. The tension that this creates may, according to the circumstances, be expressed in a variety of ways. For example, should the courts adopt a 'hands-off' approach or adopt a paternalistic, interventionalist role. Is the key objective freedom and facilitation of exchange for the parties or one of fairness, the protection of one party against the other? Are the requirements of contract-makers best served by legal certainty (real or supposed) or does justice requires flexibility in the law? Perhaps it may be said that contract theory is not, as Atiyah said, in a mess but that it has to serve so many different masters.

Preliminary conclusions

Before proceeding to a more detailed examination of issues that we have stressed as being significant, it is necessary to review the position so far:

(1)   Contract law is concerned with general principles – relating to agreement, terms and breach, frustration of the venture etc – which may operate alone or more likely together with further 'special' rules particular to the type of contract in question eg sale of goods, carriage by sea, etc.

(2)   The law is mainly judge-made (case law) but is also found to be in an increasing number of statutes, eg the Unfair Contract Terms Act, the Sale of Goods Act, etc.

(3)   The law was developed in the 19th century on the basis of the idea of freedom of contract – a concept which, with the absence of equality of bargaining strength, is inappropriate to modern imperfect markets.

(4)   Contract law has two main functions: planning and dispute-solving; business people and other parties may or may not utilise the law for these purposes.

(5)   Contract clauses may be drafted: (a) to take account of legal developments (statutory or judicial) so that the transaction is *in line with* the law, eg sex discrimination and equal pay legislation; or (b) to *avoid* the law, eg an arbitration clause seeks to keep disputes out of the courts (Ruritanian Bus Contract, clause 13); a 'force majeure' clause operates to control a situation after the occurrence of events (contingencies) which could otherwise involve the parties in a frustration of contract case (Ruritanian Bus Contract, clause 12).

(6)   The courts will, on a plaintiff's request, adjudicate upon a contractual dispute. An alleged breach, if proved, usually leads to an award of damages; however, note 5(b) above.

(7)   The business attitude to contract litigation is generally negative: cost is a major factor. On Macaulay's evidence, planning is more likely as regards definition of performances (particularly with complex products and/or payments systems: Ruritanian Bus Contract, clauses 1-10) and contingencies. Business people often plan to avoid the consequences of defective performance by the use, within legal limits, of exclusion and limitation of liability clauses.

(8)   Wide use is made in business of standard or model forms of contract especially where transactions are of a recurrent nature eg sales of mass-produced goods, local authority building projects, etc. There are, however, social dangers where standard forms are presented to parties whose lack of bargaining strength prevents them from resisting onerous clauses. Intra-business transactions may proceed in a 'legal limbo' through conscious avoidance or ignorance of the law.

(9)   Increasing statutory control of contracts must, however, increase awareness of the principles and rules of contract law, while at the same time reducing the extent to which contractual rights and duties stem from the parties' agreement.

(10) Many of the statutory and judicial measures in the field of contract over the last few decades have sought to restore some measure of equality into transactions (eg the attack on exclusion clauses and the doctrine of economic duress, see Chapter 9).

(11) The changing nature of the relationship between contract law, its political, economic and social environment, and business practice is at the heart of a proper understanding of this field of study. Changes in the context in which contract law functions have meant that the ('market individualistic') foundations of 'classical' contract law have given ground to new ('consumer-welfare') solutions in the courts.

In the remainder of this book, we will continue to be concerned with both the law and practice of contract. As in the export sales illustration, the two may go very much hand-in-hand – or they may not. At the same time we will examine the nature and importance of clauses frequently found in business contracts – price variation clauses, indemnity clauses, exclusion clauses, 'force majeure' clauses, liquidated damages clauses and arbitration clauses – and their relationship to, or standing in, the law.

We will be much concerned with problems of inequality of bargaining power, with economic pressure in contract and the role of government and the courts in producing checks and counter-balances to misuse of economic power. This will necessitate a scrutiny of standard-form contracting in both business and consumer transactions. Also, by examining government contracting and commercial arbitration, we are able to indicate other pressures on contract law to the extent that its functions are not fully utilised in those spheres of business life.

References and further reading

Adams and Brownsword (1994), *Understanding Contract Law,* 2nd edn.

Atiyah (1978), *From Principles to Pragmatism.*

Atiyah (1979), *The Rise and Fall of Freedom of Contract,* Part III, particularly chs 21 and 22.

Diamond, 'Codification of the law of contract' (1968) 31 MLR 361.

Friedmann (1972), *Law in a Changing Society,* 2nd edn, ch 4 'The changing function of contract'.

Gilmore (1974), *The Death of Contract,* Ohio State University Press.

Kessler, 'Contracts of adhesion – some thoughts about freedom of contract' (1943) 43 *Columbia Law Review* 629.

Treitel (1981), *Doctrine and Discretion in the Law of Contract.*

Questions

(1) Examine each of Friedmann's four social causes of the transformation of contract in terms of freedom and equality.

(2) The contents of contracts are frequently predetermined by statute, public authority or group pressure. Examine this statement in relation to the following cases:

    (a) *Wren v Holt* (1903);

    (b) *Willmore & Willmore v South Eastern Electricity Board* (1957);

    (c) *National Coal Board v Galley* (1958).

(3) 'All this remarkable infusion of checks, guides, directives, compulsions and prohibitions into the claim of free contracting manifests the sociological truth of what has become ... a juristic commonplace. That is that in so far as the law of contract places the coercions of the legal order behind the terms of a contract settled by private parties, the legal order may and indeed should set socially approved limits to the support which it gives to the terms which one party is in a position to impose on the other': Julius Stone.

    (a) In the light of the above, explain how and why the law in 1962 took away 'the support' which it previously gave to the railway company's terms in the case of *Thompson v London, Midland and Scottish Rly Co Ltd* (1930).

    (b) What legal device did the House of Lords use in *London and North Western Rly Co Ltd v Neilson* (1922), so as to refuse 'support' to the railway company's terms in this case?

(4) In order to obtain a clearer view at this stage of the legal meaning of frustration of contract (see Friedmann's fourth 'major factor' on p 43), read Lord Radcliffe's speech in *Davis Contractors Ltd v Fareham UDC* (1956) and be prepared to discuss it.

(5) How does the need for a balance between 'knowledge, analysis and context' apply to the study of contract law? (See the statement made by Sir Robert Goff quoted on p 3.)

PART TWO

5   Agreement: law and business practice

We are concerned in this chapter with the following questions:

(1) How do lawyers analyse the process by which the parties to a contract reach agreement?

(2) How does business practice relate to the legal analysis of agreement?

Most lawyers would say that the answer to the first question is well settled by the leading cases which provide a rational account of the negotiation and agreement process. However, others would say that the rules of offer and acceptance, on which the legal concept of agreement rests, are unsatisfactory – first because they are largely irrelevant to the conduct of business today, and second because they are often awkward tools if, and on the rare occasions when, they are called onto be used by the courts for the settlement of disputes. Who is right?

Contract law here as elsewhere works from a 19th century 'base line'. When asked, 'Is there a contract between the parties?' The lawyer's answer is that a contract comes into existence when there is an agreement between the parties which is supported by consideration. While consideration is analysed in terms of bargain or mutuality of obligation, agreement is traditionally established by the process of matching a firm offer from one party with the unqualified acceptance of the other. The relationship between offer and acceptance and the promises that generally constitute consideration is simple: the offeror's promise is set beside the acceptor's promise, the bargain is established and the contract is binding.

Critics of this view of the formation of contract assert that the offer-acceptance-consideration model presents an unrealistic, rigid and oversimplified view of business agreements. Concern is expressed therefore in terms of either the undue emphasis placed on the idea of binding promises, or on the 'ribbon-matching' offer and unqualified acceptance requirement of agreement in law. The critics complain that the degree of certainty required by the law offends against the need for a degree of flexibility in business that the law does not allow or appears not to allow. The American commentator Mooney is scornful of the traditional textbook analysis:

> We learned that there are certain expressions of mutual assent to which the law appends
> an obligation arising from the express or plainly implied 'promises' of the parties. The
> legal obligation is strictly limited to the promises. These promises are discovered in *the*
> unvarying method by which human beings contract with each other, namely by means of
> 'offers' embodying 'promises' directed by 'offerors' of particular 'offerees' who 'accept' by

> manifesting assent either by tendering a promise or an act ... Case variations were hung on
> the construct like ornaments on a Christmas tree, glittering but essentially useless.

It is argued that such an analysis grounds contract rules on a spurious operative act – the making of a promise – which, in the 'life-situation' of business, seldom occurs in the manner suggested by the normal connotations of the word 'promise'. Over-emphasis on promises reflects simplistic 'party autonomy' and 'as you promise so you shall be bound' views of contract and fails to pay attention to the realities of business negotiations, the safeguard and contingency 'buffers' which the parties themselves build into agreements, and the mass of contract terms now emanating from statutory provisions. Nevertheless, it is clearly dangerous to dismiss the idea of promise – and reliance on a man's word – altogether. However, without delving into the old case law on consideration, which has virtually no relevance to the business person's view of contract and is rarely of consequence in modern cases (as we will see in the next chapter), the concept of binding promises is of some historical significance to students of contract, and may at least remind them that a considerable period of time, during which much may happen, may elapse between formation and performance.

Also, although the courts' rules relating to agreement are based to a great extent on the relatively simple contractual situations of a century or more ago, they are not as immobile as some would suggest. It is easy enough to show that these rules are not as 'black-letter' as they sometimes appear. From a generally stated 'base line' they shade off towards a more realistic middle ground more in keeping with the complexity and merely approximate certainty of business life today. In a complicated commercial case a few years ago, *New Zealand Shipping Co Ltd v Satterthwaite & Co Ltd* (1975), Lord Wilberforce was of the opinion that:

> It is only the precise analysis of this complex of relations into the classical offer and acceptance, with identifiable consideration, that seems to present difficulty, but this same difficulty exists in many situations of daily life, eg sales at auction; supermarket purchases; boarding an omnibus; purchasing a train ticket; tenders for the supply of goods ... these are all examples which show that English law, having committed itself to a rather technical and schematic doctrine, in application takes a practical approach, often at the cost of forcing the facts to fit uneasily into the worked slots of offer, acceptance and consideration.

What is striking about this case is that a majority of their Lordships were willing to engage in an ingenious and robust analysis and application of the legal concepts of agreement and consideration in order to achieve 'commercial reality', whereas the minority stayed within the bounds of traditional analysis.

In the House of Lords in *Gibson v Manchester City Council* (1979), Lord Diplock, following an attack by Lord Denning in the Court of Appeal on an unvarying analysis of contracts into the form of offer and acceptance (see below), was willing to concede that:

> There may be certain types of contract, though I think they are exceptional, which do not fit easily into the normal analysis of a contract being constituted by offer and acceptance; but a

contract alleged to have been made by an exchange of correspondence between the parties in which the successive communications other than the first are in reply to one another is not one of these. I can see no reason in the instance case for departing from this conventional approach.

In the examination of the cases which follow, we will see that, albeit exceptionally, judges have been willing to discard strict offer and acceptance analysis and 'find' the existence of a contract in order to accommodate accepted business practice. We will also see how traditional analysis has been applied to new technological developments in electronic communications (employed by the parties); with more or less success to the 'battle of the forms' (the situation referred to when discussing Macaulay's article in Chapter 2 in which the parties consider they have an agreement but each considers that his terms apply) and to other aspects of business practice unknown at the time the law was first formulated.

Offer and acceptance: basic premise, definitions and related 'rules' or presumptions

Basic premise

The prime requisite of a contract is that the parties should have reached agreement and agreement is reached when an offer by one party is unequivocally accepted by the other. It is, however, immediately worth noting that numerous editions of Cheshire and Fifoot's *Law of Contract*, a traditional student textbook, issued this warning regarding offer and acceptance:

> It must again be emphasised that the phrase 'offer and acceptance', though hallowed by a century and a half of judicial usage, is not to be applied as a talisman, revealing, by a species of esoteric art, the presence of a contract. It would be ludicrous to suppose that businessmen couch their communications in the form of a catechism ... The rules which the judges have elaborated from the premise of offer and acceptance are neither the rigid deductions of logic nor the inspiration of natural justice. They are only presumptions, drawn from experience, to be applied in so far as they serve the ultimate object of establishing the phenomena of agreement.

The quotation above warns us against over-dependence on the 'rules' of offer and acceptance as problem-solvers where contract formation is concerned. The 'rules' must be used with extreme care in an area where considerations such as the parties' intention as revealed by their words or conduct, special circumstances, and policy may all play their part. The student's dilemma and a plea for pragmatism have been neatly put:

> The formation of contracts by offer and acceptance is an aspect of law that has always aroused considerable academic interest, primarily for the opportunity it offers to pose largely unrealistic problems that permit varied, inconclusive and interminable intellectual analysis. Generations of

students are acquainted with the noisy river that drowns the voice of the offeree as he accepts the offeror's offer (latterly a low-flying aircraft may be substituted for the clamorous flood); with the letter of acceptance that never arrives; with the epistolary revocation of offer that arrives after the letter of acceptance has been posted but before it has been delivered.

The academic approach may be criticised for a lack of pragmatism. Principles are sought by logical deductions without regard to the realities of the situation. The decisions of the courts, on the other hand, often demonstrate a reluctance to do more than decide the particular case on the particular facts, without regard for any general principles on which the decision may be securely based. The answer to the two differing approaches is, in this as in all aspects of life, a happy medium – a combination of the academic, which can help to create an intelligible and rationally defensible *corpus iuris*, and the pragmatic, which will not lose sight of the realities of the situation (Charles Lewis: see References and Further Reading).

Definitions, form and objectivity

An *offer* is an expression, by words or conduct, of a willingness to enter into a legally binding contract, and which by its terms expressly or impliedly indicates that it is to become binding on the offeror as soon as it has been accepted, usually by a return promise or an act on the part of the person (the offeree) to whom it is addressed. An *acceptance* is a final and unqualified expression of assent to the terms of an offer. Acceptance turns an offer, so defined, into agreement. As regards the *form* of the agreement, it comes as a surprise to many students to discover that only in certain cases does the law require it to be in writing. (The fact that transactions are frequently conducted on the basis of printed standard forms of contract is a matter of business expediency and is not a *legal* requirement.) Therefore a contract may be in writing, perhaps signed; it may be concluded verbally or even by conduct, or some mixture of all three: see the beginning of Chapter 7. A written contract is obviously the best evidence of its terms and, for example, as a consumer protection measure the Consumer Credit Act 1974 requires that hire purchase and other credit transactions be in writing and signed by the parties.

The legal view of agreement in also essentially *objective*: if the parties have to all outward appearances agreed in the same terms on the same subject-matter, generally neither can deny that he intended to agree. (We will see that this is subject to defences such as misrepresentation and mistake, etc.) A person's intention is that which the law (the reasonable man) will attribute to him on examining his words and conduct – which do *not necessarily* accord with what was in his mind. As discussed earlier, the subjective *consensus ad idem* theory, popular in the 19th century, that there could be no contract without a meeting of the minds of the parties ('the elusive mental element') has largely passed from the law: see, for example, the effect of the postal rules, below. In *Thake v Maurice* (1986), Mr Justice Peter Pain stated that: 'The test as to what the contract was does not depend on what the plaintiffs or the defendant thought it meant, but on what the court objectively determines that the words used meant.'

Offers, invitations to treat and other negotiating issues

Traditional analysis and an alternative approach

Where the crucial issue in a case is whether or not the parties have succeeded in concluding a binding agreement, the answer to the question traditionally rests on the court's ability or willingness in the first instance, when examining the negotiations between them, to find that one party has made an offer, for without an offer there can be no acceptance. Depending on the circumstances (there is no single approach), this may involve the court in *construing* the language used by the parties in order to establish whether, from an objective viewpoint, words used by one party show the necessary clear intention to be bound on specified terms. Or, alternatively, is there a definite promise to be bound provided the specified terms are accepted? In other words, does a statement made by one party match up to the legal definition of an offer?

As a general proposition, offers must be distinguished from other statements made at a pre-contractual stage which are known as *invitations to treat*, an old-fashioned expression (to treat with a person means to negotiate terms with him) covering statements which encourage the *other party* to negotiate further or to make a definite offer himself. It was on the basis of well-established, conventional analysis that the House of Lords in *Gibson v Manchester City Council* (1979) reached its decision in favour of the council and reversed the Court of Appeal where, as noted above, Lord Denning eschewed the traditional approach in the course of finding for Gibson and some 250 other tenants who considered that they had concluded a binding agreement to purchase their council houses from the defendants.

The dispute originally arose when the Labour council overturned the previous Conservative council's policy of selling off council houses to those tenants wishing to buy them. The scheme had been prepared on the basis of a simple form of documentation which did away with the normal legal formalities (exchange of contracts prepared by the parties' solicitors, etc) regarding such contracts. It was when the council changed political control and discontinued sales except in cases where there was a binding contract to sell that problems ensued. In *Storer v Manchester City Council* (1974), the Court of Appeal, adopting conventional offer and acceptance analysis, had decided that the simplified procedure followed by the parties (some 120 tenants, including Storer, and the council) had reached the stage at which a binding contract had been concluded and specific performance was ordered. S had applied to buy his council house, the town clerk had forwarded to him an 'Agreement for Sale' detailing the purchase price and mortgage arrangements and S had signed and returned the Agreement before the policy had been discontinued. Lord Denning stated that:

> [Mr Storer] had done everything which he had to do to bind himself to the purchase of the property. The only thing left blank was the date when the tenancy was to cease ... The corporation put forward to the tenant a simple form of agreement. The very object was to dispense with legal formalities. One

of the formalities – exchange of contracts – was quite unnecessary. The contract was concluded by offer and acceptance. The offer was contained in the letter of 9 March in which the town clerk said:

'I ... enclose the Agreement for Sale. If you will sign the Agreement and return it to me I will send the Agreement signed on behalf of the Corporation in exchange.'

The acceptance was made when the tenant did sign it, as he did, and return it, as he did on 20 March. It was then that a contract was concluded. The town clerk was then bound to send back the agreement signed on behalf of the corporation. The agreement was concluded on Mr Storer's acceptance. It was not dependent on the subsequent exchange.

The final point was this. Counsel for the corporation said that the town clerk did not intend to be bound by the letter of 9 March 1971. He intended that the corporation should not be bound except on exchange. There is nothing in this point. In contracts you do not look into the actual intent in a man's mind. You look at what he said and did. A contract is formed when there is, to all outward appearances, a contract. A man cannot get out of a contract by saying: 'I did not intend to contract', if by his words he has done so. His intention is to be found only in the outward expression which his letters convey. If they show a concluded contract that is enough.

In the later case, *Gibson v Manchester City Council* (1978), the purchasing procedure was slightly different and had not advanced as far as in *Storer*. Gibson represented the position of some 250 tenants:

G applied to the council for details of the price and mortgage terms applicable to the purchase of his council house. The City Treasurer replied that the council 'may be prepared to sell the house to you at £2,725 less 20% = £2,180. The letter gave details of the mortgage likely to be made available and asked G, if he wished to proceed, to make a formal application. This he did and the council took the house off the list of council-maintained properties. Before any further steps were taken, the policy was discontinued and the new council, as seen, resolved to proceed with sales only where contracts to sell had been concluded.

G claimed specific performance (an order that the contract be performed) on the basis that the City Treasurer's letter amounted to an offer which he had accepted. The Court of Appeal (by a majority) found in G's favour. Bearing in mind the court's decision in *Storer*, and prompted by considerations of fairness, but facing difficulties on the facts with conventional analysis, Lord Denning supported the decision as follows:

To my mind it is a mistake to think that all contracts can be analysed into the form of offer and acceptance. I know in some of the textbooks it has been the custom to do so; but as I understand the law, there is no need to look for a strict offer and acceptance. You should look at the correspondence as a whole and at the conduct of the parties and see therefrom whether the parties have come to an agreement on everything that was material. If by their correspondence and their conduct you can see an agreement on all material terms, which was intended thenceforward to be binding, then there is a binding contract in law even though all the formalities have not been gone through. For that proposition I would refer to *Brogden v Metropolitan Railway Co* (1877).

56

It seems to me that on the correspondence I have read (and, I may add, on what happened after) the parties had come to an agreement in the matter which they intended to be binding.

This approach (imbued with consumer-welfarism, see the extract from Adams and Brownsword on p 44) was, however, rejected by the House of Lords who adopted the traditional, formalist position. In Lord Diplock's words:

My Lords, there may be certain types of contract, though I think they are exceptional, which do not fit easily into the normal analysis of a contract as being constituted by offer and acceptance; but a contract alleged to have been made by an exchange of correspondence between the parties in which the successive communications other than the first are in reply to one another is not one of these. I can see no reason in the instance case for departing from the conventional approach of looking at the handful of documents relied on as constituting the contract sued on and seeing whether on their true construction there is to be found in them a contractual offer by the council to sell the house to Mr Gibson and an acceptance of that offer by Mr Gibson. I venture to think that it was by departing from this conventional approach that the majority of the Court of Appeal was led into error.

It was decided that no offer to sell had been made by the council. The City Treasurer's letter had stated that the council *may be prepared to sell* and it invited G *to make a formal application to buy.* No clear intention to be bound could be evinced on a true construction of the words used and the letter amounted to no more than an invitation to treat. It should also be noticed that two of the things that 'happened after' the correspondence (see Lord Denning, above) were that the council took the house off their maintenance list and Gibson made some alterations to the property. However, it cannot be said that the English courts recognise and protect reliance (in this case by Gibson) on *expected* contracts, although protection is afforded to reliance on agreed variations to *existing* contracts as will be seen in the next chapter. We will also see later in this chapter that Lord Denning's approach, whereby he was willing to look at the 'whole transaction' rather than insist on strict offer and acceptance analysis, has been applied in other cases and so it cannot be said that it has been entirely rejected.

Advertisements, displays of goods and policy choices

It has been stated above that the key to formation problems is to find the offer as manifested by a party's clear intention to be bound. Unfortunately in this area we have to tread carefully and may well have to qualify our previous assertion. Does a display of goods in a shop window or on the shelves of a supermarket with a price attached amount to an offer? One would think so and presumably shopkeepers who display signs reading 'Special Offers – Exceptional Bargains' and the like think so too. However, as early as the mid-19th century in the case of shop displays, the courts took a different view, which was endorsed in the supermarket case of *Pharmaceutical Society of Great Britain v Boots Cash Chemists (Southern) Ltd* (1953):

> A Boots customer selected goods from the shelves and presented them at the cash desk where she paid the price. Some of the goods were required by the Pharmacy and Poisons Act 1933 to be sold only under the supervision of a registered pharmacist. A pharmacist was present at the cash desk for this purpose. Boots were alleged to have infringed the Act.
>
> When did the sale take place? The society argued that it was when the customer put the goods into her wire basket, so accepting the offer constituted by their display on the shelves. If this were so, certain medicines and poisons would be 'sold' without supervision (and possible intervention) and therefore contrary to the Act.
>
> The Court of Appeal however disagreed and ruled that the sale took place at the cash desk. The display of the goods did not mean that they were on offer; an offer to buy was made by the customer at the cash desk subject to supervision and possible refusal. The display of goods was merely an invitation to treat.

This decision really rests on a policy choice supporting commercial convenience (for example, offers may be refused) rather than on orthodox, formalist analysis of contract formation. The issue usually arises in the context of criminal statutes and the *Boots* ruling has led to difficulties, see *Pilgram v Rice-Smith* (1977). Nevertheless, it has been applied to the display of priced goods in a shop window in *Fisher v Bell*, a case involving the alleged offence of 'offering for sale' a 'flick knife' contrary to the Restriction of Offensive Weapons Act 1959. Although the statute was clearly intended to cover the situation, it was held that the display was merely an invitation and that no offence had been committed.

It has been argued that the law would be better served to regard displays or advertisements as offers subject to the condition (sometimes found in advertisements) that stocks remain available. Parties may of course indicate that their statements do not constitute offers, eg estate agents: 'These particulars do not form, nor constitute any part of, an offer, or a contract, for sale.' Advertising takes a wide variety of forms. It is highly unlikely that it will be possible to identify an offer in a television commercial. Even where an advertisement, say in a catalogue or in the 'For Sale' columns of a newspaper, contains specific wording, a court will almost certainly, on the basis of the 'limited stocks' argument, regard the advertisement as an invitation to treat. This was 'business sense' according to Lord Parker in *Partridge v Crittenden* (1968), another statutory offence (Protection of Birds Act 1954) case in which the defendant inserted in a periodical a notice stating 'Bramblefinch cocks and hens 25s each'. If the advertisement had been construed as an offer and demand had exceeded the defendant's supply, he would at least in theory have faced any number of breach actions, as well as being guilty of an offence.

This is not to say that an advertisement can never be construed as an offer. In the famous case of *Carlill v Carbolic Smoke Ball Co* (1893), Bowen LJ stated that the advertisement in question 'was intended to be understood by the public as an offer to be acted upon' and Lindley LJ said: 'Read this how you will ... here is a distinct promise, expressed in language which is perfectly unmistakeable, that £100 will be paid by the Carbolic Smoke Ball Co to any person who contracts influenza after having used the ball three times daily, and so on.'

> The defendant company produced a medical preparation called 'The Carbolic Smoke Ball'. They inserted an advertisement in the 'Pall Mall Gazette' in which they offered to pay £100 to anyone who caught influenza after having used the Smoke Ball in a specified manner and for a specified period of time. They also stated that they had deposited £1000 with the Alliance Bank as a sign of their good faith.

> On the strength of the advertisement, Mrs Carlill bought a smoke ball from a chemist, used it as prescribed, but nevertheless caught influenza. It was held that there was a contract between the parties and that the plaintiff could recover £100.

In finding that the company's advertisement was to be construed as an offer, the court rejected the claim that it was 'a mere puff', ie vague and non-actionable sales talk. The offer was of a type known as an offer to the world at large which 'is to ripen into a contract with anyone who comes forward and will perform these conditions ... It is not like cases in which you offer to negotiate'. The offer therefore constituted an express promise to pay £100 to any party who fulfilled its terms. A *unilateral* contract, consisting of a promise in return for a stipulated *act* (as distinguished from a bilateral contract consisting of reciprocal binding promises, see Chapter 1) was created when Mrs Carlill used the smoke ball as prescribed. At that point she was to be regarded as both accepting the company's offer (that normal communication of acceptance was not required was inferred from the wording of the offer and the nature of the transaction) and providing the necessary consideration (an act which put Mrs Carlill 'to some inconvenience at the request of the defendants'). Finally, the offer was seen as a serious one, showing an intention to create legal relations and therefore imposing a legally enforceable obligation on the company. (If it is complained that the concepts of agreement and consideration were somewhat 'stretched' by this decision, it is clear that policy issues underlay the court's ruling: this was the age of 'quack' medical preparations, the defendants were rogues and they did not deserve to succeed.)

Tenders, reasonable reliance or legitimate expectation

Contracts governing important, high-cost business projects (eg major construction or engineering works or the supply of military or other equipment) are usually negotiated on a competitive tender basis, whereby interested parties are invited to bid for the contract work. The request of tenders may be communicated by an advertisement or it may only apply to a selected group of companies.

As such, the request would normally be seen as an invitation to treat and a contractor who chose to submit a tender (a priced quotation) would thereby be making an offer, which might be accepted or not. Unless the initial invitation stated that the contract would be awarded to the lowest bidder, *any* tender may be chosen on a 'value for money' basis. For example, in March 1995 the government decided to buy a mixed fleet of 35 helicopters from a British/Italian consortium and a US company at a cost of £1.2 billion rather than accept a £300 million lower bid from the US company alone. This option was taken against financial advice from the Ministry of Defence but was justified on the ground that it safeguarded 5,000 British jobs.

If a request for a tender clearly indicates that the lowest (or, where the requester is a seller, the highest) bid will be successful, it will be an offer. In *Harvela Investments Ltd v Royal Trust Co of Canada Ltd* (1986), sellers of shares invited tenders from two parties and bound themselves to accept the higher bid which complied with the 'single sum' terms of the invitation. A bid was accepted by the sellers which, although the higher, was arguably not in compliance with the seller's terms. It was held that the invitation to bid was an offer to be bound by whichever bid was the higher. This offer was made to both potential buyers and was unilateral (cf the offer in *Carlill*) as it requested (ie without creating any obligation to do so) the performance of an act, the submission of the higher bid (conforming to the seller's instructions) and which, when once performed, converted the invitation into a bilateral contract of sale to the higher bidder. As the bid which had been 'accepted' did not conform to the seller's own instructions, it was invalid. The invalid bid had stated a fixed sum (slightly lower than the other bid) but alternatively 100,000 Canadian dollars in excess of any other offer. By accepting that bid, the sellers were breaking their own 'single sum' rules and the plaintiff merited protection from such absence of good faith.

A similar situation arose in *Blackpool and Fylde Aero Club v Blackpool Borough Council* (1990), in which the judicial device of implying (or 'finding') a collateral (additional but subordinate) contract was again utilised to protect the legitimate expectations of a party during negotiations prior to the main contract, the possible conclusion of which was thwarted by the defendant council's failure to adhere to its own terms:

> The council invited tenders for a concession to operate pleasure flights from Blackpool airport, the tenders to be submitted by noon on a given day. The Aero Club (who had operated the flights prior to the licence coming up for renewal) submitted a tender in time but, due to an error on the part of a council employee, it was marked as having been received late and was consequently not considered. The concession was awarded to another bidder. The Club's claim that the council was in breach of a contract to consider all valid bids was upheld.

This was a contract governing the conduct of the tendering procedure as laid down by the council itself. As Bingham LJ observed:

> Where, as here, tenders are solicited from selected parties all of them known to the invitor, and where a local authority's invitation prescribes a clear, orderly and familiar procedure ... the invitee is in my judgment protected at least to this extent: if he submits a conforming

tender before the deadline he is entitled, not as a matter of mere expectation but of contractual right, to be sure that his tender will after the deadline be opened and considered in conjunction with all other conforming tenders.

(This case should be considered in conjunction with *Gibson v Manchester City Council*, above.)

Letters of intent, expectations and agreement

A letter of intent (sometimes called 'an instruction to proceed') states that the sender *intends* to enter into a contract with the addressee. This is a common device, particularly in the construction industry, and business people rely on such letters and are often called onto, and in fact do, commence performance on the basis of them, even through the contract has yet to be fully negotiated and concluded by the parties. Although on its true construction, such a letter probably creates no obligations on the parties, where it embodies an instruction to proceed with performance and such performance has begun, the contract when it is eventually agreed will relate back to the performance that has taken place: the contract has retrospective effect, as seen in the case of *Trollope and Colls Ltd v Atomic Power Construction Ltd* (1962):

> In February 1959 TC as sub-contractors submitted to main contractors AP a tender for civil engineering work in the construction of a nuclear power station. The tender was for a lump sum price and incorporated conditions authorising variations in the form, quality or quantity of work, such variations to be taken into account in ascertaining the contract price. The tender further incorporated a fluctuation clause relating to labour and material costs.
>
> Considerable changes were made in the work by the Central Electricity Generating Board, after the date of tender, necessitating amendment of drawings, specification and bills of quantities.
>
> TC were notified of these changes and in June they were asked to start work by a 'letter of intent': 'We have to inform you that it our (AP's) intention to enter into a contract with you for [the works]. As soon as matters outstanding between us are settled we will enter into a contract agreement with you, and in the meantime please accept this letter as an instruction to proceed with the work necessary to permit you to meet the agreed programme.'
>
> On 11 April 1960 all outstanding matters were agreed although no contract was signed. TC contended that they should be paid on a value of work done (quantum meruit) basis (see below) for the work carried out before this agreement, rather than on the basis of the original tender as adjusted by variations, since there was no binding contract on those terms.
>
> It was held that the parties having acted in the course of negotiations on the understanding and in the anticipation that, if and whenever a contract were made, it would govern what was being done meanwhile, the contract which came into existence on 11 April 1960, could rightly be supported as governing the rights of the parties as to prior work, on either of two grounds: (i) by the implication of a stipulation, necessary for the business efficacy of the contract, that the variations clauses should apply retrospectively, or (ii) that the tender constituted an offer that contemplated variation of the work and the ultimate acceptance of that

offer was, in the circumstances, an acceptance of the offer as applied to and embracing the changes requested and agreed in anticipation of the ultimate acceptance.

Megaw J concluded that there is 'no principle of English law which provides that a contract cannot in any circumstances have retrospective effect'.

A similar situation arose in the case of *Trentham Ltd v Archital Luxfer Ltd* (1993), in which performance again took place before a contract came into existence; moreover it was, according to the leading judgment in the Court of Appeal, a contract which could not 'be precisely analysed in terms of offer and acceptance'. In this latter regard, this unanimous decision of the Court of Appeal therefore again focuses attention on Lord Denning's 'alternative' approach to agreement as seen in the *Gibson* case above. Whether the contract in *Trentham* was one of the 'exceptional' types of contract which, in *Gibson*, Lord Diplock hinted might allow for a departure from the conventional approach (the transaction in *Trentham* was wholly performed) awaits an authoritative ruling from the House of Lords:

TL, main contractors engaged by a client to design and build industrial units, entered into negotiations with ALL for them to supply and install aluminium windows on a sub-contract basis. This work was completed and paid for but, following the making of arbitration awards totalling £900,000 against TL in proceedings brought by the client under the main contract for delays and defects, TL sued ALL (and others) for an indemnity. They alleged defects in the windows and thus breach of ALL's sub-contract. ALL denied the existence of any sub-contract.

No written sub-contract had come into existence but TL claimed that a binding contract was nevertheless formed on the basis of written exchanges, oral discussions and particularly the performance of the transaction by both parties.

Steyn LJ, delivering the only full judgment, held that 'in this fully executed transaction a contract came into existence during performance even if it cannot be precisely analysed in terms of offer and acceptance.' He based this decision on the following points:

1   English law adopts an *objective* approach to contract formation: 'the governing criterion is in the reasonable expectations of [in this case] ... sensible business people'.

2   Although the coincidence of offer and acceptance is the normal mechanism of contract formation, 'it is not necessarily so in the case of a contract alleged to have come into existence during and as a result of performance.' *Gibson* was cited at this point.

3   The fact that the transaction was executed (ie wholly performed by both parties) made it impossible to argue that there was no intention to create legal relations or that the contract was void for uncertainty (see below).

4   If a contract only comes into existence during and as a result of performance of the transaction, it will frequently be possible to hold that the contract impliedly and retrospectively covers pre-contractual performance: see *Trollope and Colls Ltd*.

Before moving on to examine situations such as those in *Trollope and Colls* and *Trentham* but where *no* contract can be established, it is of interest to reflect on the 'contractual' nature in the Macaulay sense (see Chapter 2) of transactions in the construction industry. Detailed planning by means of standard form contracts is the norm; such contracts deal with delay and penalties for delay, and they provide for disputes to be settled by arbitration (see Chapter 13). Decisions such as these also, in the face of formalist analysis, bring the law into line with the reality of practice in this field.

What is the position if no contract can be found in these circumstances? The decision in *Peter Lind & Co Ltd v Mersey Docks and Harbour Board* (1972) shows that where work is done and accepted, it is possible for the contractor to recover on a non-contractual, restitutionary (quantum meruit) basis at a reasonable rate for the benefit conferred on the other party. In *British Steel Corporation v Cleveland Bridge & Engineering Co Ltd* (1984) the problem arose again:

> CBE entered into negotiations with BSC for the supply of a number of steel nodes and issued a letter of intent to BSC requesting them to start work 'pending the preparation and issuing to you of the official form of sub-contract'. BSC declined to contract on CBE's terms (BSC had their own standard forms of contract), a particular 'sticking point' being the question of liability for loss caused by late delivery. Negotiations continued but no agreement was reached. Nevertheless all but one of the modes were delivered; the last one being held back firstly by BSC because they had received no payment and later as a result of a strike. It was eventually delivered.
>
> BSC sued for the value of the nodes on a quantum meruit, restitutionary basis, arguing that no contract had been concluded and CBE counterclaimed for damages of a higher amount for late delivery.
>
> It was held by Robert Goff J that the parties had not reached agreement and no contractual relationship had come into existence. Thus the work performed under the letter of intent was not referable to any contract terms as to payment and performance. BSC recovered £230,000 on its quantum meruit claim but CBE's counterclaim for £870,000 failed, there being no binding terms regarding delivery or payments for late delivery for the claim to be measured against.

What these cases reveal is that business pressure can create a dangerous 'no man's land' between practice and the conventional view of contract formation. To some extent the *Trentham* approach closes that gap and, as regards the above case, it may be that even as main contractors CBE were naive to think they could impose terms on such a powerful organisation as British Steel.

Acceptance of the offer

It is clear that, despite occasional inroads, traditional offer and acceptance analysis remains dominant when agreement issues reach the courts. Our attention will now focus on acceptance. Acceptance, denoting assent to the terms of the offer, transforms the offer into agreement and, on the basis of the 'ribbon-matching' or 'mirror image' requirement, an acceptance must correspond exactly to the terms of the offer. Criticism of this insistence on a 'perfect fit' has already been noted and, as Treitel has remarked: 'When parties carry out lengthy negotiations it may be hard to say exactly when an offer has been made and accepted ... Business people do not, any more than courts, find it easy to say precisely when they have reached agreement' but a court must 'decide whether an apparently unqualified acceptance did in fact conclude the agreement'.

It is this approximate certainty in inter-business contracts which refuses to fit neatly into the 'doctrinal handcuffs' of rigidly interpreted rules. As Macaulay shows, business people are much less strict than lawyers as regards contractual certainty; directors or managers often feel that insistence on adherence to contractual 'detail' is bad for continuing business relations and, in any case, it may be bad policy to tie oneself at the time of agreement to an uncertain future. While acceptance must be unconditional, the agreement itself may be hedged round with a variety of adjustment devices – renegotiation clauses, price variation clauses and so on – to allow for desired flexibility as performance proceeds.

Trollope and Colls and *Trentham* reveal another side to approximate business certainty created by the need for main contractors to co-ordinate the work of sub-contractors when facing completion dates. In his book, *Government Procurement and Contracts*, Colin Turpin cites an amazing statement made by the Chief of Defence Procurement in 1986: 'We know that in these major contracts everything is fine while the project is running well but when a project goes wrong everybody starts reading the contract. We want to be sure that when we read it still means what we hoped it meant at the beginning.'

Returning to the general contract 'rules', it follows that once an effective acceptance has come about (in writing, orally or by conduct), the offeror can no longer withdraw his offer. Two further 'rules' follow: (i) to be effective, the withdrawal of an offer (like the offer itself) must be communicated to the offeree (before acceptance), and (ii) acceptance of an offer is not (normally) effective until communicated to the offeror. Difficulties in this area tend therefore to centre on questions of *correspondence* ('ribbon-matching') and *communication*.

Counter-offers, inquiries and the 'battle of the forms'

An offeree's response to an offer which significantly differs from the offeror's terms is a counter-offer, which does not amount to acceptance. It is a rejection of the original offer and brings it to an end:

In *Hyde v Wrench* (1840), W offered to sell his farm to H for £1,000. H in reply said he would give £950 for it. W turned down this proposal. Later H wrote that he was prepared to pay £1,000 after all. This communication was ignored, and H sued to enforce an alleged sale at £1,000. It was held that no contract existed. H had rejected W's original offer by his counter-offer of £950 and he was unable to revive it by changing his mind and tendering a purported acceptance – which was nothing more than a new offer which W was entitled to refuse.

In *Northland Airliners Ltd v Dennis Ferranti Meters Ltd* (1970), the sellers, a company in North Wales, negotiated with the buyers, a Canadian company, for the sale of an amphibian aircraft. The sellers sent the following telegram: 'Confirming sale to you Grummond Mallard aircraft ... Please remit £5,000.' The buyers replied: 'This is to confirm your cable and my purchase Grummond Mallard aircraft terms set out your cable ... £5,000 sterling forwarded your bank to be held in trust for your account pending delivery ... Please confirm delivery to be made thirty days within this date.' The sellers did not reply but sold the aircraft to a third party at a higher price. The Court of Appeal held that there was no contract. The buyers' reply introduced two new terms, one as to payment and the other as to delivery, and the sellers were not bound to reply to this counter-offer.

However, an inquiry as to *whether* the offeror might modify his terms does not necessarily amount to a counter-offer. In *Stevenson, Jacques & Co v McLean* (1880), it was held that S could still accept M's offer of a certain quantity of iron 'at 40s nett *cash* per ton', even though he had telegraphed to M requesting details of possible credit terms. Bearing in mind that, as was known, S was buying for re-sale in an unsettled market, his words were 'nothing specific by way of [counter] offer or rejection, but a mere inquiry which should have been answered'.

The main significance today of the counter-offer rule lies in its use in litigation over the 'battle of the forms'. It is not uncommon to find business buyers and sellers who, although 'agreed' in Gurvitch's 'rapprochement' sense, are 'separated' by the express wording of their respective contractual documents. This is markedly so where standard forms are prepared by each party setting out the terms and conditions on which he will do business. In some instances, whether these forms are properly examined and understood by the parties is open to doubt. The case of *Butler Machine Tool Co Ltd v Ex-Cell-O Corporation Ltd* (1979) is illustrative of one sequence of events which gave rise to the 'battle of the forms', and to which the Court of Appeal rather unconvincingly applied traditional counter-offer analysis. The facts may be illustrated as follows:

Buyer/Ex-Cell-O		**Seller/Butler Machine**
	Inquiry	
(1) B	————————————————————	S
	Quotation: standard conditions of sale	
(2) B	————————————————————	S
	'to prevail over any terms and conditions in the buyer's order'	
	Order: standard conditions of purchase	
(3) B	————————————————————	S
	with tear-off acknowledgement slip: 'We accept your order on the terms and conditions stated thereon'	
	Acknowledgement slip returned	
(4) B	————————————————————	S
	but with covering letter referring back to quotation	
	Goods delivered	
(5) B	————————————————————	S
	and accepted	

The buyer's terms differed significantly from the seller's. On whose terms, if anyone's, was the contract made? The court held that the seller's quotation (2) was an offer, the buyer's order (3) a counter-offer: cf *Hyde v Wrench* above, and the seller's return of the acknowledgement slip (4) an acceptance of the buyer's counter-offer. The contract was therefore made on Ex-Cell-O, the buyer's terms.

The significance of this finding was that although the price quoted by Butler was £75,500, the seller's terms contained a 'price-escalation' clause (under which Ex-Cell-O was to pay at prices ruling at the date of *delivery*) but the buyer's terms did not. When the seller tried to invoke the clause, claiming a further £3,000, this dispute arose, resulting in the sellers eventual failure in the Court of Appeal. (Lord Denning drew attention to the seller's delayed delivery; perhaps costs had increased mainly as a result of this delay.) It has been said that the court's ignoring of the seller's covering letter (4) 'may be unconvincing to some, because it seems plain that the sellers did intend to re-import their terms and conditions into the bargain'. If this letter had been taken to be another counter-offer, it could be said that the buyer's acceptance of delivery (5) was acceptance by conduct of that counter-offer, in which case the seller's terms would have prevailed. Or would the buyer's lack of previous response to (4) have meant that there was *no* contract: see *Felthouse v Bindley* below, with the result that, although accepting delivery, the buyer's liability would therefore have been non-contractual – to pay a reasonable price as in the *Peter Lind* case above?

Other 'battle of the forms' cases have been decided as follows. The first reveals the 'hit or miss' nature of the outcome where, as seems likely, the relevant words or documents are not read by the parties. In *British Road Services v Arthur Crutchley Ltd* (1968), BRS delivered a large consignment of whisky to C's warehouse. The driver handed C a delivery note which incorporated BRS conditions of carriage. The note was stamped by C – 'Received under (C's) conditions'. The court held that this amounted to a counter-offer, which BRS accepted when handling over the whisky (which was later stolen). The contract was therefore concluded on C's terms.

In *Cie de Commerce et Commission SARL v Parkinson Stove Co Ltd* (1953), P sent to C (foreign sellers) an order for a quantity of steel sheets on a printed form containing the following provision: 'This order constitutes an offer on the part of (P) on the terms and conditions and at the prices stated herein and to constitute a binding contract on (P), said offer must be accepted by execution of the acknowledgement in the form attached by (C), it being expressly understood that no other form of acceptance, verbal or written, will be valid or binding on (P).'

C omitted to sign and return the acknowledgement slip attached to the form, but on receipt of the order replied to P: 'We acknowledge receipt of ... your order No. K. 4851 dated March 5, which we received today and for which we thank you.'

Subsequent correspondence left no doubt that the parties regarded themselves as bound. However, P cancelled the order. C sued for breach and P claimed that there was no concluded contract, (a) by reason of C's failure to return the acknowledgement slip, or alternatively, (b) assuming that strict compliance with the request for return of the slip was not necessary to create a contract, because C's letter of acknowledgement could not be construed as a sufficient acceptance of P's offer.

Neither argument found favour at first instance, but the Court of Appeal held that there was no concluded contract and, accordingly, that C were not entitled to damages. It was felt that C's letter of acknowledgement, which did not strictly adhere to the terms of the offer, did not amount to an acceptance of the order.

It is difficult to disagree with the case note commentator who wrote: 'It is submitted that the [French] plaintiffs may in the circumstances be forgiven if they are left with a feeling that the requirements of the English law of contract are none too easy to fulfil. It is difficult to envisage how they could have more clearly indicated their acceptance of the order, short of returning the acknowledgement slip itself.' The eventual decision is scarcely an illustration of what Pilcher J, in the court of first instance, referred to as the tendency of the courts 'always [to] lean towards giving legal effect to documents which the parties themselves regard as constituting a binding contract in law'.

Communication issues

As the *Smoke Ball* case shows, unilateral contracts call for acceptance by performance of the act requested and embodied in the offer and there is no requirement, contrary to the general 'rule' that the offeree's acceptance be communicated to the offeror (unless the offeror requires it). The general 'rule' is that acceptance is not effective – it does not create a contract – until it is communicated to the offeror. There is therefore a need for some clear and definite manifestation of acceptance of which the offeror must be apprised. Mental acceptance or mere acquiescence, without more, is not sufficient even where, in a bilateral contract situation, the offeror waives the need for communication by indicating that acceptance by silence will suffice: see *Felthouse v Bindley* (1863).

The means by which parties can communicate with each other nowadays are many and varied: face-to-face or on the telephone (with or without an answering service); by post, telemessage or telegram; by telex, fax machine or e-mail. Also as business is becoming more and more impersonal with the growth of large-scale organisations, just what is meant by effective communication of acceptance can be a difficult question. The 'rule' is only a starting point; it may not meet special circumstances. Here are some of the points that may arise.

Acceptances made by an instantaneous (as if speaking face-to-face) form of communication, eg by telephone, telex or fax, conform to the general 'rule' – they have no effect until communicated to the offeror. In *Entores Ltd v Miles Far East Corporation* (1955), the Court of Appeal held that a telexed acceptance took place *where* it was received (in England) not where it was sent (in Holland). If there is a fault, either the offeree or the offeror will be aware of the failure of communication and only when the fault is rectified and acceptance complete will there be a contract. As regards the exact *time* at which acceptance is received, in *The Brimnes* (1975) a telex withdrawal of a ship from a charterparty appeared on the charterer's telex machine between 5.30 and 6.00 pm (within office hours) on 2 April but was not read until the following day. It was held that the withdrawal was effective when it appeared on the machine. By analogy, an acceptance received during office hours would be effective when received by the telex or fax machine. The following case was based on facts similar to those in *Entores*:

> In *Brinkibon Ltd v Stahag Stahl* (1983), B, an English company, sought leave to serve on S, an Austrian company, notice of a writ claiming damages for breach of a contract to supply B with a consignment of mild steel bars. The contract was formed by means of (1) a telex message from S in Vienna to B in London, amounting to a counter-offer, and (2) another telex sent the next day by B to S which was an acceptance of that offer. It was held that the contract was made when and where the acceptance telex was received – in Vienna. Leave to serve the writ was therefore refused.

In this case the House of Lords gave a qualified endorsement of *Entores*, warning that its 'rule' could not be applied universally in view of the many variants in the use of telex. Where communication was not instantaneous (as, for example, where the message was sent out of office hours with the intention that it would be read at a later time), the position was to be resolved by reference to the parties' intentions, by sound business practice and, in some cases, by a judgment as to where the risk should lie.

If communication is not instantaneous, at what time is it effective? When all else fails, the concept of reasonableness is at hand. For example, Stone, when remarking on the 'not particularly helpful' lead given by the House of Lords in *Brinkibon*, continues:

> ... in so far as any general principle can be read into it, it would seem ... that the communication should take effect at the time when the acceptor could reasonably have expected it to be read ... There does not seem to be any reason for treating faxes differently from telex, but electronic mail, sent to an electronic 'post-box' which will only be checked once or twice a day, might well be said only to be communicated once the time for checking has passed. A similar approach might need to be used in relation to messages left on a telephone answering system. That is, the message should only be regarded as communicated once a reasonable time has elapsed to allow it to be heard by the offeror.

> If this line is taken, it is clearly to the advantage of the acceptor, in that it allows an acceptance to be treated as effective although the offeror may [he may have read or listened to the acceptance before a reasonable time has elapsed] be unaware of it (as is the case under the postal rule).

Communication: the acceptance postal 'rule' and revocation of the offer

As an exception to the general 'instantaneous rule', an offer is regarded as effectively accepted, where the post is the recognised medium of communication, as soon as the letter of acceptance is properly put into the hands of the Post Office. The issue arose in *Adams v Lindsell* (1818) in which the court concerned itself more with questions of speed, early reliance (by the offeree) and convenience rather than logic. To hold that a posted acceptance must reach the offeror before it could be effective would, in the court's view, be impractical and inefficient. (What does 'reach the offeror' mean? Whenever that is, the offeree/acceptor is then 'in the dark'.)

This communication exception (which also applies to telemessages and telegrams) can produce bizarre results. It was affirmed by the Court of Appeal in *Household Fire Insurance Co v Grant* (1879), a case which involved non-performance in relation to a contract of shareholding by an offeror who was ignorant of the fact that acceptance had taken place; the letter of acceptance having been lost in the post. It has been said that where the postal rule applies offerees are protected in all such transactions at the price of hardship to offerors in a very few of them. Certainly, the offeror is put at risk to the extent that he is bound by a contract before he is aware of the fact. To avoid this risk, the prudent offeror should, as Bramwell LJ advised in the above case, clearly state that: 'Your answer by post is only to bind if it reaches me.'

An offeror may therefore be advised to *exclude* the postal rule by the terms of his offer and insist that he will only be bound on actual receipt of a posted acceptance. In *Holwell Securities Ltd v Hughes* (1974) an offer to sell a house was made in the form of an option stated 'to be exercisable by notice in writing to the Intending Vendor'. Such a notice, properly addressed, was posted within the time limit allowed but it never reached the offeror. It was held that there was no contract as the terms of the option, on their true construction, required acceptance to be actually communicated. Indeed, the court went so far as to suppose that there *was no single or universal rule* determining the effect of a posted acceptance (cf the court's treatment of telexed acceptances in *Brinkibon*, above): the postal rule, bearing in mind all the circumstances of the case, 'probably does not operate if its application would produce manifest inconvenience and absurdity'. The question is one of practical considerations and convenience rather than deductions from a general rule. If the offeror prescribes a particular method of communication for acceptance, then this part of his offer must be complied with – or improved upon, eg by means of an acceptance by fax rather than letter.

Finally, it should be emphasised that an offeror's posted revocation of his offer (like the offer itself) is only operative when it is received by the offeree, so that it will not prevent a contract coming into existence if the latter has already posted his acceptance:

In *Henthorn v Fraser* (1892), H who lived in Birkenhead was given an option in F's Liverpool office to buy certain property within 14 days. The next day F posted a letter withdrawing the offer which did not reach Birkenhead until after 5 pm. In the meantime H had posted a letter at 3.50 pm accepting the offer. This letter was delivered at F's office after it had closed and was not opened until the next morning. The Court of Appeal held that F was entitled to specific performance.

Agreement and certainty

Even though it comes about through acceptance of an offer in compliance with the above 'rules', an agreement may not be binding on account of its vagueness or incompleteness. We have seen that business people are generally less concerned than lawyers about complete and precise expression of their contractual obligations. The issue of vagueness or incompleteness arose in the case of *Hillas & Co Ltd v Arcos Ltd* (1932), which is also a good example of a court readily putting an agreement into its business context in order to fulfil its primary role as an upholder of bargains:

Arcos (sellers) and Hillas (buyers) entered into and performed a contract for the supply of Russian timber for the year 1930, and H took up an option for A to supply further timber 'of fair specification' for delivery during 1931. A was unable to supply this timber (having sold it to a third party) and, when sued for breach, argued that the 1931 agreement was void for uncertainty.

On the basis of the parties' involvement in the Russian timber trade, the concluded contract for 1930, and expert evidence on the nature of that trade, the House of Lords felt able to construe the words 'of fair specification' with sufficient precision to establish a binding agreement between the parties for 1931 supplies.

Lord Wright stated that:

Business men often record the most important agreements in crude and summary fashion; modes of expression sufficient and clear to them in the course of their business may appear to those unfamiliar with the business far from complete or precise. It is accordingly the duty of the court to construe such documents fairly and broadly, without being too astute or subtle in finding defects; but [that] does not mean that the court is to make a contract for the parties, or to go outside the words they have used, except in so far as there are appropriate implications of law, as for instance, the implication of what is just and reasonable to be ascertained by the court as a matter of machinery where the contractual intention is clear, but the contract is silent on some detail. Thus in contracts for future performance over a period, the parties may neither be able nor desire to specify many matters of detail, but leave them to be adjusted in the working out of the contract ... As obvious illustrations I may refer to such matters as prices or times of delivery in contracts for the sale of goods.

(A footnote: Arcos, the losing defendants, were the All-Russia Co-operative Society. Their London premises were raided by the Special Branch in 1927 and found to be a cover for Soviet foreign espionage.)

Where the dividing line between certainty and uncertainty, enforceability and unenforceability, is drawn may well depend therefore on the court's ability and wish to accommodate business practice. A strictly formalist court, approaching this question in a manner similar to that in the 'ribbon-matching' *Parkinson Stove* case above, would no doubt not strive to settle an important matter that the parties had chosen to leave unsettled in their original agreement. Such a court would insist that a good contract must be a concluded bargain; one which settles everything that needs to be settled and leaves nothing to be settled by *further* agreement between the parties.

This was the approach adopted in *May and Butcher Ltd v The King* (1934) in which the parties entered into a contract whereby a government Disposals Board agreed to sell old tentage to MB over a certain period of time. The price was to be 'agreed from time to time' and disputes were to be submitted to arbitration. MB claimed that a reasonable price should be determined by the court or that a price should be fixed under the arbitration clause. The Disposable Board's contention that there was no contract was upheld by the House of Lords. Although then (as now) the Sale of Goods Act provided for a reasonable price where the contract was silent on the point, it was held that the contract was not silent because there was a provision for the parties to agree on price. Arbitration was also excluded, there being 'a failure to agree, which is a very different thing from a dispute'.

The Court of Appeal went the other way in *Foley v Classique Coaches Ltd* (1934), a decision which reflects Lord Wright's words in *Hillas* when he spoke of 'the implication of what is just and reasonable to be ascertained as a matter of machinery where the contractual intention is clear' (see above). In *Foley*:

> The contract between the parties provided that C Ltd should buy petrol exclusively from F 'at a price to be agreed by the parties from time to time'. There was also an arbitration clause in the contract which the court took to apply to any failure to agree as to price. After three years C Ltd, believing they could get better petrol elsewhere, repudiated the agreement on the basis that it was incomplete. F brought this action, claiming a declaration that the agreement was binding, damages for breach, and an injunction restraining C Ltd from buying petrol other than from F. The court found in F's favour, being impressed by the fact that (a) the parties had for three years clearly believed that they had a contract, and (b) they had provided machinery for dealing with any failure to agree as to the price. It was held that the petrol should be supplied at a reasonable price.

A similar position emerges when considering two cases involving leases.

In *King's Motors (Oxford) Ltd v Lax* (1969), it was decided that an option in a lease for a further period of years 'at such rental as may be agreed on between the parties', was, at least where there was no relevant arbitration clause, void for uncertainty. Thus the landlords could terminate the lease although the option had been duly exercised. Uncertainties of this kind may prove to be a loophole through which an unwilling party can escape from an agreement. However, in *Sudbrook Trading Estate Ltd v Eggleton* (1983), a lease gave the tenant an option to purchase the premises 'at such price as may be agreed on by two valuers, one to be nominated' by each party. The landlord refused to appoint a valuer. The House of Lords held that the option in effect provided a formula enabling *a reasonable* price to be fixed (without further agreement between the parties). The ancillary machinery for determining that price having broken down, the court felt able to substitute its own machinery. It was stressed that with a partly performed agreement, 'the court would strain to supply the want of certainty': see also *Didymi Corporation v Atlantic Lines and Navigation Co Inc* (1988).

It is well known that agreements for the sale of land (including property) are usually made 'subject to contract' and as such are incomplete and are not binding until formal contracts have been exchanged by the parties (normally via their legal representatives). This 'safeguard' for parties who are often in a property 'chain' (buyers can have title investigated and mortgage facilities settled) is frequently more than offset by extreme inconvenience when a party opts out of such an agreement. In a period of rapidly rising house prices, as occurred in the 1970s, the practice of 'gazumping' put extreme pressure on buyers when sellers refused to complete unless the buyer would agree to a price higher than that originally agreed. What was at the time described as 'a social and moral blot on the law' came under close scrutiny by both the courts (see *Cohen v Nessdale Ltd* in 1981) and the Law Commission. However, the Commission concluded that 'gazumping' was (as later proved) a short-term phenomenon and any change in law or practice would not in general benefit buyers.

In recent years, 'agreements to agree' have re-emerged in the form of 'negotiation contracts' – agreements to negotiate. In *Courtney and Fairbairn Ltd v Tolaini Brothers (Hotels) Ltd* (1975) the Court of Appeal felt unable to recognise a contract to negotiate. The parties (hoteliers and property developers) agreed to negotiate but negotiations broke down on the fundamental question of price. The developers claimed the loss of profits they would have made if they had been employed as builders for the motel project. The action failed: an agreement to negotiate is too uncertain to have binding force.

The outcome was the same in *Walford v Miles* (1992), a House of Lords decision concerning an oral agreement reached by the parties during negotiations for the purchase of M's business 'subject to contract'. Following M's sale of the business to a third party, W brought an action for breach of an oral 'lock-out' contract constituted by M's promise not to negotiate with or consider offers from third parties in exchange for a letter of creditworthiness from W's bank stating that W would be able to meet the agreed price of £2 million.

The 'lock-out' agreement contained no time limit and their Lordships considered that M had in no legal sense locked himself *into* negotiations with W. Arguments claiming that the agreement contained an implied term that M would continue to negotiate in good faith with W for a reasonable period of time failed to impress the court. The agreement was uncertain and not binding. In Lord Ackner's view, 'the concept of a duty to carry on negotiations in good faith is inherently repugnant to the adversarial position of the parties when involved in negotiations'. Shades of Gurvitch's concept of 'separation' (see Chapter 2), as each party while looking for agreement seeks the best deal for himself. It may be doubted that Lord Ackner's analysis was entirely appropriate to describe the relationship between these parties which envisaged close co-operation ('rapprochement' or common purpose) between them, M having agreed to continue working in the business as W lacked expertise in the field in question.

This decision has not met with unanimous approval. Adams and Brownsword see it as based on 'a formalist concern for certainty of terms in conjunction with a robust market -*individualism*'. *Walford v Miles* was applied by the Court of Appeal in *Pitt v PHH Asset Management Ltd* (1993). P was twice 'gazumped' when PHH withdrew from an agreement for the sale of a property 'subject to contract'; the defendants on each occasion having received a higher offer from a third party. Nevertheless, PHH later agreed to sell to P and they promised not to consider any further offers in return for P's promise to exchange contracts *within two weeks* of receipt of the draft contract. It was held that this was a binding 'lock-out' agreement which PHH, who had again withdrawn, had broken. The key factor which distinguishes this agreement from the one in *Walford v Miles* is the specified time limit, which provides the requisite degree of certainty, and to which both parties must adhere. Otherwise it would appear that certainty will only be found, and reliance protected, where performance has already taken place: as in such cases as *Hillas*, *Foley* and *Trentham*.

Agreement: a special case

Public procurement, tenders and European Community law

Government contracts are very big business; some companies exist solely on the basis of such contracts. As noted in Chapter 4, the total value of government procurement contracts for goods and services, including public works, was approximately £15 billion in 1982. Later figures estimated that Ministry of Defence expenditure on arms and equipment (defence procurement) stood at over £9 billion. All governments require procurement policies and public purchasing contracts in the European Community in 1986 were valued at 530 billion ECU (£350 billion).

The purchasing policies and practices of national governments within the Community (and elsewhere) have inevitably favoured national suppliers to the detriment of suppliers from other Member States. Although such discrimination constitutes an impediment to trade *between* Member States and leads to a costly closure of national markets to foreign competition (thus preventing the creation of a genuinely integrated Common Market), it is normal to find governments justifying their position in terms of the maintenance of national levels of employment and economic activity (see the helicopter example on p 60).

Since Britain joined the European Community (now Union), we have become subject to EC rules designed to liberalise trade between the Member States. Although the rules on free movement of goods tend to strike at *national legal restrictions* (eg import duties, import bans and a variety of other measures) which prevent or impede private sector import-export contracts, these restrictions can also impact on public procurement contracts. For example, any measure by which national public authorities effectively discriminate against imported goods in the award of procurement contracts is contrary to Article 30 of the EC Treaty. Competition must proceed on the basis of quality not national origin:

Case 45/87 *Commission v Ireland (Re Dundalk Water Supply)*

The contract specification for tender for a public works contract for the Dundalk water supply augmentation scheme included a clause stipulating that pressure pipes must be certified as complying with Irish Standard 188 of 1975 as drafted by the Irish Institute for Industrial Research and Standards. An Irish company, in response to an invitation to tender, submitted a tender providing for the use of pipes manufactured by a Spanish firm. These pipes had not been approved and certified by the IIRS but they complied with internationally recognised standards and were suitable for the Dundalk scheme. The absence of IIRS approval was given as the ground for the local authority proceeding no further with the Irish/Spanish bid.

74

The EC Commission in Brussels acted on a complaint and the matter came before the European Court of Justice in Luxembourg. It was held that Ireland was in breach of Article 30 by restricting the contract only to tenderers proposing to use Irish materials, thereby excluding suitable products lawfully made in other Member States complying with different standards. (Pipes, any pipes, might be rejected on quality grounds but the use of Irish standards was in breach of Community law by impeding the importation of pipes into Ireland.)

Apart from Article 30, most government procurement contracts are also governed by EC legislation in the form of directives. General programmes adopted for guidance prior to the adoption of the legislation spoke of the need to eliminate restrictions, including rules and practices of Member States only applicable to foreign firms, which 'exclude, limit or impose conditions on the capacity ... to submit offers or to participate, whether as main or sub-contractor, in contract awards by the state or other legal persons constituted under public law'.

Purchasing agencies throughout the Community are bound by the directives (on the basis of the *national* law which implements them) and the emphasis is on widespread publication of invitations to tender, 'open' tender procedures whereby all interested suppliers can present an offer, the definition of technical specifications by reference to European (not national) Standards and remedies for injured contractors or suppliers (injunctions, damages) available in national courts against public bodies acting contrary to Community and/or national rules.

Conclusions

As we have seen, the law relating to the mechanics of contractual agreement is, according to Lord Diplock in *Gibson v Manchester City Council* (1979), 'well settled, indeed elementary' although 'there may be certain types of contract, though I think they are exceptional, which do not fit easily into the normal analysis of a contract as being constituted by offer and acceptance'. It follows from this view that the well-polished 'rules' are considered quite capable of satisfactorily meeting the demands made on them from time to time by the business world. We have seen that they should be regarded not as 'black-letter' rules to be rigidly applied, but rather as presumptions that are flexible and adaptable to new situations. Of course, some judges will see more flexibility in the 'rules' than others, and some judges will consider a case to be 'exceptional' which others will see as conventional.

References and further reading

Adams, 'The battle of the forms' (1983) JBL 297.

Adams and Brownsword (1992), *Understanding Contract Law*, ch 4 (first part) and ch 5(3).

Adams and Brownsword, 'More in expectation than hope: the Blackpool Airport case' (1991) 54 MLR 281.

Ball, 'Work carried out in pursuance of letters of intent – contract or restitution' (1983) 99 LQR 572.

Cumberbatch, 'In freedom's cause: the contract to negotiate' (1992) 12 OJLS 586.

Evans, 'The Anglo-American Mailing Rule ...' (1966) 15 ICLQ 553.

Fennell and Ball (1994), 'Welfarism and the renegotiation of contracts', in Brownsword *et al* (eds), *Welfarism in Contract Law*, Dartmouth.

Gardner, 'Trashing with Trollope: a deconstruction of the postal rules' (1992) 12 OJLS 170.

Howarth, 'Contract, reliance and business transactions' (1981) JBL 122.

Jones, 'Claims arising out of anticipated contracts which do not materialise' (1980) 18 University of West Ontario LR 447.

Lewis, C, 'The formation and repudiation of contracts by international telex', (1980) LMCLQ 433.

Lewis, R, 'Contracts between businessmen: reform of the law of firm offers and an empirical study of tendering practices in the building industry' (1982) 12 *British Journal of Law and Society* 153.

McKendrick, 'The battle of the forms and the law of restitution' (1988) 8 OJLS 197.

Rawlings, 'The battle of the forms' (1979) 42 MLR 715.

Simpson, 'Quackery and contract law: the case of the Carbolic Smoke Ball' (1985) 14 *Journal of Legal Studies* 345.

Stone (1994), *Contract Law*, ch 2, Cavendish Publishing.

Questions

(1) According to Lord Wilberforce (see p 52), there is difficulty involved in the precise analysis of various situations of daily life into the 'classical offer and acceptance'. What difficulties exist with regard to

(a) sales at auction,

(b) boarding an omnibus,

(c) bankers' commercial credits?

(2) Best-Buy Stores published the following advertisement in a newspaper:

Saturday, 9 am sharp. 3 brand new fur coats worth £500.

    First come, first served, £1 each.

John queued all night Friday and was first to the cash desk on Saturday at 9 am. The assistant refused to sell him a fur coat for £1 on the ground that the offer had been intended only for women. Is John entitled to the coat?

(3) X writes to Y on 1 November offering to sell 500 bottles of 'Nouveau Beaujolais' at £2 per bottle and stating that the offer 'will remain open only until 5 pm on 5 November'. Y receives the letter at 9 am on 5 November and immediately tries to telephone X. X, however, is out and therefore Y leaves a message on X's answering machine asking X if he would agree to £1.85 per bottle.

Later the same morning, Y changes his mind and sends X a telemessage stating: 'Disregard earlier phone call. I accept your offer at £2 per bottle.' X returns to his office at 1 pm and, on hearing Y's telephone message, he immediately sells the wine to Z. At 2 pm X receives Y's telemessage. Discuss the legal position.

(4) On 1 April 1995, Monumental Marble Masons Limited wrote to Decor and Fittings Limited the following letter.

Dear Sirs,

We have the following remainders in Italian Marbles which we are pleased to offer to you as one of our regular customers, in whole lots, delivery to be taken at our Tomb Street Yard, at the prices marked below, which we are sure you will agree are well below current market rates for these excellent quality marbles. This special offer is open for acceptance up to the end of the month. Do not miss this splendid opportunity to lay in a stock which cannot fail to improve in value, even if you have no immediate use in mind.

Offer in whole lots – Delivery to be taken at our yard

Lot No.1 Piastraccia – 45 No. slabs 3/4" thick by 3'6" x 1'9" at £75

Lot No.2 Rosso Levanto – 58 No. slabs 1/2" thick by 4'6" x 1'6" at £35

Lot No.3 Botticino – 37 No. slabs 3/4" thick by 4'0" x 1'9" at £75

Lot No.4 etc, etc

Yours faithfully,

Decor and Fittings Limited received the letter by post on 3 April and replied on 4 April as follows:

Dear Sirs,

Thank you for your offer of marble remainders in yours of the 1st instant. We will be pleased to take delivery of Lot No.3, 37 Botticino slabs 4'0" x 1'9" x 3/4", and we enclose herewith our cheque for £75. Please advise the soonest that we can collect from your yard.

Yours faithfully,

The letter was posted on the evening of 4 April, but due to a misdirection by the Post Office it did not arrive at Monumental Marble Masons' office until Monday 14 April. In the meantime, on Friday, 11 April, Shop and Salon Services Ltd, who had received a similar letter from MMM, called at the Tomb Street Yard, paid £100 cash and collected both Lot 2 and Lot 3. MMM immediately dispatched a telemessage to Decor and Fittings Limited and the three other firms to whom they had sent their offer, saying: 'Our letter of 1 April Lots 2 and 3 withdrawn from offer'. Decor and Fittings Limited did not man their offices on Saturday, so that the telemessage was not delivered until Monday 14 April. When MMM received Decor and Fittings' letter and cheque on 14 April, they immediately returned the cheque by post and confirmed details of their telemessage. Advise Decor and Fittings of their rights, if any.

(5) On two occasions prior to 6 May, and on 6 May, D Ltd ordered and received shipments of film from P Ltd. On each of these occasions D Ltd had used a purchase order form which stated: 'ALTERATION OF TERMS: None of the terms and conditions contained in this Purchase Order may be added to, modified, superseded or otherwise altered except by a written instrument signed by an authorised representative of Buyer and delivered by Buyer to Seller, and each shipment received by Buyer from Seller shall be deemed to be only on the terms and conditions contained in this Purchase Order except as they may be added to, modified, superseded or otherwise altered, notwithstanding Buyer's act of accepting or paying for any shipment or similar act of Buyer.'

P accepted each order by sending an acknowledgement form which stated: 'IMPORTANT: Buyer agrees he has full knowledge of conditions printed on the reverse side hereof, and that the same are part of the agreement between buyer and seller and shall be binding if either the goods referred to herein are delivered to and accepted by buyer, or if buyer does not within ten days from date hereof deliver to seller written objection to said conditions or any part thereof.'

The reverse side of P Ltd's acknowledgement form contained a general arbitration clause binding both parties to submit any dispute arising under the contract to arbitration. A dispute arose over the 6 May transaction and P Ltd brought an action to require that D Ltd submit the dispute to arbitration. Discuss the legal position.

(6) 'In stressing objective certainty and completeness the requirements of traditional contract have perpetuated the idea of a contract as a rationally complete and discrete transaction' but 'most contracts are part of a wider relationship composed of previous dealings, other contracts or shared business standards, which are ignored by this objective, individualised approach': Ball (see References and further reading).

6 Contractual intention, consideration and estoppel

Intention to create legal relations

It is a part of the modern law of contract that an agreement, albeit supported by consideration, is not a binding contract unless it is accompanied by an intention to create legal relations. This is a feature of the law which, together with others, was imported from continental legal thought in the 19th century (see Chapter 2) and gradually accepted by the courts. No doubt the idea of 'a concurrence of intention' in the parties was attractive at a time when the law concentrated on party autonomy – and two wills becoming one in true *consensus*. Nevertheless, attribution of such an intention *to the parties* is, in the vast majority of cases, essentially unrealistic. Do parties actually turn their minds to this question? It is very doubtful if they do. Macaulay's findings suggest the opposite and, as Atiyah points out: 'The "intention of the parties" does not mean the real intention of these particular parties. It means that intention which reasonable parties would have had in those circumstances.'

The test of intention is therefore almost invariably *objective*; not subjective because the parties themselves rarely show, indeed need not show, any such positive intention. To put it another way, it is not actual but 'constructive' intention that settles the matter if (as is not often the case) the question is in issue. It is the court which decides – working from *presumptions* as to the presence or absence of such an intention. Where transactions of a business, or a predominantly business, nature are concerned, there is a presumption that legal relations are intended – and that such agreements are therefore binding. For merely social and domestic arrangements there is presumed to be no intention to create legal relations. In *Albert v Motor Insurers' Bureau* (1972), Lord Cross stated that: 'It is not necessary in order that a legally binding contract should arise that the parties should direct their minds to the question and decide in favour of a legally binding relationship. If I get into a taxi and ask the driver to take me to Victoria Station it is extremely unlikely that either of us directs his mind to the question whether we are entering into a contract.'

There is no doubt that there are strong elements of policy and expediency behind the intention doctrine. It enables the court to hive off and exclude from jurisdiction 'unwanted' agreements. Thus, as regards most purely domestic agreements, it is, in Atiyah's view, 'probably true that in these cases the result depends not so much on the lack of intention to create legal relations, as on the courts' view that it would be unseemly and distressing to allow husbands and wives, while still living together, to use the court as an arbiter for their matrimonial differences'.

In *Balfour v Balfour* (1919) the defendant husband, while on leave with his wife from his work in Ceylon, agreed to pay her £30 a month maintenance while she remained in England for medical treatment. Later the husband suggested that his wife not rejoin him abroad, and eventually she obtained a divorce. This action concerned the husband's failure to pay monthly sums prior to the divorce. The Court of Appeal held that the agreement, made by a husband and wife 'in amity', was not a binding contract but a merely domestic arrangement which, in the absence of indications to the contrary, the parties did not intend to give rise to legal relations. (It is also highly unlikely that the wife provided consideration.) As regards the policy element, Atkin LJ was of the opinion that 'the small courts of this country would have to be multiplied one hundredfold if these arrangements were held to result in legal obligations'!

It is worthy of note, when examining the husband and wife relationship, that we are back with Weber's prime illustration of the 'status' contract – the 'total' relationship which differs from the 'purposive' contract with its limited commercial aims. One can hear echoes of this distinction in Atkin LJ's words: 'Agreements such as these are outside the realm of contracts altogether ... The consideration that really obtains for them is that natural love and affection which counts for so little in these cold courts ... and the principles of the common law ... find no place in the domestic code.'

An agreement between a husband and wife no longer 'in amity' – as where the husband has already deserted the wife – which relates to the future arrangement of their financial affairs may well be held to be binding: see *Merritt v Merritt* (1970). There is only a narrow dividing line between the domestic and the business nature of some of these agreements (and a binding *business* agreement may clearly be made between spouses, eg a wife may employ her husband or sell property to him).

For agreements made within a business framework, the basic presumption made by the court, which has the agreement there before it to be construed, is that legal relations are intended. (A feature of the research done by Macaulay and others is the finding that the business community's prime concern is with good, continuing *business* relations, and that, in as much as they consider the matter at all, business people seek to avoid legalism and litigation. However, this is not to say that their agreements, once brought before a judge or arbitrator, will not be found binding on them, as we saw with 'battle of the forms' cases.)

It is possible – though rarely found – for business parties actually to think about legal relations and to *exclude* the intention to be bound by an express statement to that effect in the agreement itself, as in *Rose and Frank Co v Crompton & Bros Ltd* (1923). However, they must do this in the clearest possible terms before the court will allow that the basic presumption has been overturned: see *Edwards v Skyways Ltd* (1964). A 'binding in honour only' clause inserted into an agreement and insisted on by a party with overpowering bargaining strength could operate as a massive exclusion of liability clause.

There are other business agreements which the courts have refused to enforce on the ground of an absence of constructive intention. The most important example is the industrial collective bargaining agreement, which has developed in significance and complexity since the formative days of contract's 'classical' period. It is therefore not surprising that contract concepts in general, and intention in particular, which might have been appropriate to the private bargains of the 19th century, have failed to transplant into this new and specialised area of bargaining.

Collective bargaining agreements are negotiated by trade unions and employers (or associations of employers) over such matters as wage rates and conditions of work. We have already noted, in Chapter 1, that contract law has to a large extent been supplanted in the employment area in modern times by a growing mass of 'special' statutory measures and voluntary codes of practice making up, at least in part, the field of labour law. This is true of collective agreements, which are now covered by the Trade Union and Labour Relations (Consolidation) Act 1992. On the assumption that litigation is not the best way of promoting industrial relations, the Act keeps the courts away from such an agreement by laying down that it is ,'conclusively presumed not to have been intended by the parties to be a legally enforceable contract' unless it is in writing and expressly provides to the contrary. Few, if any, collective agreements contain such express provision, and the Act continues to express government policy in this sensitive and controversial area. The point was clearly made by the Royal Commission on Trade Unions in 1968:

> This lack of intention to make legally binding collective agreements, or better perhaps, this intention and policy that collective bargaining and collective agreements should remain outside the law, is one of the characteristic features of our system of industrial relations which distinguishes it from other comparable systems.

However, before statutory intervention, in the case of *Ford Motor Co Ltd v Amalgamated Union of Engineering and Foundry Workers* (1969), the enforceability or otherwise of a collective bargaining agreement was left to rest on the common law position. Although one might think such an agreement was a *business* agreement (and therefore presumed to be binding), it seems that it was regarded more as a 'special case'. By means of what has been called 'artificial and unusual reasoning', the judge's search for the parties' intentions took him to 'the climate of opinion voiced and evidenced by the extra-judicial authorities' and 'the background adverse to enforceability'; factors which, among others, led to a decision that the agreement was not enforceable. Criticism of this case centred not on the policy issue of whether or not collective agreements *ought* to be binding, but on the nature of 'constructive' intention and its application by the judge in this particular instance. It should finally be noted that terms of such unenforceable collective agreements can become binding when incorporated into individual contracts of employment: see *National Coal Board v Galley* (1958).

Although the question of intention to create legal relations is not a very important aspect of contract law, it is, like several others, a controversial issue if one penetrates below the surface. Some commentators argue that it could be abolished, and the cases to which it has been applied could or should have been decided on a different basis. On the other hand, the decisions to be found in the reports represent – unless they have been overruled – the law as it stands.

Intention and comfort letters

In *Kleinwort Benson Ltd v Malaysia Mining Corporation* (1989), MMC set up a wholly owned subsidiary, Metals Ltd, to trade in tin on the London Metals Exchange. MMC also sought a loan of £5 million from KB, a merchant bank, to supplement Metals' existing capital. Before making the loan, KB asked MMC for a guarantee of their subsidiary's indebtedness to them. MMC declined to do this but said that the loan would be covered by their comfort letter. KB replied that this would be 'no problem' but the rate of interest charged would be slightly higher.

MMC's comfort letter stated that 'It is our policy to ensure that the business of Metals Ltd is at all times in a position to meet its liabilities to you.' MMC also said they would not reduce their current financial interest in Metals Ltd until the loan had been repaid.

In 1985 the world tin market collapsed and Metals Ltd went into liquidation with the loan (now £10 million) unpaid. KB sued MMC for the full amount on the basis of the comfort letter, which they maintained had contractual effect.

The Court of Appeal held that the correct test to determine the status of a comfort letter was to ask whether a promise was being made, rather than the test applied at first instance of whether there was an intention to create legal relations. The letter amounted to a policy statement only and did not form the basis of a contract.

A guarantee is a binding promise to pay another's debts if he fails to pay. Ralph Gibson LJ, on a 'true' construction of the relevant parts of the comfort letter, considered that MMC were accepting 'a moral responsibility only' to pay its subsidiary's debts. This implies that appropriate wording could establish a promissory obligation. (Which would appear to make the comfort letter a guarantee or the equivalent.) The facts of this case do not fit easily into the concept of a clear rebuttal of the presumption that business agreements are binding. They raise difficult questions of risk and reliance. In *Banque Brussels Lambert v Australian National Industries Ltd* (1989), the wording of the comfort letter was such as to enable the Australian court to find a promissory obligation (and a breach of contract).

What is the status of a comfort letter within the business community? The New South Wales court considered them to be little different from letters of guarantee. (So why would MMC provide one but not the other?) If the Court of

Appeal had 'found' a promise to pay (as the court of first instance did), it would at least have avoided antipodean criticism to the effect that its decision was commercially unrealistic:

> There should be no room in the proper flow of commerce for some purgatory where state-ments made by a business people, after hard bargaining and made to induce another busi-ness person to enter into a business transaction would, without any express statement to that effect, reside in a twilight zone of merely honourable engagement. The whole thrust of the law today is to attempt to give proper effect to commercial transactions. It is for this rea-son that uncertainty, a concept so much loved by lawyers, has fallen into disfavour as a tool for striking down commercial bargains.

Consideration

Contract as bargain and exchange

In Chapter 1 we identified consideration with the idea of bargain and exchange by means of the simple illustration of the car sold for £5,000. We also noted that the law regards mutual *promises* (eg of a car and of payment for it) as considera-tion, sufficient to bring into being a binding, albeit executory, contract. The link between the parties' promises and offer and acceptance was also made. In Chapter 2 we saw how consideration came to set limits on promissory liability, 'bare' promises not supported by consideration – not part of an agreed bargain – being regarded as lying outside the field of contract law.

It should be obvious that, in the simplest terms, the vast majority of contracts involve one party doing something for the other in return for payment. Property is sold or leased; plant and equipment, goods or 'know-how' are sup-plied; labour and services, such as carriage and insurance, are provided. Business and consumer bargains or exchanges are struck and carried through to completion. The contract law textbooks reveal almost three centuries (from 1602 to 1884) of 'leading' cases on consideration, cases concerning a variety of legal propositions (and exceptions thereto) regarding the nature of this contractual requirement as 'the sign and symbol of bargain'.

However, for an introductory study of the law as it operates *today*, it is doubt-ful if full attention need be given to the extensive and complicated accumulation of 'old' case law on consideration. Points from such cases do still arise but more often than not, as will be seen, in the context of cases which demonstrate moves in judicial thinking *away from* strict bargain theory. These are particularly cases in which the strict *quid pro quo* requirement has either been loosened or bypassed in situations where the parties have agreed *to vary an existing bargain*.

Support for a 'playing-down' of consideration can be found in recent extra-judicial statements. Sir Frederick Lawton has said that: 'Students always seem to spend a lot of time on the formation of contract, consideration and mistake but little on the discharge of contract and remedies, with which the practitioner is usually concerned. Occasionally problems arise as to whether there has been a contract and whether the parties were thinking of the same subject matter; but in all my time in the law I have never met a problem about consideration.' In a similar vein, Lord Denning expressed the view that the effect of the development of promissory estoppel since 1947 'has been to do away with the doctrine of consideration in all but a handful of cases. During the 16 years while I have been Master of the Rolls I do not recall any case in which it has arisen or been discussed.' Taking these statements as our cue, we will confine ourselves to an examination of consideration's main features and then proceed to a closer look at promissory estoppel and another move away from traditional requirements.

In 1915 in *Dunlop v Selfridge*, Lord Dunedin said he was content to adopt from a work of Sir Frederick Pollock the following definition of consideration: 'An act or forbearance of one party, or the promise thereof, is the price for which the promise of the other is bought, and the promise thus given for value is enforceable.' Thus *acts* (supplying goods under a contract of sale, or delivering them under a contract of carriage, etc) or *forebearances* (say, the giving up of all or a portion of interest or rent due), or *promises* of such are the main constituent elements making up the necessary 'something of value in the eyes of the law' to be given for a promise to make it binding. Informal, gratuitous promises (ie those not under seal) lack the required reciprocity needed to make them enforceable – nothing is given for them.

Generally speaking, 'value in the eyes of the law' means *economic* value. The economic value of goods received, services rendered, or cash paid is obvious; and mutual or 'bargained for' promises can be said to have value in that they establish commercial reliance and expectation of fulfilment. Although, as was stated in one case, 'natural love and affection' do not amount to consideration, the courts are willing to acknowledge merely nominal (economic) consideration which has usually been stipulated for so as to make an agreement binding: 'The adequacy of the consideration is for the parties to consider at the time of making the agreement, not for the court when it is sought to be enforced', as Lord Blackburn said in 1873. The operation of the doctrine of consideration within classical freedom of contract principles called for a bargain, but not necessarily a good bargain in business terms; parties were *free* to set their own price on their promises.

Nowadays, when courts are more sensitive to imbalances of bargaining strength between parties, and the use of excessive commercial pressure or undue influence, a grossly inadequate consideration may militate against a court's sense of 'fairness in exchange'. For example, in *Lloyd's Bank Ltd v Bundy* (1975), although Lord Denning stated that 'no bargain will be upset which is the result of the ordinary interplay of forces', the court struck down a contract of guarantee by which the defendant, an elderly farmer not well versed in business affairs, mortgaged his house as security for the debts of his son's business at a time when the company was already in dire financial straits, and not long before its eventual collapse. It was felt that, in the circumstances, 'the considera-tion moving from the bank was grossly inadequate' and, at the late stage at which the guarantee was given, 'all that the company gained was a short respite from impending doom'. The concept of free bargaining still plays a part on judi-cial thinking but judges and legislators can and do exercise control over consid-eration in a variety of ways. We have noted the 'legislative bargain' in the con-text of carriage of goods by sea (see p 20), and, for example, both rents and interest rates can be similarly regulated.

Executory, executed and past consideration

The 'bargain' view of contract, rooted in the idea of reciprocity, means that promises (or, in the case of a unilateral contract, a promise and an *act*) must be given in return for each other. Hence the oft-repeated statement that considera-tion may be executory, executed but not past. In a bilateral contract, considera-tion initially consists of mutually supporting promises: a promise is a promise *and* the consideration for the other party's promise (so making both parties promisors and promisees). At this stage the contract is said to be *executory*. Performance of the act (or the forbearance) embodied in such a promise amounts to *executed* consideration: the promise is performed.

Thus it is said that something wholly performed *before* a promise is made can-not amount to consideration: it is *past* consideration and there will be no con-tract. For example, A renders a service for B and afterwards B promises to pay £100 for it. In a business context it may be argued that if B originally requested the service it must have been understood by the parties that payment would be forthcoming, and the later express promise to pay merely confirms and quanti-fies an earlier implied promise on B's part: see *Re Casey's Patents* (1892).

In *Pao On v Lau Yiu Long* (1980) the defendants sold shares to the plaintiff who promised not to put them on the market for at least 12 months. (The defen-dants, who retained a large block of shares, had required this, as they did not wish to see the value of their holding depressed by a sudden sale of the plain-tiff's shares.) The defendants later promised to indemnify the plaintiff against any loss he might incur if the shares fell in value during the year. The Privy Council was willing to marry together the plaintiff's promise not to sell (albeit given as part of the original contract of sale) and the defendants' subsequent promise to indemnify. It has been said that the plaintiff was 'only getting what he was really, morally and commercially, entitled to'. The case also supports the growing idea that, in appropriate circumstances, the court should have regard to a *continuing commercial relationship* between parties rather than concentrating on 'discrete' transactions or arrangements within that relationship.

Consideration and existing contractual duties

Pollock's definition of consideration focuses attention firmly on the exchange or *quid pro quo* (something for something) aspect of contract. The payment of a 'price' (an act, a forbearance or the promise of such) in return for the other's promise also connotes the idea of detriment – but also benefit. Parties must not only be receivers but must also contribute or give value as recognised by the law. Although courts may be willing in appropriate circumstances to 'find' consideration and therefore a contract, eg *Carlill v Carbolic Smoke Ball Co* or, as in *Gore v Van der Lann* (1967) where a senior citizen's 'free' bus pass was held to form the basis of a contract, it has not until recently been the case that a court has been willing to answer the following question in the affirmative: Can the performance of, or the promise to perform, an act which the promisor is *already* under a contractual duty to the promisee to carry out, amount to consideration?

The position can be outlined as follows: A agrees to carry out certain obligations for B at a fixed price. B later agrees to pay A *more* money if he promises to perform (or performs) his (A's) existing obligations. Is B's promise binding? The traditional view, in line with the definition of consideration and the cases which embody it, must be that B's promise is not binding because it is not supported by additional (or sufficient) consideration from A. We are looking at two stages: an original contractual agreement followed by a variation of it. The variation, it would seem, can only stand if A (in return for B's later promise) agrees to do *more* for B. This would be an accord (a new agreement) and satisfaction (additional consideration). But B provides no additional consideration. However, a further question remains. Why should B promise additional payment? The answer, at least where both A and B are business parties, is that it must be of some advantage to B to do so. Should the courts take account of this?

The 'old' case law is, as said, unhelpful:

In *Stilk v Myrick* (1809), a crew had been engaged to sail a vessel from London to the Baltic and back at the rate of £5 a month. Following the desertion of two of the 11 crew members, the captain promised to share the deserters' wages among the remaining crew if they would work the ship back to London.

The owners refused to honour the captain's promise when the ship returned. It was held that the seamen's claim failed for lack of consideration. The crew were already bound by their contract to meet the normal emergencies of the voyage and were doing no more than their duty in sailing the ship back. (In *Hartley v Ponsonby* (1857), 17 out of 36 crew deserted and the voyage became very hazardous. It was held that the remaining crew had in consequence been discharged from their original contract and were free therefore to enter a new one at higher wages.)

One report of *Stilk v Myrik* stresses the danger that a shift in bargaining power (as afforded the crew) could lead to instances of extortion. While this policy argument is not taken to be reason for the decision (there was no evidence of extortion; the captain offered the extra wages), it is of interest in view of later developments.

In the 1950s, in two cases where a party – in return for a promise – merely promised to perform an existing legal (but not contractual) duty, Lord Denning nevertheless felt able to find that such a promise was good consideration:

> I have always thought that a promise to perform an existing duty, or the performance of it, should be regarded as good consideration, because it is a benefit to the person to whom it is given: *Ward v Byham* (1956) in which the existing duty was statutory.

And in *Williams v Williams* (1957):

> Now I agree that, in promising to maintain herself while she was in desertion, the wife was only promising to do that which she was already bound to do. Nevertheless, a promise to perform an existing duty is, I think, sufficient consideration to support a promise, so long as there is nothing in the transaction which is contrary to the public interest.

The focus has now been switched from bargain to *practical (though not exchange) benefit* to the person to whom the promise is given (*Ward*), and to the possibility of public policy reasons for not enforcing the promise (*Williams*). These points re-emerge in the following case which, like *Stilk v Myrick*, concerns an existing *contractual* duty.

> In *Williams v Roffey Bros and Nicholls (Contractors) Ltd* (1991), R, as main contractors entered into a contract with a housing association for the refurbishment of a block of flats. R sub-contracted the carpentry work to W for £20,000. Part way through the work, W was in finan-cial difficulties because he had (a) tendered too low and (b) had failed to supervise his workmen properly. There was a distinct possibility that W could not complete on time or would stop work altogether.
>
> Facing a penalty clause in the main contract for late completion, R agreed to pay W a further £10,300 at a rate of £575 per flat completed. The carpentry work on eight more flats was completed but, with only a further £1,500 having been paid by R, W stopped work and sued for damages in respect of the eight completions. R argued that W had provided no consider-ation to support their promise of additional payment – the *Stilk v Myrick* argument – and W was merely doing what he was already obliged to do.
>
> The Court of Appeal held that R were bound by their promise. In the view of Glidewell LJ, 'the present state of the law on this subject can be expressed in the following proposition:
>
> (i) If A has entered into a contract with B to do work for, or to supply goods or ser-vices to, B in return for payment by B, and
>
> (ii) at some stage before A has completely performed his obligation under the con-tract B has reason to doubt whether A will, or will be able to, complete his side of the bargain, and
>
> (iii) B thereupon promises A an additional payment in return for A's promise to per-form his contractual obligations on time, and

(iv) as a result of giving his promise B obtains in practice a benefit, or obviates a dis-benefit, and

(v) B's promise is not given as a result of economic duress or fraud on the part of A, then

(vi) the benefit to B is capable of being consideration for B's promise, so that the promise is legally binding.'

The benefits obtained (or disbenefits avoided) by the main contractors were agreed as (i) seeking to ensure that the plaintiff continued work and did not stop in breach of the sub-contract, (ii) avoiding the penalty for delay in the main contract, and (iii) avoiding the trouble and expense of engaging other people to complete the carpentry work. This case certainly stretches the limits of consideration and an application of the above six points perhaps allows *Stilk v Myrick* to be distinguished. What is crucial is that the promisor gains some tangible (if not exchange) benefit from the rearrangement and that no economic duress (wrongful pressure, see Chapter 9) or fraud is exerted to give rise to that promise.

Stepping back from the detail, it could be said that this decision can be explained in terms of freedom of contract. Both parties are business contractors. The main contractor, when giving a his promise of additional payment, is making the best of a bad job. In his estimation it is less disadvantageous to pay the sub-contractor more than to run the very real risk of paying the client even more under the terms of the penalty clause in the main contract. On this basis, the court leaves the parties to their rearrangement. The position is similar where the principle of promissory estoppel excludes the need for consideration at all: see the *High Trees* case below (and on penalty clauses, see 'Liquidated Damages Clauses' in Chapter 13).

This view of the case can be seen, in more technical language, in the words of Russell LJ: 'Consideration there must be but in my judgment the courts nowadays should be more ready to find its existence so as to reflect the intention of the parties to the contract where the bargaining powers are not unequal.' Over 60 years ago, the American realist lawyer, Karl Llewellyn (who insisted that a true understanding of business law's purpose assumes an understanding of the facts of business life) summed up the position as follows and in so doing leads us to the next issue:

Four troublesome classes of cases remain ... A third and hugely important class is that of either additional or modifying business promises made after an original deal has been agreed upon. Law and logic go astray whenever such dealings are regarded as truly comparable to new agreements. They are not. No business man regards them so. They are going-transaction adjustments, as different from agreement – formation as are corporate organisation and corporate management; and the line of legal dealing with them which runs over waiver and estoppel is based on sound intuition.

Consideration and promissory estoppel: exchange or reasonable reliance

Our discussion of consideration has centred on the idea of bargain or exchange as a reasonable basis for an explanation of the doctrine. Bargain, as we have seen, excludes from the province of contract formation – if not modification – promises which have not been 'paid for'. In *Williams v Roffey*, the modification of the contract enabled Roffey to obtain benefits (or obviate disbenefits). Although Williams merely promised to continue his original obligations, the practical benefit to Roffey was sufficient to make his promise binding.

Alternatively, what is the position if the variation of the contract involves one party C *giving up* some of his rights, whereas the other party D provides no further consideration to support C's promise? In neither case is there a true exchange at the variation stage. In the second situation C is indeed a gratuitous promisor. Should C's promise be enforceable? Fifty years ago, in the *High Trees* case (below), this question was addressed and, in the face of seemingly over-whelming 'exchange' arguments to the contrary, was answered in the affirmative. The effect of the doctrine of *promissory estoppel* is to hold a promisor such as C to his word – to prevent (or stop) him from going back on his promise – where it would be unjust or inequitable for him to do so.

The practical result of the establishment and development of promissory estoppel in the post-war years (and similarly now the effect of *Williams v Roffey*) is an increasing number of cases where agreements are being enforced which are strictly not contracts (albeit they vary existing contracts) owing to a lack of consideration from one of the parties. The pathway to an understanding of promissory estoppel is quite difficult to negotiate. Let us start by asking a question which falls within the scope of our second paragraph above: 'If D owes money to C (arising out of an existing legal, say contractual, relationship) and, in reliance on C's promise to forgo payment of the full amount, D proceeds to pay merely the balance, can D hold C to his promise should C change his mind and seek to revert to the original position?'

In common law, D's failure to provide consideration to support C's promise is fatal. D is in fact doing *less than* he was originally bound to do. This position was established as early as *Pinnel's Case* (1602) in which it was stated that payment of a lesser sum on the day in satisfaction of a greater was no satisfaction of the whole. This 'rule in *Pinnel's Case*' was affirmed by the House of Lords in *Foakes v Beer* (1884):

> F owed £2,000 to B who sued and obtained judgment. F needed time to pay and it was eventually agreed that B would take no further proceedings (say, in bankruptcy) in return for an immediate payment of £500 plus specified instalments until the whole judgment was satisfied. After the £2,000 was paid, B claimed £360 interest on the judgment debt. The court upheld her claim – F's payment of the lesser (capital) sum did not discharge the greater

(capital plus interest) debt. B could recover the full amount; even if she had promised to forgo interest (it was not mentioned in the agreement), F had provided no consideration for that promise.

The 'remorseless logic' of the common law can be summarised as follows:

(1)   A legal (usually contractual) relationship exists between C and D.

(2)   A new agreement is made – C promises or assures D that he will accept *less than* is due to him (this is a forbearance).

(3)   C's promise is *not* supported by consideration from D, therefore –

(4)   there is no *accord and satisfaction* (new agreement supported by consideration) to discharge the original contract.

(5)   C can therefore retract his promise, insist on his strict legal rights, and sue for the larger sum – the full, original debt.

Despite its logic, the common law rule has never been free from criticism. The commercial position allows for at least two possibilities. Financial compromise, involving the waiving of part of a debt, may be good business sense especially in times of cash-flow problems. In *Foakes v Beer* itself, Lord Blackburn, reluctantly acquiescing in the majority view, stated that:

> I think it is not the fact that to accept prompt payment of a part only of a liquidated demand, can never be more beneficial than to insist on payment of the whole. And if it be not the fact, it cannot be apparent to the judges ... What principally weighs with me ... is my conviction that all men of business, whether merchants or tradesmen, do every day recognise and act on the ground that prompt payment of part of their demand may be more beneficial to them than it would be to insist on their rights and enforce payment of the whole. Even where the debtor is perfectly solvent, and sure to pay at last, this often is so. Where the credit of the debtor is doubtful it must be more so.

However, it is not necessarily solely a case of allowing a creditor to renege on his promise; the villain of the piece may be a debtor whose reluctance, or worse, drives the creditor into accepting less than is due. That an unscrupulous debtor should be bound to pay in full was recognised in *D & C Builders Ltd v Rees* (1966) – either by use of the common law rule or by applying ideas of unfair pressure or duress (see below).

In any event the rule in *Pinnel's Case* is now so hemmed in by exceptions that there must be few cases today in which the principle is in fact applicable. The main exceptions are as follows:

•   *At common law*

A good accord and satisfaction can be achieved (so as to exclude the rule) by a *variation* in the debtor's performance – a variation in the method, time or place of payment by the debtor to support the creditor's promise to waive part of the debt: eg payment of a smaller sum in a different currency (not, however, a cheque or bill of exchange for a smaller sum in the same currency, see *D & C Builders Ltd v Rees*), or payment before the due day, or at a different place. (The variation must perhaps originate with the creditor – and be to his advantage.) Provision by the debtor of something different in kind (eg a car instead of £2,000) also falls under this heading.

- *In equity*

Since 1947 it is by means of an equitable evasion that the rule in *Pinnel's Case* has been largely eroded. In that year, in the *High Trees* case, it was established that a promise by a party not to enforce his full legal rights (see point 2 in the list on p 91) has – although it is *not* supported by consideration (point 3) – a degree of binding effect in equity.

This doctrine of *promissory estoppel* operates in the following way and subject to the following requirements:

(a) There must be a *pre-existing legal relationship* giving rise to rights and duties between the parties (eg a lease with a right to agreed rent).

(b) One party later makes a clear *promise* or assertion that he will *not fully enforce his existing rights* against the promisee (eg he will not insist on the full rent). He may do this for a variety of reasons; it may be sound business sense in changing circumstances.

(c) The *effect* of promissory estoppel is to *prevent* (or *stop*) the promisor from denying this promise – from retracting it and insisting on his strict legal rights under the existing contract – even though:

(d) the promisee provides *no consideration* for the promise, ie there is no accord and satisfaction. However

(e) it must be intended that the promise be *relied upon*, and the promisee does in fact rely upon it. (According to Lord Denning, in *Alan & Co Ltd v El Nasr Co* (1972), this does not mean detrimental reliance: 'The nearest to consideration is that the other must have been led to alter his position. This only means that he must have been led to an act differently from what he would otherwise have done' eg he pays the agreed lower rent.) The effect is to make it

(f) *inequitable* for the promisor to go back on the promise he has given. As Atiyah has stated: 'Where there is no bargain involved, it is the mere action in reliance on the promise which usually makes it just to enforce the promise.'

(g)   However, it is generally considered equitable to allow the promisor, on giving *reasonable notice*, to insist on a *resumption* of his strict rights. (This will not be possible and the promise will become 'final and irrevocable if the promisee cannot resume his position' before the promise was given.)

(h)   Where his rights are only suspended, the promisor can sue to enforce his original rights as to *the future*, but he cannot recover any balances 'owed' while his forbearance took effect. The promisee can use the *promise as a defence* to such an action.

(i)   However the *promisee himself cannot sue* on the promisor's promise (to waive his full rights) as he provided no consideration for it: the doctrine is a 'shield and not a sword' – it does not create new rights so as to abolish the doctrine of consideration by the back-door.

As with contract itself, the overall effect of the doctrine is to 'hold a man to his word' – as regards his forbearance or waiver of rights – at least for a time. Unlike contract, no consideration moves from the promisee – there is no bargain – but the equity lies in the promisee's reliance on the other's word.

The modern genesis of promissory estoppel lies in the case of *Central London Property Trust Ltd v High Trees House Ltd* (1947) decided by the then Denning J. He was able to manoeuvre round the *Foakes v Beer* decision by reviving the equitable basis of another decision of the House of Lords in *Hughes v Metropolitan Railway Co* (1877). In that case Lord Cairns stated that if one party leads the other 'to suppose that the strict rights arising under the contract will not be enforced, or will be kept in suspense or held in abeyance, the person who otherwise might have enforced those rights will not be allowed to enforce them where it would be inequitable having regard to the dealings which have thus taken place between the parties'.

In the *High Trees* case itself:

In 1937 CLPT let a block of flats in London to their subsidiary company HTH for 99 years at a ground rent of £2,500 pa. In 1940 as a result of bombing raids many of the flats were empty and CLPT agreed to reduce the rent to £1,250 pa because the original rent could not be paid by HTH out of the profits they received from the flats. (HTH provided no consideration to support CLPT's promise to forgo half the ground rent.) By 1945 the flats were again fully let, and the receiver of CLPT wrote to HTH claiming £625 future payment of rent at the full rate and 'arrears' of almost £8,000. These friendly proceedings were later instituted.

Denning J accepted the claim for full rent from mid-1945; the 1940 agreement being merely a temporary expedient and the conditions giving rise to it having disappeared. The judge however added that CLPT could not have sued for the full rent in the period covered by the 1940 agreement because of the equitable doctrine in *Hughes v Metropolitan Railway*. (If a claim for arrears had actually been made, HTH would have been able to use CLPT's promise as a defence to the action. They would thus not have been trying to prove the existence of a contract, varying the original one. They could not do this in any case as they had provided no consideration: see *Combe v Combe* (1951) below.)

The *High Trees* decision (which was taken no further) has since found basic acceptance with the House of Lords, subject to some uncertainty about its limits. Academic lawyers, however, have continued to question not only the limits but the basis of this erosion of *Foakes v Beer* and the rule in *Pinnel's Case*. Some writers seemed satisfied if its effect is taken to be a mere suspension of the rights of the creditor – who, on giving notice, can withdraw his promise to waive his strict rights. (In *High Trees*, notice was given but the £1,250 pa agreement was in any case stated to be only 'for the duration' of the war. *Tool Metal Mftg Co Ltd v Tungsten Electric Co Ltd* (1955) is a House of Lords decision dealing with periodic payments of royalties under a licence to use a patent and *suspension* of full payments to the owner; reasonable notice reviving the original terms of the licence.)

In essence, the judicial differences have been between Lord Denning, who sought to extend the doctrine as forcibly as possible, and the House of Lords who have given warnings about the need for 'coherent exposition'. Lord Denning did not accept that the doctrine is limited to the mere suspension of rights: 'the principle may be applied ... so as to preclude the enforcement of them.' (Lord Cairns's statement of 1877 does refer to rights not being enforced *or* being kept in suspense.)

As seen, further argument is said to relate to the promisee's actions following the promise. Must he act to *his detriment* for the doctrine to apply? It is perhaps true to say that this is the wrong approach. The key is *reliance*. All that is necessary is that the promisee places reliance on the promise and acts upon it, eg pays rent at £1,250 per annum or, as in *Charles Rickards Ltd v Oppenheim* (1950), where the seller, who had been promised further time in which to make delivery beyond the agreed date, continued to make efforts to perform the contract.

Another development comes with the suggestion that promissory estoppel *can* provide the basis of a cause of action, ie not merely act as a defence available for the party to whom the promise was made if and when sued by the promisor. The leading case for the 'defence only' rule is *Combe v Combe* (1951):

The parties were married in 1915 but separated in 1939. The wife started divorce proceedings and in 1943 was granted a decree nisi. The husband then promised her £100 pa tax free as permanent maintenance. (The wife did not apply to the Divorce Court for maintenance but this was not a forbearance at the husband's request. She had a larger income than the husband and that court would most probably not have made an order in her favour.) The decree was made absolute, but no payments were made by the husband. In 1950 the wife sued for £600.

At first instance, the court held that, although the wife had provided no consideration for it, the husband's promise was binding on the basis of the *High Trees* decision. However, on appeal, it was made clear, by Denning LJ, that to allow the wife to *base her action solely* upon such a promise was to ignore the necessity of consideration. The promisee could not sue on such a promise and the husband's appeal was allowed.

The 'promissory estoppel as a cause of action' proposition is a relatively new and controversial addition to an already complex and controversial topic. For example, is it not arguable that the plaintiff sub-contractor in *Williams v Roffey*, when claiming extra payment from the defendant, was using estoppel as a 'sword' to base his action.

One of the requirements for the application of promissory estoppel is that it must be inequitable or unjust for the promisor to go back on the promise they have given. The principle is an equitable one and its use is in the court's discretion. It was on this ground that Lord Denning based his judgment in *D & C Builders v Rees* (1966):

> D & C, a small firm of builders, did work for R at a cost of £482. Having pressed for payment for several months, they eventually and reluctantly agreed with R's wife, who knew they were in financial difficulties, to accept £300 'in completion of the account'. Mrs R told them that if they refused to take the lesser sum, they would get nothing.

> D & C later sued for the balance of the original debt. Their promise to accept £300 (not supported by consideration from R) was of a type to raise the estoppel principle but it was necessary to take account of 'the dealings which have thus taken place between the parties'. Mrs R had held the plaintiffs to ransom; her conduct amounting to unfair pressure in the circumstances.

> It was therefore not inequitable to permit D & C to go back on their promise and recover the whole debt. (Note that the wrongful pressure or economic duress point was also crucial in *Williams v Roffey* but there was no evidence of it in that case.)

In 1994 the Court of Appeal decided a case which not only revived Lord Blackburn's disquiet in *Foakes v Beer* regarding a mismatch between the rule in *Pinnel's Case* and regular business practice, but also presented an opportunity to bring the prevailing argument in *Williams v Roffey* to bear upon that early 17th century decision. Nevertheless, the opportunity was not taken; the rule remained (subject to its exceptions): part payment of a debt is no consideration. It was analytically possible for the Court of Appeal to find that a benefit to the creditor (as explained by Lord Blackburn, above) was sufficient consideration, but the court decided that it was bound by the House of Lords decision in *Foakes v Beer*:

> In *Re Selectmove Ltd* (1995), the company owed large sums in unpaid tax and national insurance contributions (NIC) to the Inland Revenue who presented a petition to wind up the company. (The Revenue would be preferred creditors in a winding up.) The company alleged a later agreement by which the Revenue would not take such action on the debt if the company (a) paid future tax and NIC as they fell due and (b) paid off arrears at £1,000 per month. (In return for these forbearances, S Ltd were in effect only doing what they were already obliged to do.) The company made late payments of both new demands and arrears instalments.

> It was held that if there was an agreement, it was unenforceable for lack of consideration and a plea of promissory estoppel could not stand. It was not inequitable for the Revenue to

go back on its promise not to enforce the debt as S Ltd had broken its promise to pay new demands as they become due.

The court was sympathetic to the *Williams v Roffey* argument that a promise to perform an existing obligation to the promisee may amount to good consideration if there are practical benefits to the promisee. The rearrangement – whereby the company had been kept out of liquidation, paying off its debts over a period – had indeed gone forward and was apparently the outcome the Revenue preferred. The picture is similar to that painted by Lord Blackburn in *Foakes v Beer* but of course Lord Blackburn had nevertheless joined the other Law Lords in that case in affirming the rule in *Pinnel's Case*. In addition, Lord Hanworth in *Vanbergen v St Edmund's Properties Ltd* (1933) had repeated the 'well established principle that a promise to pay a sum which the debtor is already bound by law to pay the promisee does not afford any consideration to support the contract'.

The upshot is that *Williams v Roffey* does not apply where the pre-existing obligation is an obligation to pay, as opposed to an obligation to supply goods or services because otherwise *Foakes v Beer* would have no application. It must be the case that further developments are required to eliminate the 'rough edges' that presently exist in this area of the law. Taking a cue from Professor Llewellyn (see p 89), it may be that the answer is to abolish the requirement of consideration for contract renegotiations and let the presence or absence of economic duress be the test of enforceability.

Privity of contract: contracts and third party beneficiaries

Whereas the doctrine of consideration is concerned with establishing the line between enforceable and unenforceable promises, the doctrine of privity determines, among other things, *who* may enforce a promise. In *Dunlop Pneumatic Tyre Co Ltd v Selfridge and Co Ltd* (1915), see also p 204, the Lord Chancellor, Viscount Haldane, stated that 'in the law of England certain principles are fundamental. One is that only a person who is a party to a contract may sue on it.' Like other fundamental contract principles this one appears to be simple, even obvious, and in the vast majority of cases privity causes no problems. Only two parties are involved and each agrees to perform stipulated obligations for the benefit of the other. Each may enforce the other's promise. However, as enunciated by Viscount Haldane, the main privity rule means that a person may not enforce a contractual promise, even when that promise is made in his favour, if he is not a party to the contract.

In *Dunlop v Selfridge*, S's promise was made in favour of D (a promise not to sell D's tyres below a certain price) but that promise was made as part of a contract between S, a retailer of D's tyres, and his supplier, who had bought the tyres from D and resold them to S. D was not a party to that contract and so could not enforce S's promise. Clearly here privity interfered with manufacturer

D's marketing strategy. The company was unable to enforce its resale price maintenance policy against S at a time when RPM, which is essentially anti-competitive, was not itself unlawful.

Another way of looking at this case is on the basis of the related rule that consideration must move from the promisee. D provided no consideration to support S's promise (made to his supplier). Looked at from this perspective, Lord Dunedin, although agreeing with the decision, felt compelled to state that:

> I confess that this case is to my mind apt to nip any budding affection which one might have had for the doctrine of consideration. For the effect of that doctrine in the present case is to make it possible for a person [S] to snap his fingers at a bargain deliberately made, a bargain not in itself unfair, and which the person [D] seeking to enforce it has a legitimate interest to enforce.

It is possible to go much further with a discussion of privity. The doctrine, established in the mid-19th century and resting on 'clear-cut' views of agreement (consent) and consideration (bargain) seems eminently logical at first sight. It has spawned other third party problems but more significantly, in the face of commercial inconvenience and injustice in the changing circumstances and values of the 20th century, it has produced a wide range of evasions and exemptions. (See Adams and Brownsword, 'Privity of contract – that pestilential nuisance' in References and further reading.

One example of a statutory exception is to be found in s 148(7) of the Road Traffic Act 1988 which allows third parties to sue on the benefit of motor vehicle insurance policies. As regards general reform of the doctrine of privity, the Law Commission in a 1991 consultation paper proposes that reform should take the form of a detailed legislative scheme granting third parties the right to enforce contracts made for their benefit. Third party plaintiffs would only include those on whom the parties to the contract expressly or impliedly intended to confer an enforceable legal obligation.

References and further reading

Contractual intention

Brown, 'The letter of comfort – placebo or promise?' (1990) JBL 281.

Hedley, 'Keeping contract in its place: *Balfour v Balfour* and the enforceability of informal agreements' (1985) 5 OJLS 391.

Hepple, 'Intention to create legal relations' (1970) CLJ 122.

Tettenborn, 'Commercial certainty: a step in the right direction' (1988) CLJ 346.

Unger, 'Intent to create legal relations, mutality and consideration' (1956) 19 MLR 96.

Consideration and promissory estoppel

Adams and Brownsword, 'Contract, consideration and the critical path' (1990) 53 MLR 536 (*Williams v Roffey*).

Atiyah (1989), *An Introduction to the Law of Contract*, 4th edn, ch V1.

Denning (1979), *'High Trees'*, Part Five of *The Discipline of the Law*.

Dugdale and Yates, 'Variation, waiver and estoppel – a re-appraisal' (1976) 40 MLR 680.

Gordon, 'Creditors' promises to forgo rights – a study of the *High Trees* and *Tool Metal* cases' (1963) CLJ 222 (an article setting out to demolish promissory estoppel).

Peel, 'Part payment of a debt is no consideration' (*Re Selectmove*) (1994) 110 LQR 353.

Phang, 'Consideration at the crossroads' (1991) 107 LQR 21.

Thompson, 'From representation to expectation: estoppel as a cause of action' (1983) CLJ 257.

Wilson, 'A reappraisal of quasi-estoppel' [1965] CLJ 93 (a reply to Gordon's article, see above).

Privity of contract

Adams and Brownsword, 'Privity of contract – that pestilential nuisance' (1993) 56 MLR 722.

Law Commission, *Privity of Contract: Contracts for the Benefit of Third Parties* (1991) Consultation Paper No 121.

Questions

(1) (a) What is meant by the term 'presumption'? How may a presumption concerning the intention of the parties be rebutted? Is the presumption relating to the enforceability of business agreements a realistic one?

(b) In *Rose & Frank Co v Crompton & Bros Ltd* why was the 'honour clause' not applicable to contracts of sale entered into in pursuance of the distribution agreement?

(c) A and B have been negotiating the settlement of a dispute between them. As a result A agrees to pay B £500 on an *ex gratia* basis. Can B sue A for performance of this promise?

(2) 'Consideration is a perfectly adequate test of liability in contract, the so-called doctrine of intention to create legal relations is superfluous.' Discuss this statement in the light of decided cases.

(3) White has been friendly for several years with Black, who is senior partner for a local firm of accountants and tax advisers. He telephones the firm and requests advice concerning his income tax return. At his appointment, Brown, another partner, gives advice and agrees to prepare White's return to the Inland Revenue. Nothing is said about a fee for these services. Brown prepares the return and lodges it with the local tax office. A week later White receives a bill for £100 from the accountants.

On learning that the usual fee for such services is £60, White goes back to the firm and remonstrates with Brown regarding the account. At length Brown agrees to accept £60 for the work done. White promises to send a cheque but, after four months, he has paid nothing. Discuss the legal position.

(4) In *Ajayi v Briscoe (Nigeria) Ltd* (1964), Lord Hodson defined the principle of promissory estoppel as one in which one party to a contract in the absence of fresh consideration agrees not to enforce his rights – in such a case an equity is raised in favour of the other party.

Discuss, with appropriate illustrations, the qualifications to which Lord Hodson stated that the equity was subject:

(a) that the other party has altered his position;

(b) that the promisor can resile from his promise on giving reasonable notice;

(c) that the promise only becomes final and irrevocable if the promisee cannot resume his position.

(5) Explain the doctrine of promissory estoppel in terms of its being

(a) a moral principle;

(b) the bending of a rule of higher generality;

(c) good business sense.

(6) 'An agreement to do an act which the promisor is under an existing obligation to a third party to do, may quite well amount to consideration and does so in the present case: the promisee obtains the benefit of a direct obligation which he can enforce': Lord Reid in *The Eurymedon* (1975). Discuss.

(7) On 1 December Colin agrees to construct a swimming pool for Dave at a price of £3,000, completion by, and payment on, 1 June. Colin subsequently purchases tiles from Eric, the price of £500 to be paid on 1 April.

Colin has miscalculated the costs of construction and by March is in considerable financial difficulties. He explains his plight to Dave who reluctantly agrees to increase the price of the pool to £3,400, of which £400 is to be paid on 1 April. At the same time, Colin says to Eric, 'You'll have to accept £400 on 1 April; I won't be able to pay you any more'. Dave pays Colin £400 and Eric reluctantly accepts this sum as 'full settlement' for the tiles.

By 1 June the pool is completed but Dave pays Colin only £2,600. Eric now claims an additional £100 from Colin. Advise Colin.

(8) Consider the relationship between, and the results achieved in the following cases from three different jurisdictions:

(i)   the English case of *Gibson v Manchester City Council* (1979);

(ii)   the Californian case of *Drennan v Star Paving Corp* (1958);

(iii)   the Australian case of *Walton's Stores (Interstate) Ltd v Maher* (1988).

(These cases are dealt with by Collins, *The Law of Contract*, Wheeler and Shaw, *Contract Law: Cases, Materials and Commentary* and others.)

7   Contractual terms and breach

Express and implied terms

As we have seen, contract law is not usually concerned with the form into which the parties put their agreement. Many business agreements, such as cif export sales, building contracts and hire purchase agreements, are, or are based on, standard printed documents. A contract may be entirely in a written form, or it may be partly written with the remainder orally expressed. Many agreements are wholly oral and indeed certain contractual obligations may simply be implied from the parties' conduct, eg I take a newspaper from an unattended pile and place 20 pence into a tin. A mixed bag of factors such as economy, convenience, certainty, security or speed tends to dictate contractual expression and, as one aspect of freedom of contract, the law itself rarely demands a particular form.

The multiplicity of forms that a contract may take is well illustrated by the case of *Evans & Son (Portsmouth) Ltd v Merzario Ltd* (1976):

> For several years M made the transport arrangements for the importation of machinery by E from Italy. The course of dealing between the parties was based on the printed standard conditions of the freight forwarding trade, clause 4 of which read: 'Subject to express instructions in writing given by the customer, the Company reserves to itself complete freedom in respect of means, route and procedure to be followed in the handling and transportation of goods.' It was not disputed that the terms of the standard form had, by the course of dealings, become part of each individual contract made by the parties.
>
> After eight years it was proposed that the machinery should be carried in containers, and M's manager, in the course of discussions in Portsmouth with E's manager, assured him: 'If we do use containers, they will not be carried on deck' (where the machinery might go rusty). Containers were used and invoices, referring as usual to the standard conditions and containing new charges, were sent. Nothing was put in writing about the containers being carried below deck.
>
> A container carried on deck fell into the sea and was lost. The court held that E was entitled to damages for breach of contract on two grounds, one of which being that the oral assurance amounted to an express term of the contract, which was partly in writing, partly implied by conduct and partly oral. The new oral term and clause 4 of the printed conditions being inconsistent, the court held that the individual assurance overrode the standard form.

This case was mainly concerned with express terms: what was written or said by the parties and what was written in the printed form which they adopted. Other contractual issues – as noted in Chapter 1 – centre on the question of *implied terms*, which are just as binding as express terms and are implied and incorporated into contracts from a variety of sources. Although government policy, through the medium of statute law, is the most important source of implied terms, say as regards consumer protection, the courts themselves possess the power to imply terms into a contract. We have already seen, in the context of certainty, how a court will imply a reasonable contract price in certain circumstances. Similarly, terms may be implied from business practice and other sources.

The courts will not make a contract for the parties, so when and on what basis will they 'find' a term which has not been expressed? Judges and academics have gone to great lengths to identify certain categories or groups of implied terms. Opinions vary as to how many categories there are, probably because, as Lord Wilberforce has said, they are not so much distinctive categories but shades on a continuous spectrum. Professor Treitel considers that implied terms can be divided into three categories: terms implied in *fact*, terms implied in *law* and terms implied by *custom or usage*.

Terms implied in fact

Such terms are implied on the basis of what the parties *must* have intended. Therefore such terms can only be implied if *both* parties, had they applied their mind to the matter now in issue, would have considered it to be necessary:

> *Prima facie* that which in any contract is left to be implied and need not be expressed is something so obvious that it goes without saying; so that if while the parties were making their bargain, an officious bystander were to suggest some express provision for it in the agreement, they would testily suppress him with a common 'Oh, of course!' (*MacKinnon LJ* in *Shirlaw v Southern Foundries (1926) Ltd* (1939)).

For example, in a charterparty it would, if necessary, be implied that the vessel on hire was seaworthy. In the *Hong Kong Fir Shipping* breach case (to be discussed shortly), Diplock LJ makes the point that: 'No doubt there are many simple contractual undertakings, sometimes express, but more often because of their simplicity ("It goes without saying") to be implied.'

'It goes without saying' because the term is an established usage within the business context into which the contract takes it place.

The 'officious bystander' test has on occasion been merged with another, 'business efficacy' test:

> A term can only be implied if it is necessary in the business sense to give efficacy to the contract; that is if it is such a term that it can confidently be said that if at the time the contract was being negotiated some one had said to the parties, 'What will happen in such a case?', they would both have replied, 'Of course, so and so will happen; we did not trouble to say that; it is too clear (Scrutton LJ in *Reigate v Union Manufacturing Co* (1918)).

It is probable that in practice the two tests amount to much the same thing. In *Banco de Portugal v Waterlow & Sons Ltd* (1932) a term was implied into a contract for the printing of bank notes for the Portuguese central bank that the London printers should not allow use of the plates to get into unauthorised hands. In any event, 'the touchstone is always necessity and not *merely* reasonableness'. It must be necessary common sense to imply the term because the parties themselves – a *subjective* test – would have agreed to it. In *Trollope & Colls Ltd v NW Metropolitan Regional Hospital Board* (1973), Lord Pearce stated that: 'The court will not ... improve the contract which the parties have made, however desirable the improvement might be ... If the express terms are perfectly clear and free from ambiguity, there is no choice to be made ... the clear terms must be applied.'

Terms implied in law

The implication of these terms does not, as is the case with terms implied in fact, depend on the common intention of the parties. Instead, they should be seen as duties arising out of certain types of contracts; they are 'legal incidents of those ... kinds of contractual relationship'.

Terms are implied by law as a matter of *policy* and in many instances the implication of the term is really the imposition of a legal duty. In *Liverpool City Council v Irwin* (1977), Lord Wilberforce stated that:

> ... the court is here simply concerned to establish what the contract is, the parties not having fully stated the terms. In his sense the court is searching for what must be implied ... The question to be answered ... is what is to be the legal relationship between landlord and tenant as regards these [missing] matters.

In *Shell UK Ltd v Lostock Garage Ltd* (1977), Lord Denning said that terms implied in law are to be found in 'those relationships which are of common occurrence ... seller and buyer, owner and hirer, master and servant, landlord and tenant, carrier by land or sea, contractor for building works, and so on. In all those relationships the courts have imposed obligations on one party or the other, saying they are implied terms ... The House in *Liverpool City Council v Irwin* ... examined the existing law of landlord and tenant ... to see if it contained the solution to the problem; and, having found that it did not, they imposed an obligation on the landlord to use reasonable care.'

> In *Liverpool City Council v Irwin* (1977), the Council's obligations under their 'conditions of tenancy', in respect of a 15-storey tower block of flats which had rapidly and drastically deteriorated, were absent from the document. The contract being incomplete, the court implied terms 'such as the nature of the contract itself implicitly required'. These included the Council's duty to take reasonable care as regards repair and usability of common parts. However, the tenants also had their responsibilities as reasonable tenants. The tenant's appeal failed (as it had done in a unanimous Court of Appeal); it not having been shown that the Council was in breach of the implied duty.

Policy considerations form the basis for the implication of terms in law. The court may be seen to be regulating the contract in terms of distributive justice so that one party does not take advantage of the other. In Lord Denning's opinion, one must look to see what would be reasonable in the circumstances in the general run of such cases '... and then say what the obligation shall be'.

In various sectors of business and commerce, terms implied judicially as legal duties have come to acquire the status of general rules, eg in building contracts (the contractor will supply good and proper materials), in contracts for the carriage of goods by sea (the carrier will provide a seaworthy vessel), and in contracts for the sale of goods (the goods sold must be reasonably fit for their purpose). As we will soon see, some of these 'standardised' implied terms came to be put into statutory form.

Terms implied by trade usage

The willingness of a court to imply terms from *business practice* is a clear illustration of the point that it may be unwise to regard a contract's express terms in isolation; the better course, in appropriate circumstances, is to set them firmly within an overall framework or context of business conduct and relationships:

> In *British Crane Hire Corpn Ltd v Ipswich Plant Hire Ltd* (1975), BC supplied a dragline crane to IP. It being a matter of urgency, the agreement was made by telephone and nothing was said about the conditions of hire. Later BC sent their printed conditions to IP but before they were signed the crane sank in marshy ground. The conditions were similar to those used by all firms in the plant hire business – including IP – and they laid down that the hirer was liable to indemnify the owner of equipment against all expense in connection with its use. When sued for the cost of recovering the crane, IP claimed they were not liable under BC's conditions because they had not been incorporated into the oral contract.

> The court held that as IP knew that such conditions were in common use in the business, BC were entitled to conclude that IP were accepting the crane on their conditions, which had therefore been incorporated into the contract on the basis of the common understanding of the parties.

In this case, a term was implied or incorporated into a contract because it was reasonable and in common use in a trade to which both parties belonged. Similarly, terms may be incorporated into contracts between parties who have established a regular, previous course of dealing, whether or not they are in the same line of business. This has already been seen in the *Merzario* case as regards the printed standard conditions of the freight forwarding trade. Similarly in *Kendall & Sons v Lillico & Sons Ltd* (appeals from *Hardwick Game Farm v Suffolk Agricultural Poultry Producers Association*) (1969):

> Poultry feeding stuffs were sold orally on the Bury St Edmunds Corn Exchange by HGF to SAPPA. The next day HGF sent a confirmation note to SAPPA on the back of which were HGF's conditions of sale, including one that the buyer took responsibility for latent defects. It was established that the parties had regularly contracted in this way over a period of

years, and so it was held that the note's written terms could properly be incorporated into the oral contract.

In *Spurling v Bradshaw* (1956), B had stored goods with S for many years. He delivered eight barrels of orange juice to S's warehouse. A few days later he received as usual a printed acknowledgement that contained a series of clauses on the back. When the barrels were later found to be empty, B refused to pay the storage charges and when sued he counter-claimed for negligence. To this S pleaded a clause in the acknowledgement document which stated that S was exempt from liability for 'any loss or damage occasioned by the negligence, wrongful act or default' of themselves or their servants.

B argued that as the document was sent to him only after the conclusion of the contract, the clause was inoperative. On evidence that in previous dealings he had received a similar document but had never bothered to read it, the court held that he was bound by it. (This case would now be covered by the Unfair Contract Terms Act, see Chapter 9.)

As was stated in a similar case: 'It is the consistency of a course of conduct which gives rise to the implication that in similar circumstances a similar contractual result will follow.'

Finally it will be recalled that in *Hillas & Co Ltd v Arcos Ltd*, discussed in Chapter 5 in the context of certainty, details from a previous contract between two parties engaged in the timber trade were available to 'fill out' and provide sufficient certainty for a subsequent agreement to be declared binding.

Statutory intervention

We have already noted in Chapter 4 the tremendous expansion of the mixed economy and welfare state functions of the state which, particularly since the end of the Second World War, has led to vastly increased governmental involvement in business and social affairs: it has led to a 'multitude of statutory terms of contract, substituted for, or added to, the terms agreed between the parties'. It is this erosion of freedom of contract by statute which is mainly responsible for the transformation of contract from a private to a public act and, in a sense, contract is now as 'mixed' as the economy itself. For a variety of social welfare reasons, statutes may now compel us to make certain contracts (eg for motor insurance coverage) or, more commonly, regulate the terms of contracts (eg hire purchase agreements, rent controlled tenancies, contracts of employment.)

Statutory intervention often stems from the need for Parliament to restore some semblance of balance to the contractual relationship in question. Where freedom of contract has degenerated into freedom to oppress owing to an imbalance of economic power between the parties, the legislature has tended to move in on behalf of the weaker party by way of statutorily implied contractual terms. An excellent illustration of this process concerns contracts for the carriage of goods and the description given by Professor Gutteridge as far back as 1935 deserves to be quoted at length:

No part of English commercial law has undergone greater or more fundamental changes than that which concerns the rules governing the carriage of goods. The primary cause of this has been the development of means of communication and transit due to modern inventions, but another influence which has been at work is the desire to secure world-wide uniformity in the rules of carriage by sea and by air which are necessarily international in character. The growth of the law is also marked throughout by the struggle which has taken place between the carriers in an attempt to escape liability for negligence, and the goods owners who have been at a disadvantage when faced with the uncertainty and expense of litigation in which their opponents have been great and wealthy corporations in whose hands the business of carriage has become concentrated during the last 50 years.

The judges, for their part, have striven to restrain the attempts of the carriers to obtain contractual exemption from responsibility by refusing to recognize such exemption when accompanied by negligence, deviation or unseaworthiness, and this has resulted in a considerable volume of case law which, in its turn, has been followed by further attempts by the carriers to escape liability. The intervention of the legislature became necessary and resulted in such important measures as the Carriage of Goods by Sea Act 1924, the Railways Act of 1921 and the Carriage by Air Act 1932. On the other hand, it has become evident that the interests of the community call for a balancing of the interests of the goods owners and those of the carriers in order to avoid excessive charges for carriage, and the Acts of Parliament which have just been mentioned ... have been framed so as to relieve the carrier, to the utmost extent which is commercially possible, from the more hazardous features of his responsibility.

It is probably correct to say that no other part of our commercial law reflects, in a similar degree, the interplay of purely economic considerations and those of legal theory (*Contract and Commercial Law 1885-1935*).

Regulation or 'a balancing of interests' (the search for equilibrium between Gurvitch's 'rapprochement' and 'separation', see Chapter 2) through the imposition of implied obligations on a party possessing stronger bargaining power has a long history in the sale of goods field. As with carriage, first the courts acted alone, the legislature intervening later.

Sale of goods and protection for buyers

The maxim *caveat emptor* – let the buyer beware – has its English origins in the system of trading common to the markets and fairs of the Middle Ages, where the goods were on open display and where they could be examined, tested and bought on the spot. The buyer was assumed to rely on his own judgment. Professor Llewellyn has described later developments in this way:

Out of this we move gradually into a credit and industrial economy ... Markets widen with improved transportation – internal waterways, railroads. This means reliance on distant sellers ... Industrialization grows out of and produces standardization ... a certain predictability and reliability of goods. Contracts made by description, or by sample, which is a form of description, or by specification, which is an elaborate description, become the order of the day. Contracts come increasingly to precede production ... The law of seller's obligation *must* change, to suit.

At the time of predominantly face-to-face contractual situations, a buyer might obtain a remedy if, on receiving defective or worthless goods, he could prove breach of an express promise made by the seller or if he could prove fraud. Later, when goods came to be dealt in mainly by way of description to a buyer a hundred or a thousand miles away, or, in the case of packaged or canned goods, merely sold over a shop counter, the law of seller's obligation as to quality did gradually change. In *Gardiner v Gray* in 1815 and *Jones v Bright* in 1829, the court was willing to infer or imply promises as to quality into the sale – promises or terms as to merchantability and fitness for the buyer's purpose.

The Sale of Goods Act 1893, which codified the law as it existed at that time, represents something of a halfway house between the opposing ideas of 'caveat emptor' and consumer protection. The decision in *Jones v Bright*, to the effect that if goods are sold for a particular purpose it is impliedly understood that they will be fit for that purpose, reappeared in s 14(1) of the Act. However, it did so only as an exception to the underlying principle of *caveat emptor*, and the right which it afforded the buyer was hedged round with qualifications:

> 14 ... there is no implied warranty or condition as to the quality or fitness for any particular purpose of goods supplied under a contract of sale, except as follows ... (1) Where the buyer, expressly or by implication, makes known to the seller the particular purpose for which the goods are required, so as to show that the buyer relies on the seller's skill or judgment, and the goods are of a description which it is in the course of the seller's business to supply (whether he be the manufacturer or not), there is an implied condition that the goods shall be reasonably fit for such purpose, provided that in the case of a contract for the sale of a specified article under its patent or other trade name, there is no implied condition as to its fitness for any particular purpose.

Although subsequent case law reveals that the courts interpreted the requirements of s 14(1) in a manner favourable to the buyer, the greatest stumbling block to the fulfilment of real consumer protection was to be found in s 55 of the Act: 'Where any right, duty or liability would arise under a contract of sale by implication of law, it may be negatived or varied by express agreement.' Therefore, by clinging to the notion of freedom of contract, the legislature set its statutory seal of approval on freedom to exploit. By means of tightly worded, small-print exclusion clauses in their contracts, sellers of goods, backed by economic power brought about through monopoly or combination, were able to negative whatever protection was afforded the buyer by means of s 14(1) and similar provisions in the Act and so deprive buyers of their legal remedies.

The following cases illustrate some of the important features of the law relating to the implied obligation of fitness for a particular purpose:

In *Cammell Laird & Co Ltd v Manganese Bronze and Brass Co Ltd* (1934), B ordered two ship's propellers to be made by S to B's design and specifications but the thickness of the blades was left to the skill and judgment of S. The unsuitable thickness of one of the blades caused undue noise when the propellers were used. It was held that S were in breach of s 14(1), the defect relating to a part of the work which fell within S's sphere of judgment.

In *Baldry v Marshall Ltd* (1925), B asked motor dealers for a car that would be suitable for touring purposes and they recommended an eight-cylinder Bugatti. B found that it was not suitable and the court held that the dealers were in breach of s 14(1). As regards the trade name proviso in that section the court stated that it would only protect the seller if the buyer specified goods under their trade name in such a way as to indicate that he was satisfied that they would answer his purpose and that he was not relying on the seller's skill and judgment.

When s 14 was re-drafted in 1973 under the Supply of Goods (Implied Terms) Act, s 14(1) became s 14(3) and the proviso was excluded. Thus, unless actual use of a patent or trade name clearly shows the absence of reliance, the condition of fitness for purpose will be implied into the contract providing the other requirements of the sub-section are met. Section 55 of the 1893 Act has also been changed by subsequent legislation and it is now clear that exclusion clauses in contracts for the sale of goods which seek to negative or vary the seller's implied obligations (as to fitness for purpose, etc) will be of no effect in consumer transactions and in other cases will be subject to a test of reasonableness.

The complex question of exclusion clauses will be fully examined in Chapter 9, but the following case illustrates how such a clause operated to deprive a buyer of her rights:

In *L'Estrange v Graucob Ltd* (1934), L signed a sales agreement for the purchase of an automatic cigarette machine which contained the following clause: 'This agreement contains all the terms and conditions under which I agree to purchase the machine specified above and any express or *implied condition*, statement or warranty, *statutory* or otherwise not stated herein is hereby excluded.' (Emphasis added.) The machine failed to work properly. L's claim for breach of s 14(1) failed; G being protected from a claim for breach of the implied obligation of fitness for purpose.

The increasing prevalence and severity of such clauses (particularly in the related field of hire purchase) meant that eventually parliament was prevailed upon to amend the law – as it did in 1973. This was a major advance in the protection of buyers' (and HP buyers') rights and the implied term is no longer, for parties contracting as consumers, in the shadow of the exclusion clause: see now the Unfair Contract Terms Act 1977.

The Sale of Goods Act 1893 together with its subsequent amendments has now been consolidated in the Sale of Goods Act 1979 (as further amended in 1994). Similar implied terms regarding quality in such contracts as those for work and materials, exchange and hire are to be found in the Supply of Goods and Services Act 1982. This Act also provides that there is an implied term that the supplier of *services* will carry out the service with reasonable care and skill: see *Wilson v Best Travel Ltd* (1993) concerning package holidays.

Judicial approaches to breach of contract

In the previous section we have considered the express or implied nature of contractual terms. We have also previously seen that contract planning often covers four main issues: definition of performances, effect of defective performance, effect of contingencies and use or non-use of legal sanctions. Breach of contract implies non-performance or defective performance and so relates directly to the first issue, whilst its effect may be accounted for in the second (eg 'defective parts shall be replaced').

Clauses in a contract which relate to defective performance, contingencies and sanctions are of a secondary or procedural nature, eg 'if there is a strike then ...' or 'the parties agree to arbitrate any dispute arising ...'. Terms which describe performances are of a different, primary or substantive nature and indicate what the contractual obligations are, how they will be fulfilled and, perhaps impliedly, the required quality of performance: for a discussion of primary and secondary rights in the context of breach, see Lord Diplock in *Photo Production Ltd v Securicor Transport Ltd* (1980).

There is therefore a clear relationship between breach of contract and contractual terms which define performances. In this section we are concerned with two approaches taken by the courts to breach, and in discussing this issue it should be appreciated that, whilst it is important to have regard to the business community's general preference for amicable negotiation or arbitration of disputes, the law reports reveal a continuing stream of breach cases, not a few of them on appeal from arbitration tribunals. These cases clearly involve situations where the parties' planning (if any) and co-operation have broken down completely. The role of the law is to clear up the mess, which it primarily seeks to do by ordering compensatory payments – damages – to be made to aggrieved parties, although in some circumstances a further right – to terminate the contract – is also recognised.

The operation of this right of a party to terminate the contract in the face of what he considers to be a breach by the other can give rise to a problem. For example, X agrees to pay Y for the performance of certain services. In the early days of performance Y fails, in X's judgment, to match up to the terms of his obligations. Can X dispense with Y's services? It has been put this way: 'In what event will a party be relieved of his undertaking to do that which he has agreed to do but has not yet done?' In our example: in what event will X be relieved of his obligation to pay Y? When has X a right to terminate the contract? If X terminates when no such right is available, it is clear that he himself is liable to an action or counter-claim by Y.

The English courts approach these questions concerning the right to terminate in two ways, *which may or may not give the same answer in a given case*. The first, (perhaps) longer-standing approach is what is known as *term-based*: the right to terminate is related to the nature of the term broken. A distinction is made between major terms, known as conditions, breach of which allows for termination (and damages) and minor terms – warranties – the breach of which does not allow for termination but only a claim for damages. From the mass of case law in this area, a condition has been variously described as an 'essential' term or one that 'goes to the root of the contract' and the breach of which is 'fairly considered by the other party as a substantial failure to perform the contract at all'. The Sale of Goods Act 1893 defined a warranty as a term which is 'merely collateral to the main purpose of the contract'. Essential or major terms allow for termination, minor terms do not.

This appears to be a very straightforward approach but the question remains: How precisely does a court, or a businessman, or his legal adviser go about making the distinction between the major and the minor terms in a given contract? As Atiyah has said, 'Terms do not usually bear on their face the answer to this question.' The answer given by lawyers is that one must construe or interpret the contract *as at the time it was made* and infer from it the possible intention of the parties. In 1893 Lord Justice Bowen said that it was necessary to look at the contract in the light of the surrounding circumstances and make up one's mind whether the intention of the parties would best be carried out by treating the provision as a warranty or as a condition.

This is apparently as far as the courts have got in laying down guidelines for the predication or evaluation of terms, and there is some degree of obscurity about how this approach to breach operates.

In *Behn v Burness* (1863), by a charterparty dated 19 October 1860, it was agreed that the plaintiff's ship, 'now in the port of Amsterdam ... and ready for the voyage, should, with all possible dispatch, proceed to Newport', where the defendant would load her with coal for Hong Kong. At that time, however, the vessel was, in fact, detained by bad weather at Niewdiep, 62 miles from Amsterdam, which she did not reach until 23 October. When the vessel reached Newport, Burness, the charterer (who had by then presumably made alternative arrangements) refused to load his coal and thereby repudiated the charterparty. He was sued for wrongful termination by the shipowner. It was held that Burness was justified as Behn was in breach of an essential term – the clause stating the 'whereabouts of the vessel' at the time of agreement.

As Williams J stated: 'Now the place of the ship at the date of the contract, where the ship is in foreign parts and is chartered to come to England, may be the only datum on which the charterer can found his calculations of the time of the ship's arriving at the port of loading ... A statement is more or less important in proportion as the object of the contract more or less depends upon it. For most charters, considering winds, markets and dependent contracts, the time of a ship's arrival to load is an essential fact, for the interest of the charterer. In the ordinary course of charters in general it would be so: the evidence for the [charterer] shows it to be actually so in this case.'

The 'whereabouts of the vessel' clause was a condition, it had been broken by the plaintiff, and the defendant was justified in terminating the contract.

This decision and other cases involving the breach of similar 'essential' terms in regular commercial use led, through the operation of the doctrine of precedent, to the understanding that such terms were always to be regarded as conditions. The 'once a condition, always a condition' result was applauded as introducing a strong element of certainty into business contracts; the consequences of breaking such terms being readily apparent from the case law.

Later, this development could be confirmed by reference to statute law. As we have seen, certain obligations of a seller of goods, such as the merchantability (now 'satisfactory quality') of those goods and their fitness for a particular purpose, are implied conditions by reason of the Sale of Goods Act. Breach of such an obligation gives the buyer a right to reject the goods as a matter of statute law. We have therefore reached a point where (i) the breach of an essential term gives a right to terminate the contract, and (ii) some terms are always to be classified as conditions on the basis of precedent or statutory authority.

An unsatisfactory feature of this position is, however, revealed by the decision in *Arcos Ltd v Ronaasen & Son* (1933):

A quantity of timber staves, described in the contract as being 1/2 inch thick, was bought for the purpose of making cement barrels. Most of the staves delivered were 9/16 inches thick. Although the discrepancy in no way impaired their suitability for the contract purpose, it was held that the buyer might nevertheless reject the timber. The seller was in breach of the implied condition, to be found in s 13 of the Sale of Goods Act 1893, that the goods delivered must correspond to the contract description. The fact that the buyer's motive in rejecting the goods was to allow himself the chance to buy elsewhere in a falling market did not affect the decision.

This case clearly illustrates that breach of an 'essential' term can give a right to terminate although performance is only marginally defective, the consequences for the 'injured' party are only slight, and he is abusing the right to terminate. (As regards the sale of goods, a 1994 amendment to the Sale of Goods Act 1979 has rectified this position for sellers who are dealing with buyers who are not dealing as consumers. If the seller's breach concerning description, satisfactory quality or fitness for purpose is so slight that it would be unreasonable for the buyer to reject the goods, the breach is not to be treated as a breach of condition but may be treated as a breach of warranty.)

In 1962 the whole question of terms and breach was reopened in the case of *Hong Kong Fir Shipping Co Ltd v Kawasaki Kisen Kaisha Ltd*, where the 'term-based' approach was seriously challenged. In the leading judgment of the Court of Appeal, Diplock LJ stated that what was critical was not the nature of the term broken but the nature of the event arising from the breach. If the consequences for the injured party were sufficiently serious – such as to deprive him of substantially the whole benefit which it was intended that he should obtain – then he was entitled to terminate the contract. If they were not so serious, then he could only claim damages:

> K chartered a vessel from H for 24 months. The ship developed engine trouble and was laid up for repairs for 20 weeks out of the first seven months of the contract. Although she was made seaworthy at the end of that period, the charterers terminated the contract. The owners, H, claimed damages for wrongful repudiation. The court held that H's breach of the seaworthiness clause had not given rise to consequences serious enough for K to terminate. Amongst other things, the charterparty still had a further 17 of the original 24 months to run. K were only entitled to claim damages and H won the case. (The main reason why K threw up the contract was that freight rates had fallen dramatically and they could charter another vessel at a much lower rate.)

On the basis of this 'seriousness of consequences' approach, the seaworthiness clause in this case only amounted to a warranty. However, had the court found the consequences of its breach to be such as to deprive K of substantially the whole benefit from the contract, termination would have been justified and the clause would therefore have had the status of a condition. Diplock LJ put it this way:

> There are, however, many contractual undertakings of a complex character which cannot be categorised as being 'conditions' or 'warranties' ... of such undertakings all that can be predicated is that some breaches will and others will not give rise to an event which will deprive the party not in default of substantially the whole benefit which it was intended that he should obtain from the contract; and the legal consequences of the breach of such an undertaking, unless provided for expressly in the contract, depend upon the nature of the event to which the breach gives rise and do not follow automatically from a prior classification of the undertaking as a 'condition' or a 'warranty'.

Terms which are conditions *or* warranties depending on the consequences flowing from their breach have been variously described but are best known as *innominate* (literally, having no name). Diplock LJ was of the opinion that 'the emphasis in the earlier cases ... upon the breach by one party of his contractual undertakings ... tended to obscure the fact that it was really the event resulting from the breach which relieved the other party of further performance of his obligations'. (The late arrival of Behn's ship to pick up the cargo of coal for Hong Kong?)

In another of 'the earlier cases' *Bettini v Gye* (1876), the court was at pains to look at the contract and the circumstances to see 'whether the particular stipulation goes to the root of the matter, so that a failure to perform it would render the performance of the rest of the contract by the plaintiff a thing different in substance from what the defendant has stipulated for'. Thus the court speculated at some length as to what the effect of the plaintiff's breach would have been, had not the defendant, in this case wrongfully, terminated the contract. It would therefore appear that, before the 'once a condition, always a condition' case law development and a similar trend established by the Sale of Goods Act 1893 with its list of implied conditions, the remedy available might depend to some extent on the effect of the breach rather than solely on 'a prior classification' of the term broken. Citing other 19th century cases, Treitel endorses this point, speaking of an original 'application of a general, open-textured rule under which the extent of the injured party's remedies depended on the seriousness of the breach'.

Even in this century, pre-1962, the 'seriousness of consequences' approach can be found. In *Aerial Advertising Co v Bachelors Peas Ltd* (1938), AA's pilot flew low over Salford main square during the two minutes silence on Armistice Day (11 November 1937) towing an advertising banner reading 'Eat Batchelors' Peas'. This was greatly offensive to many of the thousands assembled in the square. 'The result was disastrous,' said Atkinson J. 'We will never buy your goods again' was the nature of the reaction conveyed to BP. The court held that BP were released from further performance of the contract; it was commercially wholly unreasonable for them to continue work with it.

The majority of breach cases of this kind since the *Hong Kong Fir* decision have been decided according to the 'seriousness of consequences' approach, although in *The Mihalis* Angelos (1971), a majority of the Court of Appeal reverted to the 'once a condition, always a condition' line, at least as regards an 'expected ready to load' (on or about a certain date) clause in a charterparty – a clause in common usage for a very long time.

In *Schuler AG v Wickman Machine Tool Sales Ltd* (1974), the parties had themselves stipulated that a certain clause in their agreement was a condition:

S, a German company, made panel presses used mainly by car manufacturers. By a written agreement, they appointed W as English agents and distributors for their products. One of the clauses of the contract, the only one to use the word 'condition', provided that it should 'be condition of this Agreement that' W should send representatives to visit six very important customers once a week. W was in breach of this clause but S did not at that time seek to end the contract, and it was held that these breaches had been waived. Later W were guilty of some very minor breaches of the clause and S terminated the agreement. On appeal from the arbitrator, Mocatta J held that the use of the word 'condition' meant that S could terminate if there was any breach of that term, however slight and however long ago, provided only that it had not been waived.

Following further appeals, the House of Lords held that the parties could not have intended the agreement to mean that a failure by W to make one out of a possible 1,400 visits could entail an immediate right to terminate the distributorship. Lord Wilberforce dissented in strong terms. The clause was a condition. It was wrong to assume 'that both parties to this contract adopted a standard of easygoing tolerance rather than one of aggressive, insistent punctuality and efficiency. This is not a assumption I am prepared to make, nor do I think myself entitled to impose the former standard upon the parties if their words indicate, as they plainly do, the latter. (The effect of this decision is that S were in breach, having wrongfully repudiated.)

In the Court of Appeal, Edmund Davies LJ made these comments regarding *the rights of the parties to classify* the clauses of their agreements:

> Is it a sufficient indication of the contracting parties' intention as to the grave manner in which the breach of one of their agreed terms is capable of being treated that they have described it as a 'condition'? Other expressions may be insufficient – to take but one example, the undertaking of an opera singer to be in London 'without fail' at least six days before the commencement of his engagement was held by Blackburn J in *Bettini v Gye* to give rise only to ... compensation in damages. But if a term is described as a 'condition', is that enough of itself to make clear what the innocent party's rights are if it be breached? The following passage ... provides their answer to that question:

> 'Now it is clear that the common law allows the parties to a contract to indicate expressly the consequences to be attached to any particular breach; though this they must do, not merely by pinning the labels 'condition' or 'warranty' to their clauses, but by stating the effect with sufficient clarity. It is also clear that, in default of such indication, it is for the court to decide the legal result of a breach.' (Cheshire and Fifoot, *The Law of Contract* (7th edn) p 132; see now 12th edn, p 154.)

In *Cehave NV v Bremer Handelsgesellschaft mbH* (1976), the Court of Appeal held that breach of a stipulation in a cif contract that goods were 'shipped in good condition' did not entitle the buyer to reject the goods unless the extent of the breach went to the root of the contract. Part of a £100,000 shipment of citrus pulp pellets was not in good condition and the buyers purported to reject the whole consignment. It was held that the provision as to shipment in good condition was an 'intermediate term', the breach of which in this case did not justify the buyer's termination of the contract. His proper remedy was in damages for the amount by which the value of the goods was reduced by their damaged condition.

By 1976 it appeared that the 'seriousness of consequences' approach would, by weight of recent authority, push the 'term-based' solution into relative obscurity. Only in *The Mihalis Angelos* had the Court of Appeal regarded the interests of certainty – as established through a line of precedents – as paramount. In that case, Megaw LJ stressed that:

> One of the important elements of the law is predictability. At any rate in commercial law there are obvious and substantial advantages in having, where possible, a firm and definite rule for a particular class of legal relationships ... It is surely much better both for shipowners and charterers (and incidently for their advisers) when a contractual obligation of this nature is under consideration – and still more when they are faced with the necessity of an urgent decision as to the effects of a suspected breach of it – to be able to say categorically: 'If a breach is proved, then the charterer can put an end to the contract.'

The argument that the 'seriousness of consequences' approach dilutes commercial certainty is often raised. Upon what data does a business person make the decision to 'throw up' a contract? To terminate or not to terminate? What is the state of the market? What alternative ways of proceeding are available? What advice does he or she ask for and receive? – there are plenty of decisions now on both approaches. If he or she is wrong, will the other party sue? Paying damages might be less expensive than keeping the contract alive. Certainty in business and the law is elusive.

In 1976 a further clue as to the way the law would develop was seemingly given in the House of Lords by Lord Wilberforce. He was of the opinion that some of the earlier cases, such as the *Arcos Ltd v Ronaasen* type of decision, were 'excessively technical and due for fresh examination'. He continued:

> The general law of contract has developed along much more rational lines in attending to the nature and gravity of a breach or departure than in accepting rigid categories which do or do not automatically give a right to rescind, and if the choice were between extending cases under the Sale of Goods Act 1893 into other field, or allowing more modern doctrine to infect those cases, my preference would be clear.

Nevertheless, in 1981 in *Bunge Corpn v Tradax Export SA*, the House of Lords reached a decision which, in line with *The Mihalis Angelos* (and *Behn v Burness*), re-emphasises the requirements of commercial certainty:

> T agreed to sell 15,000 tons of soya bean meal to B. The first shipment was to be delivered in June, beginning on a day chosen by the buyers, and to be fob (free on board) a vessel provided by the buyers at a US Gulf port selected by the sellers. The buyers were to give at least 15 days' notice of the ship's readiness to load. The notice was given four days late and T alleged that this breach allowed them to terminate the contract (as regards the June shipment); the clause as to notice being a *condition, any breach* of which justified termination. It was held, rejecting B's claim that the term was 'innominate', that this time stipulation in a mercantile agreement was 'of the essence' and was indeed a condition in the sense alleged.

Where now does the balance lie between the 'term-based' approach (and certainty) and the *Hong Kong Fir* approach (and flexibility)? It is suggested that the following terms will be found to be conditions – without recourse to the question of the seriousness of the consequences of the breach:

(i) statutorily implied conditions (an *Arcos* type of decision can now be avoided following the 1994 amendment of the Sale of Goods Act 1979);

(ii) a term which 'has to be performed by one party as a condition precedent to the ability of the other party to perform another term', eg notice to enable loading to commence on time, as in *Bunge*. The key factor here would appear to be the strict need for *co-operation* between the parties. Without it the contract will not work;

(iii) perhaps other mercantile terms well-established as conditions by precedent;

(iv) terms clearly and reasonably designated as conditions by the parties themselves in the contract: see also *Lombard North Central plc v Butterworth* (1987).

Fundamental breach

Cases particularly from the mid-1950s onwards threw up a new category of breach known as fundamental breach. On the basis of the *Hong Kong Fir* approach to breach, a fundamental breach usually had disastrous consequences for the innocent party to the extent that, comparing the performance promised with actual performance, he was deprived of all, or substantially all, he had bargained for. However, such a description scarcely distinguishes fundamental breach from other breaches which justify termination of the contract.

The key to fundamental breach lay in the fact that it was only met in any significant sense in exclusion clause cases. The reason for this was that it was created as a judicial device to defeat clauses as wide-ranging and unfair as one which protected the defendant company in *L'Estrange v Graucob*. In this case the exclusion clause was in 'regrettably small print', in 'a part of the document where it easily escaped notice' and printed on brown paper. It read: 'any express or implied condition, statement or warranty, statutory or otherwise not stated herein is hereby excluded.'

Therefore if, in later supply of goods cases, the court was able to find what was called a 'radical departure' from the contemplated performance – rather than a serious misperformance of an agreed obligation – it felt able to assert fundamental breach rather than breach of condition and so deny a supplier the protection of a clause which excluded liability for breach of, for example, the implied conditions to be found in the Sale of Goods Act.

In one case, *Karsales (Harrow) Ltd v Wallis* (1956), it was held that there had been a fundamental breach where a car in good running order had been agreed upon, whereas when it was delivered it would not go *at all*:

> W inspected and drove a secondhand Buick in excellent condition. He made arrangements to acquire it on hire-purchase under an agreement that excluded liability for breach of conditions and warranties. The car was later towed (the only means of propulsion by now) to his house at night. Many parts had been replaced by old and defective ones. When W refused to pay instalments, he was sued! The court held that the breach was fundamental, K could not rely on the exclusion clause, and W had a complete defence.

The doctrine of fundamental breach was brought to bear not only in supply of goods cases but also in others relating to the provision of services and work and materials. However, a major legal controversy arose as to the way in which it operated. Some judges (notably Lord Denning) considered it to be a rule of law to the effect that once a fundamental breach was found, the clause, *no matter how it was worded, automatically* failed to protect its user from liability. Other judges laid down that the doctrine of fundamental breach operated as a rule of construction. This meant that the exclusion clause was not automatically extinguished by the breach but stood to be read or construed in the light of the breach, even though it was rarely if ever taken to have been intended by the parties to be applicable to a fundamental breach.

From this it can be seen that, given the willingness of the court to find a fundamental breach, an unfair exclusion clause would have been defeated whichever approach was used. However, the controversy was more than a storm in a legal tea cup, and the distinction between the two approaches is important because it is only the rule of construction approach which accords with the long-established general rules relating to breach of contract. These rules lay down that a party faced by a serious breach (eg a breach of condition) has, as we have discussed, a *right* to treat the contract as at an end. In other words he has an election: he may terminate and sue for damages or he may affirm the contract but nevertheless sue for damages (eg treat a breach of condition as a breach of warranty). He may even ignore or waive the breach as seen in *Schuler v Wickman* above.

Therefore, before a serious breach situation can give rise to termination of the contract, the injured party must (expressly or impliedly) elect to bring the contract to an end as regards unperformed primary obligations. (The breach may be of such a nature that the question of election is made redundant; in practical terms further performance is impossible.) He may, for financial reasons – say, the difficulty of finding an alternative supplier – decide not to terminate (cf *Williams v Roffey Brothers*).

The rule of law approach to fundamental breach distorted these rules by claiming that such a breach automatically deprived the wrongdoer of the benefit of his exclusion clause, the contract in which it was to be found having ceased to exist. After several differences of legal opinion, it is now settled, following the decision of the House of Lords in *Photo Production Ltd v Securicor Transport Ltd* (discussed in Chapter 9) and the passing of the Unfair Contract Terms Act 1977, that (i) to the extent that the concept of fundamental breach remains, as regards the injured party's rights, they remain the same as for other serious breach situations, ie to elect to terminate or to affirm; (ii) to the extent that exclusion clauses are not invalidated by the 1977 Act, the question of whether they provide protection for suppliers of goods or services, etc is one of *construction* of the clause and the contract containing it. These developments will be more fully discussed in Chapter 9.

References and further reading

Brownsword, 'Retrieving reasons, retrieving rationality? A new look at the right to withdraw for breach of contract' (1992) 5 JCL 83.

Bojczuk, 'When is a Condition Not a Condition?' (1987) JBL 353.

Devlin, 'The treatment of breach of contract' (1966) CLJ 192.

Greig, 'Condition – or warranty?' (1973) 89 LQR 93.

MacDonald, 'Express and implied terms and exemptions' (1991) 107 LQR 555.

Phang, 'Implied Terms Revisited' (1990) JBL 394.

Phang, 'Implied terms in English law: some recent developments' (1993) JBL 242.

Reynolds, 'Discharge of contract by breach' (1981) 97 LQR 541.

Weir, 'The buyer's right to reject defective goods' (1976) CLJ 33.

Questions

(1)   (a)   For what reasons are terms implied into contracts (a) from the Sale of Goods Act 1979, (b) from a previous course of dealing?

      (b)   On what basis were terms implied into the lease in *Liverpool City Council v Irwin* (1977)?

(2)   'The legal right to terminate a contract may well be of no significance.' Explain this statement in relation to the case of *Godley v Perry* (1960).

(3)   (a)   In *Arcos Ltd v Ronaasen* (1933) the seller was held to 1/16 inch and told that if he had wanted a margin, he should have provided for it. In *Tradax Int SA v Goldschmidt SA* (1977), the seller provided for a margin but exceeded it by 1/10 per cent. The buyer was not, however, allowed to reject the goods. How do you reconcile the decisions in these two cases?

      (b)   Explain why the failure of one party to open a banker's confirmed credit allowed the other party to repudiate the contract in *Trans-Trust SPRL v Danubian Trading Co Ltd* (1952).

(4)   Does Diplock LJ in *Hong Kong Fir* intend that the classification approach should be abandoned totally in favour of a test relating to the seriousness of the effects of a breach of contract?

(5)   In December 1992 A Ltd contracted to supply Z Ltd each month in 1993 with 500 gallons of a chemical needed by Z Ltd in their factory. The contract stipulated that delivery should take place in the first day of each month in 1993. Z Ltd use the chemical in their production of washing-up liquids. The first 500 gallons were delivered on time, but the second instalment arrived a fortnight late. Z Ltd told A Ltd that they would not accept any more late deliveries because this was causing delay in their own factory, and when the third delivery failed to arrive on 1 March, Z Ltd telephoned A Ltd and cancelled the whole order. By this time Z Ltd had entered into a lucrative contract to produce dishwashing machine powder, for which the chemical is not needed. Advise A Ltd, who have no other market for the chemical.

(6)   Discuss the following statements:

   (a)   'In penalising wickedness the *Hong Kong* rule rewards the incompetent; like other moralism it operates unfairly.'

   (b)   'When the right to reject depended on the nature of the term in the contract which was broken, the innocent party simply had to go to the filing cabinet, consult the contractual document and then decide whether the term broken was a very serious one or not.'

   (c)   'Many people put forward their contractor's breach as a ground of release when they actually want to quit for wholly different, and legally inadequate, reasons, such as a movement in market or exchange rate, or a change in their own requirements or resources. This may be good business, but it seems a poor show.' (Weir: see References and further reading).

(7)   'For the most part, the relationships between the classification and the consequential approaches, their underlying principles, and the contractual ideologies are quite clear. The proportionality and bad faith principles are consumer-welfarist, and are currently served by the consequential approach. The certainty principle and the principle of sanctity of contract are market-individualist, and are better served by the classification approach': Adams and Brownsword, *Understanding Contract Law*. Discuss.

8 Standard form contracts

Uses, abuses and bargaining power

We have already encountered standard form contract documents on several occasions: for example the sales agreement in *L'Estrange v Graucob Ltd*, the standard conditions of the freight forwarding trade in *Evans (Portsmouth) Ltd v Merzario Ltd* and the documents in the *Butler Machine Tool* 'battle of the forms' case. In the USA, and there is no reason to believe the position is different here, it has been said that:

> Standard form contracts probably account for more than 99 per cent of all the contracts now made. Most persons have difficulty remembering the last time they contracted other than by standard form; except for casual oral arrangements, they probably never have. But if they are active, they contract by standard form several times a day. Parking-lot and theatre tickets, package receipts, department store charge slips, and gas station credit card purchase slips are all standard form contracts.

It is clear therefore that standard forms of contract are to be found in operation in both the inter-business and the consumer contract fields. In the Parliamentary debate prior to the passing of the Unfair Contract Terms Act in 1977 (which specifically recognises the existence of 'written standard terms of business'), the point was made that: 'It is probably the case that most contracts are based on standard conditions to some extent irrespective of the relative bargaining strength of the parties.' There is no statutory definition of a standard form contract in this country but in Israel the legislature has defined it as 'a contract ... all or any of whose terms have been fixed in advance by, or on behalf of, the person supplying the commodity or service ... with the object of constituting conditions of many contracts between him and persons undefined as to their number or identity.' (It is not necessarily only a *supplier* who draws up such a contract. If this were so, there would be no 'battle of the forms'.)

It was not considered advisable to attempt to define 'standard form contract' in the Unfair Contract Terms Act, but to leave the question when it arose to the judiciary. Section 3 of the Act is concerned with, among other things, the reasonableness or otherwise of an exclusion clause where 'written standard terms of business' are used – indicating thereby situations in which there has probably been a lack of genuine negotiation between the parties. A Scottish case, *McCrone v Boots Farm Sales Ltd* (1981), raised the issue of what is a 'standard form contract', and, without attempting a comprehensive definition, Lord Dunpark was of the opinion that the phrase was 'wide enough to include any contract, whether wholly written or partly oral, which includes a set of fixed terms or conditions which the proponer [offeror] applies, without material variation, to contracts of the kind in question'. (This was a case involving a consumer and a business entity, the latter drawing up the contract terms.)

In an earlier case, *Schroeder Music Publishing Co Ltd v Macaulay* (1974), Lord Diplock gave his views on the nature of standard form contracts at some length:

> Standard forms of contracts are of two kinds. The first, of very ancient origin, are those which set out the terms on which mercantile transactions of common occurrence are to be carried out. Examples are bills of lading, charter-parties, policies of insurance, contracts of sale in the commodity markets. The standard clauses in these contracts have been settled over the years by negotiation by representatives of the commercial interests involved and have been widely adopted because experience has shown that they facilitate the conduct of trade. Contracts of these kinds affect not only the actual parties to them but also others who may have a commercial interest in the transactions to which they relate, as buyers or sellers, charterers or shipowners, insurers or bankers. If fairness or reasonableness were relevant to their enforceability, the fact that they are widely used by parties whose bargaining power is fairly matched would raise a strong presumption that their terms are fair and reasonable.

> The same presumption, however, does not apply to the other kind of standard form of contract. This is of comparatively modern origin. It is the result of the concentration of particular kinds of business in relatively few hands. The ticket cases in the nineteenth century provide what are probably the first examples. The terms of this kind of standard form of contract have not been the subject of negotiation between the parties to it, or approved by any organisation representing the interests of the weaker party. They have been dictated by that party whose bargaining power, either exercised alone or in conjunction with others providing similar goods or services, enables him to say: 'If you want these goods or services at all, these are the only terms on which they are available. Take it or leave it.'

This account enables us to develop some important points:

(1)   The basic reason underlying the widespread use in present-day business of the standard form of contract is the need to 'facilitate the conduct of trade'. This may be because the parties regularly enter into complex technical and legal relations (as in the fields of, for example, international trade, civil and mechanical engineering and building) or because the dealings in question throw up a multiplicity of transactions involving to some significant degree the standardised and mass-produced products, services and marketing techniques which are a common feature of modern business.

(2)   The standard form contract is to be found in use in both inter-business and business-consumer dealings.

(3)   In the inter-business field, standard form contracts may be well established as 'models', negotiated by, or on behalf of, parties of approximately equal bargaining power over a lengthy period of time (eg the cif international

contract of sale, such as the Ruritanian Bus Contract in Chapter 3, or the JCT form of building contract, see below). Where this is so, they can be *presumed* by the courts to be fair and reasonable. Nevertheless it is not uncommon for a powerful business organisation to impose its 'written standard terms of business' upon one possessing less bargaining strength, as s 3 of the Unfair Contract Terms Act recognises – see Chapter 9.

(4) Consumers do not prepare standard form contracts. In this field such contracts are prepared by, or on behalf of, suppliers of goods or services on a 'take-it-or-leave-it' basis. The inequality of bargaining strength normally found to exist between the parties may be the result of a business concentration of market power (monopolistic or oligopolistic) or because the interests of smaller firms are regulated by a trade association.

(5) Where the use of standard form contracts is accompanied by inequality of bargaining power, there is a greater likelihood of their being used as instruments of economic oppression because their terms can be weighted in favour of the interests of the stronger parties who prepare them. Here there is no presumption that such contracts are fair and reasonable; they are more likely to be subjected to legal regulation. Where there is an absence of genuine agreement and choice, the law must recognise the overriding 'separation' of the parties' interests (in the Gurvitch sense) and seek to achieve a fairer balance between them. To do this is to recognise, in particular, consumer interest in a choice of goods and services of reasonable quality obtainable at reasonable prices and on fair terms.

(6) As implied in point 1, the use of standard form contracts does achieve clear economies in transaction costs where, for example, a firm is dealing on a large scale in mass-produced products or standard services on a regular basis. A multiplicity of transactions all on a similar footing calls for a standard document, not for individually negotiated agreements. To the extent that savings are passed on to the consumer, this must count as a benefit. However, weighing against this advantage are problems regarding communication of information, relating to the crucial rights and duties of the parties, in the 'small print' of standard form documents. In inter-business dealings, the 'battle of the forms' is one example of parties either ignoring or being unaware of terms designed to regulate their relationship. It is clear that business parties often proceed without reading the details embodied in their contract: it has been said that the standard form of building contract 'works very well in practice so long as it is not read' – or subjected to legal analysis by the courts!

It must be clearly understood that standard form contracts often run to a great many pages and individual clauses to more than a page. And there are thousands of such contracts in use at the present time. It is well known that the consumer may have no time to read standard form clauses (they may merely be referred to in the contractual document and be contained in another document elsewhere), and if he did read them he would probably not understand them – in any case he must take them or leave them. Assuming that there is someone in the organisation providing the consumer with such a contract who is aware of its wording and legal significance, we have here an example of what economists call 'information asymmetries' – one party knows more about the contract than the other, see for example *Thompson v LMS* (1930). This problem calls for both increased consumer awareness and added legal safeguards relating to such matters as the form and layout of consumer contracts, simplified wording, and rules concerning reasonable notice of terms, etc.

(7) Charges of 'unfairness' in standard form consumer transactions, particularly as regards the use of exclusion clauses, have their basis in the various factors discussed under the previous heading. Superior bargaining strength is often possessed, and oppressively brought to bear, by suppliers of goods and services; the consumer often has no freedom of choice – except between one standard form, or another which is similarly weighted against him; a 'maze of small print' usually means that onerous clauses are either not read or not understood – they are not agreed to in any real sense.

Legislation passed in recent years has removed some of the more obvious causes of social concern, such as high and hidden interest rates in credit transactions. Changes have also been imposed (or suggested) relating to the form, layout and language of consumer documents. In the next chapter we will examine the operation of the Unfair Contract Terms Act 1977, the present highwater mark in the legal struggle against unfair exclusion, and limitation, of liability by business parties.

(8) The clear purpose of an exclusion clause in a consumer transaction is to enable the business person to eliminate risk, ie the risk of financial loss through the payment of damages following claims brought against him. In commercial transactions – where bargaining strength approximates to equality – exclusion clauses are less common, although limitation of liability clauses (which in effect apportion the risk of loss between the parties, who can insure accordingly) are more frequently found. In fact, in standard form dealings between business organisations, there is a general tendency towards a more sophisticated and wide-ranging concern with risk and its avoidance or apportionment than is to be found in consumer transactions. The parties, through the use of settled, agreed devices, display a willingness to combine to avoid or minimise common 'enemies' – business risks and the risks of litigation. To this extent, Gurvitch's element of 'rapprochement' is at work, drawing the parties together, emphasising com-

mon interests rather than 'separation' and conflict. 'Force majeure' clauses – often linked to insurance coverage – enable parties to take account of the occurrence and costs of contingencies. They also enable them to forestall litigation on the tricky question of frustration of the venture (see Chapter 12). Arbitration clauses and liquidated damages clauses (see particularly Chapter 13) are similar devices widely used for the avoidance of 'juridical risk', ie that expensive litigation will 'go the wrong way'.

The issues raised in this outline are at the heart of much of the remaining part of this book.

Building and engineering contracts

In an introductory book such as this it is neither possible nor appropriate to attempt even a general survey of the law and practice of standard form contracts. However, it is important that students become familiar with them to some extent. In this short section, our object is to examine some particular aspects of building and engineering contracts as they come before the courts.

In broad terms, building and engineering standard forms display many similarities, reflecting in each case a high degree of planning of the transactional 'face' of these complicated technical operations – in the absence of the comprehensive statutory control that it is to be found with most commercial contracts. This planning attempts to establish, in detail, the nature and scope of the rights and duties of the parties – the employer/purchaser and the contractor – and also extends to cover the position of third parties, the architect or consulting engineer and sub-contractors. A practical *difference* between the two areas, which we will try to explain later, is the presence of a steady stream of building contract litigation and a dearth of decisions on engineering standard forms.

We will now focus on two issues:

(i)   building contracts and their interpretation by the courts, with particular reference to variation by means of an agreed extension of time for completion of the works by the contractor;

(ii) engineering standard forms and the operation and judicial interpretation of indemnity clauses providing for one party to reimburse the other against loss.

Building standard forms

In the course of a decision reached in 1956, Lord Denning stated that: 'This case raises an important question under the standard form of contract issued under the authority of the Royal Institute of British Architects and the National Federation of

Building Trades Employers. This form is used in a great many building contracts and, like other standard forms, it has come to resemble a legislative code.'

This remark, following upon those of Lord Diplock, throws further light not only on the nature of standard form contracts but also on judicial functions in relation to them. First, most building contracts rest not on private negotiations, but on the adoption of a settled formula or model. Second, a model, such as the RIBA form (known since 1977 as the JCT contract), devised and revised over a period of time by representatives of all interested parties (builders, architects, surveyors, sub-contractors and local authorities, ie the Joint Contracts Tribunal) rapidly assumes the status of an authoritative 'everything within' as regards the building operations that it covers (although terms may be implied). However, although managers and site operators are assumed to be familiar with the contract, and work proceeds more or less in adherence to its terms, it is often the case that the task of resolving disputes arising out of the execution of the works brings out difficult questions of interpretation, ie what the words of the standard clauses which relate to the dispute actually mean. Questions as difficult, as Lord Denning implies, as those met when the court is faced with the more usual task of statutory interpretation.

Legal insistence on clarity and precision in a contractual document may well not wholly accord with the looser, more flexible approach to the implementation of the aims of such a document as favoured by builders, architects and others on site. The RIBA form of contract was described as a 'farrago of obscurities' in one case, and in 1970 an experienced commentator on building contracts wrote that 'it seems to me that the stage has now been reached where architects and others recommending the RIBA standard forms to their clients in unmodified form should be held liable for professional negligence if damage or loss to the employer ensues'. Since then the new improved 'JCT 80' standard form has been published (in six, varying, editions to suit the requirements of the parties). It is a form agreed on by the *whole industry* and does not create a situation where the party is contracting on the *other's* 'written standard terms of business'.

Engineering model forms of contract are rarely to be found in the courts but the law reports reveal that builders (construction companies), whose forms are similar, are frequently involved in formal dispute-solving. This is probably because the benefits of standardisation, particularly the apparent consensus the form provides, are often lost in practice. The various editions of the 'JCT 80' form are rarely used as printed. Amendments are made, unwanted clauses are deleted and new ones are added. Problems of interpretation more readily arise and inappropriate contracts are regularly used. If the dispute goes to formal arbitration for resolution, it may well end up in the courts on an appeal on a point of law.

It is often possible to settle a dispute arising out of the execution of the works on an *ad hoc* basis without reference to the contract documents or the law. Alternatively, the contractor, employer and architect (who is not a party to the contract) may on a relatively informal basis seek to come to an agreed interpretation of the standard form. If no agreed interpretation can be found, resort may be had to the contract's arbitration clause. This in turn may eventually mean that litigation is necessary for a final authoritative ruling if one of the parties thinks that the arbitrator erred in his application of the law. This outcome, at least, has the merit of producing directly relevant case law on builders' standard forms – so long as the decisions are in tune with current practice. Decisions can result in amendment of the forms, as can legislative changes, particularly those of a financial nature (eg the government's introduction of Value Added Tax).

The courts have been concerned with the problem of ascertaining the meaning and legal significance of documents for centuries and the task of construing standard form-building contracts, in use now for over a 100 years, is merely part and parcel of a general judicial function. A case may require the court to establish the true meaning of an individual clause, or the relationship between two printed clauses, or a printed clause and a written addition. It may involve a question of whether or not a term may be implied into the contract, or the application of an exclusion or limitation of liability clause. In such cases the substantive rules of contract law may play little part or operate only on a secondary level. But this is not to say that they are never invoked in building cases; as in other standard form cases it may be the rules relating to the formation of contracts (eg *Trollope and Colls*, Chapter 5) or frustration of contract (eg *Davis Contractors v Fareham UDC*, Chapter 12), or some other part of contract law which plays a decisive role.

The case in which Lord Denning said that the standard form of building contract had come to resemble a legislative code, *Amalgamated Building Contractors v Waltham Holy Cross UDC* (1952), is a good example of judicial interpretation in operation. Where, under an agreed clause, a contractor asks for an extension of time to complete the works, because of, for example, inclement weather or shortages of materials (events beyond his control), it is generally the architect who has to certify the length of extension allowed. Delay in completion beyond that time usually involves the contractor in paying an agreed sum by way of liquidated damages to the employer or building owner (unless a further extension is granted):

W, the building owners, employed AB, the contractors, to build 202 houses at a price of £230,000. The contractors were given possession of the site on 7 November 1946, but the formal contract was not entered into until 15 June 1948. Under it the contractors agreed to complete the work by 7 February 1949 and there was a provision for liquidated damages in the event of delay at the rate of £50 a week. On 19 January 1949 AB applied for a 12-month extension because of labour and materials difficulties. The architect did no more than acknowledge this request. The work was not completed until 28 August 1950.

On 20 December 1950 the architect wrote letters, in one of which he stated that he extended the time for completion from 7 February 1949 to 23 May 1949, and in the other he certified that the whole of the contract should have been completed by 23 May 1949. W claimed liquidated damages at £50 a week for the period from 23 May 1949 to 28 August 1950. AB resisted this claim, stating that they were not liable to pay liquidated damages at all – on the face of it an extraordinary assertion but one which is explained in the course of the judgment.

Lord Denning came to the following conclusions:

The validity of the claim for liquidated damages depends on the wording of the contract of 15 June 1948. Clauses 16, 17 and 18 provide that the contractors '(16) ... shall thereupon begin the works forthwith and regularly and diligently proceed with the same and shall complete the same on or before the date for completion stated in the said appendix subject nevertheless to the provisions for extension of time contained in Clause 18 of these conditions. (17) If the contractor fails to complete the works by the date stated in the appendix to these conditions and the architect certifies in writing that in his opinion that same ought reasonably so to have been completed, the contractor shall pay or allow to the employer a sum calculated at the rate stated in the said appendix as liquidated and ascertained damages ... (18) If in the opinion of the architect the works be delayed (i) by force majeure, or (ii) by reason of any exceptionally inclement weather ... or (ix) by reason of labour and material not being available as required ... then in any such case the architect shall make a fair and reasonable extension of time for completion of the works ...'

The work was completed on 28 August 1950. Four months later the architect wrote the two important letters of 20 December 1950. In one of them the architect wrote to the contractors: 'I have now been able to give consideration to the question of extending the time of the above contract. The present expiry date is 7 February 1949, and I have decided that an addition of 15 weeks, bringing the completion date to 23 May 1949, would be a fair and reasonable extension. After careful consideration I cannot see any reason why your whole contract should not have been completed by this date.'

That letter is said to be an extension of time. On the same day the architect wrote another letter, this time to the building owners: 'In accordance with Clause 17 of the RIBA form of contract, I certify that in my opinion the whole of the contract should have been completed by 23 May 1949.'

Those are the two letters which are relied on, the one under Clause 18 and the other under Clause 17, making, as the building owners say, liquidated damages payable for the period from the time when the works ought reasonably to have been completed, 23 May 1949, to the date of completion, 28 August 1950.

The contractors say that the extension of time was invalid. It seems strange that contractors should say that the extension (which was in their favour) was invalid, but they do so because, if the extension time was invalid, they will be able to avoid paying the liquidated damages altogether. The building owners are not able to rely on the original contract time, 7 February 1949, because they have not a certificate under Clause 17 that the works ought reasonably to have been completed by that date. In order to make good their claim to liquidated damages, they must show that the time was validly extended under Clause 18 to 13 May 1949.

The point in the case is therefore: Was the extension, given on 20 December 1950, extending the time to 23 May 1949, valid or not? The contractors say that the words in Clause 18 – 'The architect shall make a fair and reasonable extension of time for completion of the works' – mean that the architect must give the contractors a date at which they can aim in the future, and that he cannot give a date which has passed. I do not agree with this contention. It is only necessary to take a few practical illustrations to see that the architect, as a matter of business, must be able to give an extension even though it is retrospective. Take a simple case where the contractors, near the end of the work, have overrun the contract time for six months without legitimate excuse. They cannot get an extension for that period. Now suppose that the works are still uncompleted and a strike occurs and lasts a month. The contractors can get an extension of time for that month. The architect can clearly issue a certificate which will operate retrospectively. He extends the time by one month from the original completion date, and the extended time will obviously be a date which is already past. Or take a case of delay, such as we have in this case, due to labour and materials not being available. That may cause a continuous delay operating partially, but not wholly, every day, until the works are completed. The works do not stop. They go on, but they go on more slowly right to the end of the works. In such a case, seeing that the cause of delay operates until the last moment, when the works are completed, it must follow that the architect can give a certificate after they are completed. These practical illustrations show that the parties must have intended that the architect should be able to give a certificate which is retrospective, even after the works are completed.

The other members of the Court of Appeal being in agreement, it was held that the extension of time was valid and the contractors were therefore liable to pay liquidated damages of £50 a week for the period 23 May 1949 to 28 August 1950. Behind this decision appears to be the opinion of the architect that labour and materials difficulties were only partially to blame for the delay in completion; the rest of the delay being the fault of the contractor. Nevertheless, it is clearly desirable that, wherever possible, an extension or extensions of time should be granted prospectively not retrospectively.

We will now turn to consider some aspects of engineering standard form contracts.

Engineering standard forms

In an article on engineering contracts written in 1965 it was categorically stated that 'the long-established and universally accepted norms ... have greatly simplified contracting procedure; they have entirely abolished litigation and arbitration throughout the industry'. Let us take a closer look at the engineers and their standard form contract.

Over the last 70 years the Institution of Mechanical Engineers have sponsored and recommended to the industry certain standard form conditions of contract which are from time to time revised in the light of practice. They are as follows: (1) Model Form A for Home Contracts – with Erection; (2) three varieties of Model Form B for Export Contracts (Delivery; Delivery with Supervision of Erection; and Delivery to and Erection on Site of Electrical and Mechanical Plant); and (3) Model Form C for the Sale of Electrical and Mechanical Goods other than Electrical Cables (Home – without Erection).

The majority of engineering projects are, however, of such an individual nature that they must be governed by specially agreed and therefore, to some extent, 'tailor-made' contracts. Nevertheless, it is highly likely that these contracts will be modelled on the general conditions. Also, large-scale operators in the industry may well produce their own 'in-house' models, eg the (now privatised) British Steel Corporation's CC1 General Conditions of Purchase, see below. Contractors argue that an operator's own model will be weighted in the operator's own favour but these conditions will generally follow the appropriate recommended model.

The basic object of these contracts, where the engineer erects or installs the plant, is to enable the purchaser at an agreed date to take over and operate the plant, which has been completed and tested in accordance with the contract. In practice, engineering contracts are frequently of a complex technical nature and the time required for completion may be lengthy. (The general remarks that follow are equally applicable to building standard forms and operations.) Rarely is the contractor in a position to undertake all the work required, in which case a number of sub-contracts will have to be tied in to the main contract. Perhaps the two most difficult problems relating to sub-contracts are delay and the weighing of a sub-contractor's possible liability against his contribution to the total venture. The component supplied by a sub-contractor engaged in the building of an aircraft may be of little financial significance but if defective it may be the cause of a major disaster. As with building contracts it is significant that another third party, the consulting engineer, is given extensive duties to perform under the contract. (His position is generally the same as that of the architect in building contracts.) He issues instructions to the contractor and also acts as arbitrator in disputes between contractor and purchaser.

The model forms exhibit a high degree of contract planning, which is all the more necessary as, as we have said, there is no statutory code, such as the Sale of Goods Act, to regulate the relationship between the parties. The models are therefore the norm, which becomes 'tailor-made' only by a careful process of incorporation, variation and addition of terms to suit the parties' project. The fact that these forms have 'abolished litigation and arbitration throughout the industry' means that the functions of contract lawyers in the engineering sector is almost exclusively that of planning, non-litigious interpretation and periodic revision of the model forms so that the rights and duties of the parties, and third parties, may be clearly established. These rights are obviously in large part of a contractual nature but they also relate to the ownership of property (the land on which the work is being carried out, the plant itself, or patent rights, etc), or they may be, as regards damage or personal injuries incurred in the course of executing the contract, statutory or tortious rights vesting in the parties themselves, or third parties (see the discussion of indemnity clauses below).

Some idea of the high degree of planning that is exhibited in engineering contracts may be gained by reference to the following Table of Clauses from the British Steel Corporation's General Conditions of Contract for use in procurement and erection of plant at site in the United Kingdom (BSC CC1). Incidents and contingencies of all kinds are covered here, so that ideally every aspect of the contractual relationship is regulated and any on-site problem or dispute can be resolved if necessary, by reference to the contract and its attached drawings, specifications and quantities.

Table of clauses

Detailed analysis of these clauses is clearly beyond the scope of a book of this kind. However, clearer appreciation of the contract is possible albeit at a superficial level: first it is apparent that the clauses progress in a general way through a chronological pattern appropriate to the operations involved. For example: '(5) Programme for execution and termination of the Works ... (18) Delivery ... (24) Care of the Works ... (30) Completion ... (36) Payment'.

Second, clause headings take on added meaning if viewed in terms of the duties, liabilities and rights of the parties, plus the functions and authority of the consulting engineer. Also it can be seen that Macaulay's four main planning issues (definition of performances, effect of defective performance, effect of contingencies, and dispute-solving and sanctions) are again in evidence. Nor is it too difficult to establish a relationship between certain key clauses and their contract law background: clauses 12 and 16 and breach; clauses 28 and 48 and contract variation; clauses 26, 27, 33 and 47 involving defective performance and contractor's liability; clause 28 involves 'force majeure' contingencies (calling for variation or perhaps frustration of the contract); clause 41 (amongst others) deals with dispute-solving and clause 29 with agreed sanctions. Some of the issues involved in clause 28 'Extension of time for completion of the Works' and clause 29 'Liquidated Damages' have already been explored when examining similar clauses in the *Waltham Holy Cross building* case.

Clause 26 of the BSC contract ('Liability for damage to property and injury to persons') is an indemnity clause:

26.1 The contractor shall indemnify the Purchaser against all losses, liabilities, claims, costs and expenses that may result from loss of or damage to any property ... or injury or death to any person (who shall be deemed to include any employee of the Purchaser) that may arise out of or in connection with the execution of the Contract other than loss, damage, injury or death resulting directly from the act or omission of the Purchaser.

26.3 The Contractor shall insure in his own name against all those risks the subject of the Contractor's indemnity in Clause 26.1 with insurers, and on terms approved by the Purchaser ...

The general purpose of such a clause is to enable one party (here, the purchaser BSC) to recover from the other (the contractor) any loss incurred as a result of claims against him by third parties who suffer loss, damage, injury or death arising out of the performance of the contract.

The execution of engineering (and building) contracts involves a strong element of risk and parties to them, by means of indemnity and other clauses, go to some lengths to attempt to establish where any loss contingent upon such risks shall fall (see point 8 on p 123). One might initially think that a purchaser is in no real position to incur liability for loss or injury to third parties in the context of such a clause. However, although the contractor (or a sub-contractor) is the party in all probability directly responsible, a purchaser is by no means immune from third party claims of this kind. The purchaser will probably be owner/occupier of the site on which the work is being carried out and as such owes duties to others under such statutes as the Health and Safety at Work Act (and regulations thereunder) and the Occupier's Liability Act. He may have his own employees working 'in connection with' the contract for whom he is vicariously liable, and he may even be vicariously liable for the acts or omissions of the contractor himself, even though he is not an employee.

Although the wording of inter-business indemnity clauses varies, parties *claiming* indemnities usually exclude from their scope damage or injury, etc to third parties resulting directly from *their own* acts or omissions or those of their employees (as do BSC at the end of clause 26.1). Even where a party claiming an indemnity *does* attempt by some form of words to transfer to the other party loss caused by his own or his employees' negligence, he will need to use very precise language to achieve this result because the courts will construe his words on the presumption that it is 'inherently improbable that one party to a contract should intend to absolve the other party from the consequence of his own negligence'. He will probably need to state in clear express terms that his own and his employees' negligence is subject to indemnification.

In practice, the plaintiff third party is often in a position to claim that both the contractor and the purchaser are liable for his damage or injury. If the court holds the purchaser partly responsible, his indemnity against the contractor will be of no use to him unless he has clearly made his liability subject to transfer under the clause (see the *Walters* and *Smith* cases below).

None of the following cases is based on the BSC indemnity clause. In the first one the claim was against the purchaser/factory occupier alone – who then recovered from the contractor:

> In *Murfin v United Steel Companies Ltd* (1957) US engaged Power Gas on work at their factory – the latter to indemnify the former 'against every claim against US under any statute or common law for ... (b) death ... arising out of or in connection with the carrying out of PG's work and from any cause other than the negligence of US or their employees'. A sub-contractor's employee was electrocuted in the factory owing to the absence of insulating screens. It was held that US were liable in damages for breach of the Electricity (Factories Act) Special Regulations but were entitled to be indemnified by the contractor because US's 'negligence' as excepted from the indemnity did not include breach of statutory duty. (The contractor may have been able to recover from the sub-contractor under an indemnity in their contract.)

Wherever liability eventually rests, this will or should mean that the insurance company of the party responsible will bear the loss (see BSC clause 26.3). For example, X recovers £10,000 damages against P (the purchaser/site owner). C (the contractor) must indemnify P in full. This means that C's insurance company must indemnify P's insurance company who have already met P's liability for the damages awarded.

In *Walters v Whessoe Ltd & Shell Refining Co Ltd* (1960), WH were constructing a tank for S at their refinery. S's employees left an oil drum containing dangerous vapour on the site whilst WH's men were away at the weekend. One of those men, W, was later killed because an earthing fault on his welding machine caused escaping vapour to explode. In an action brought by W's widow, S was held 80% and WH 20% responsible. S sought to recover their share from WH under an indemnity clause in the contract. It was held that indemnity clauses should not be construed so as to include the consequences of the negligence of the party to whom the indemnity was given, unless those consequences were expressly covered.

In *Smith v South Wales Switchgear Ltd* (1978) X, an employee of Y, engaged on the overhaul of equipment in Z's factory was seriously injured owing to Z's negligence. X recovered from Z who claimed an indemnity from Y under a wide ranging clause in their contract. Z failed because (a) the clause did not specifically refer to negligence, and (b) it was construed as applying only to liabilities incurred by Z for (vicarious) acts or omissions of Y in connection with the contract work. (Eg X whilst in the factory injured A, a visitor or one of Z's employees, who successfully sued Z, the factory occupier.)

Government as a contracting party

In Chapter 4 we took account of what Friedmann, writing in 1972, numbered as one of the main social causes for the transformation of contract in the 20th century. This was 'the tremendous expansion of the welfare and social services function of the state in all common law jurisdictions'. One of the legal corollaries of this development was 'a vast increase of contracts where government departments or other public authorities are on one side, and a private party on the other'. (By 'private' party, Friedmann refers to a party, eg a company in the private, as opposed to the public or state, sector of the economy or to an individual acting, for example, as a consumer.)

We also saw that in its role as contractor, the state functions both as a purchaser of goods and services (government procurement) *from* the private sector and as a supplier, particularly through the agency of public authorities, of basic services such as electricity supply and rail transport *to* the private sector. (As we will see, some of these services have been returned to the private sector by the government.) Let us examine these two sides of government contracting in a little more detail; for specialist treatments the reader is directed to the books by Harden and Turpin listed at the end of the chapter.

Government procurement

In principle the general law of contract applies to government procurement. There is no special branch of 'government contract law' in this country, no legislative code as for consumer credit or fair trading, and administrative law is largely irrelevant. In fact, the complaint has been made that *no* adequate law has been evolved on public contracts. Any question of the 'adequacy' of the private law rules of contract is also largely redundant, certainly as regards dispute-solving and remedies. As with the engineering sector discussed earlier, this is a field dominated by standard contractual documents, prepared on behalf of the government authority involved, any disputes arising very rarely being settled in the courts. It has been said that: 'The government contract is an instrument of a power relationship, and only vaguely resembles the consensual agreement extolled by Maine and Adam Smith. The significant decision is that of the government in setting the terms and conditions of the proposed agreement.' In Turpin's view:

> The classical law of contract which was formulated by 19th century judges was 'a law of the market ... This law in general did not, and does not, make provision for the peculiar circumstances of government procurement, the unique relationship between the government and its principal contractors, or the specific issues of the public interest that arise in government contracting'. The need for particular legal rules adapted to the requirements of government procurement has been met in the United Kingdom by the regular use of appropriate standard conditions of contract.

Government procurement contracts are, in broad terms, an expression of economic and social policies and the contractor is the instrument whereby services and functions are executed. However, government expenditure (of tax-payer's money) on goods and services raises questions of public accountability and, although the relationship between the government and its major suppliers used to be described as a partnership with its basis 'the fair and reasonable price', the current economic climate, together with a number of cases where the private sector has 'ripped off' the government, has led to changes. European Community rules have led to more competitive tendering and a more 'free market' approach to procurement. Hard bargaining, best value for money and the attainment, not the over-shooting, of contract targets, are now the order of the day.

Nevertheless, government contracts remain almost exclusively based on standard or model forms, their clauses largely independent of any particular contract. Where, as we have seen, such models are the outcome of co-operative planning on the part of all interests, it is claimed that fairness and impartiality will dominate the transactions based on them. Such is claimed by the drafters, and revisers, of engineering and building contracts, but in practice the presence of 'employer power' and industrial giants will again tend to tilt the balance of bargaining power. Such is the case also where the government is concerned: the appropriate government form (eg GC/Works/1 or GC/Stores 1) will be used and work will be done or goods supplied on its terms with little likelihood of scope for modification by the contractor.

As is so for any standard form document, the government forms are *drafted* with reference to the general law of contract and relevant statutory measures such as the Sale of Goods Act. This is clearly necessary to guarantee their effectiveness and 'clout'; contract law may move into the background and outside the courts in the settlement of claims. Turpin again:

135

... the general law of contract has only a subsidiary or contingent application to government contracts ... Although an awareness of the rules of the law of contract influences in these ways the departments engaged in the contracting process, government procurement is a notable instance of those sectors in which, in the words of a distinguished scholar [Julius Stone], 'the coercions of law are ... only in the background.

This framework can indeed be very loose and work often proceeds not on the basis of the general law of contract or the terms of the particular contract itself, even if it has been formally signed, but rather on the basis of informal understandings and 'inarticulate practices' established through regular contact between the parties – see again, for example, the case of *Trollope and Colls Ltd v Atomic Power Constructions Ltd* in Chapter 5.

Although most disputes arising out of government contracts are settled informally, since the passing of the Crown Proceedings Act 1947 it has been possible for civil proceedings to enforce any contractual obligations to be instituted by or against any 'authorised' government department in its own name. The remedies that are available to the parties in the event of a breach of government contract are (a) as provided by the general law, eg damages and termination of the contract in the case of serious breach; (b) as provided by the contract itself; and (c) special 'administrative' remedies available only to the government. The remedies provided by the law of contract are, it would appear, never invoked, but their presence and availability may well, as stated earlier, influence the course of an extra-legal settlement. Remedies provided in the contract itself often rest on clauses which stipulate what conduct shall constitute breach. For example, SC 14(1) of the GC/Stores/1 standard form provides that if the contract articles (the supplies) 'or any proportion thereof' are not delivered within the time or times specified in the contract, the government department concerned may 'without prejudice to any other remedies, by notice to the Contractor determine the Contracts either as respects the Articles which have not been delivered in accordance with the Contract at the time of such determination, or as respects all the Articles to which the Contract relates other than those delivered in accordance with the Contract before that time'.

If the government should choose to act under SC 14 it may, on the face of it, terminate the contract even if the contractor's default relates to a single instalment of goods, which are not delivered on time or are rejected and not replaced on time. Such a clause apparently makes a minor breach (of warranty) grounds for termination, a remedy which we have seen is only available under the general law for a serious reach, eg a breach of condition. Such a clause is however understandable in the context of bargaining strength – after all, it is the government which drafted the contract in the first place. Similarly, it is economic power which lies behind the 'administrative' remedies of which the government departments avail themselves from time to time. 'Profit reduction' involves cutting the contractor's originally agreed profit by the department adjusting the contract price downwards. 'Profit disallowance', on the other hand, involves the withholding of bonus or incentive payments which a contractor would have earned by efficient performance.

Departments may decide to apply these remedies not only where the contractor is in breach, but also as a sanction for inefficient or dilatory performance which falls short of breach. Profit reduction, as opposed to the cancellation of efficiency allowances, may be impossible to justify either by resort to the general law or the standard form agreement. Turpin cites the following passage from a report of the Comptroller and Auditor General as regards a profit reduction of over £36,000 which was levied by the Ministry of Supply in 1958 upon a contractor who had undertaken the development of a guided weapon:

> The Ministry stated in this connection that the profit penalty was not an assessed compensation for extra costs which had been incurred through delays for which the contractor was responsible. General dissatisfaction with a contractor's work on such a development project was in the main a matter of opinion and impossible to express in monetary terms which could be relied upon for forming a claim against the contractor; but the Ministry had insisted on a reduction in profit as an expression of their dissatisfaction, in spite of the contractor's specific rejection of the suggestion that his effort and achievements did not warrant normal recognition.

It is clear, even from this brief survey, that government-procurement contacts are a rather special area, having only vague links with the general principles of contract law. From procurement policy to 'administrative' remedies, the contracting process is directed from somewhere along the corridors of power. Contract law may be loosely taken into account as regards the drafting and reviewing of the standard forms, but in the absence of litigation or other forms of public hearing, apart from occasional references in *Hansard*, fears of misuse of the system, as highlighted by various corruption trials in the 1970s, may well remain. It is difficult to imagine any general rules or principles of government contracts emerging; the special consideration of balancing 'value for money' against 'public interest', which must loom large in most cases, would seem to suggest that *ad hoc* judgments will continue to determine the course of government policy.

Public sector (and privatised) provisions of services: the case of electricity supply

In the late 1940s, as part of its programme for the nationalisation of key sectors of the economy, the Labour government removed the supply of a number of crucially important basic materials and services from private sector organisations into the control of public corporations. These corporations, created by statute, were not responsible to shareholders but ultimately to government in terms of national economic policy. The profit motive was subordinated to 'public interest'. Sectors of the economy so affected included coal, steel, gas, electricity and rail transport. We will concentrate on electricity, which is supplied to industry (both public and private sectors) and to private households.

As from 1 April 1948, the Central Electricity Generating Board became responsible for bulk electricity supply to Area Boards. These Boards distributed electricity to consumers and within their areas took the form of statutory monopolies. As the following case shows, the nature of the transactional relationship between supplier and consumer depended on the terms of the relevant statute, here the Electricity Act 1947:

> In *Willmore and Willmore (Trading as Lissenden Poultry) v South Eastern Electricity Board* (1957), the plaintiff poultry farmers claimed for damages against the Board, alleging that the Board was in breach of its contract to supply current adequate to operate infra-red electric lamps used by the plaintiffs in rearing chicks.
>
> Periodic failures to meet overall demand had resulted in voltage variations and a large number of chicks had become chilled and died. Conceding that if the Board had been bound by contract to supply suitable current for the lamps, they would have been liable to pay damages, the court nevertheless held that the supply of electricity was not based on contract at all but was provided in pursuance of the Board's statutory duty.
>
> The supply for which the plaintiffs applied was expressed in the application form to be 'subject to the conditions imposed by statute, order or regulation'. The only remedy available was by way of proceedings for a statutory penalty.

With government procurement, we have seen that contractual remedies are not resorted to, here they were not available. Nor, at least as regards electricity supply, has the position changed following the privatisation of the industry under the Electricity Act 1989. This Act removed electricity supply from state ownership and control and placed it back in the hands of regionally based private sector companies (eg Yorkshire Electricity Group plc).

> In *Norweb plc v Dixon* (1995), it was stated that a general agreement for the supply of electricity between a tariff customer and a privatised electricity supplier under the 1989 Act was not a contract. The creation of the relationship and the fixing of its terms was not consistent with the creation of a contract. The supplier was *obliged by the Act* to supply if requested to do so (subject to limited exceptions). The tariff was fixed by the supplier under the terms of the Act and there was no scope for bargaining by the consumer. The supplier was exercising the power conferred on it by the Act. The rights and liabilities of the parties were governed by statute and not by contract.
>
> In the circumstances of this case, the Act also gave the supplier the power to recover any charges due to it with no need to have recourse to contract. (The *Willmore* decision was cited with approval in this context.)

The court did concede that it was possible under section 22 of the 1989 Act for parties to negotiate a *special* agreement, necessary to meet the particular requirements of a consumer, and on such terms as might be specified in such agreement. It was clear from the Act itself that in such a case the electricity supply was provided on a contractual basis. No special agreement existed between Norweb and Dixon.

Since privatisation, the interests of consumers as regards prices, terms and quality of supply are provided for by statute-based regulatory agencies and not by the law of contract. For example, the Office of Electricity Regulation (OFFER) is an independent body set up by Parliament to protect the interests of electricity consumers. It is not a part of supply organisation. Problems which cannot be resolved satisfactorily with the supplier can be referred to the regional OFFER. If no solution is found, the matter may be considered by the regional consumer committee. Such a committee's decisions are not binding but decisions taken by the head of the regulatory mechanism, the Director General of Electricity Supply, have the same effect as a county court judgment: see *R v Director General of Electricity Supply, ex parte Redrow Homes (Northern) Ltd* (1995).

In several sectors (eg gas supply), the number of consumer complaints has risen dramatically since privatisation. As Collins (*The Law of Contract*, 1993) concludes: 'The real substance of the issue of the scope of contracts in this context should turn on whether the statutes regulating public utilities provide adequate alternative means of redress for consumers, so that the exclusion of contractual rights is the price paid for the advantages of the statutory scheme for complaints.'

References and further reading

Standard form contracts

Kessler, 'Contracts and power in America', in Black and Mileski (eds) *The Social Organisation of Law* (Academic Press); originally in (1943) 43 *Columbia Law Review* 629.

Rakoff, 'Contracts of adhesion: an essay in reconstruction' (1983) 96 *Harvard Law Review* 1173.

Slawson, 'Standard form contracts and democratic control of law-making power' (1971) 84 *Harvard Law Review* 529.

Treibilcock (1980), 'An economic approach to unconscionability', in Reiter and Swan (eds) *Studies in Contract Law* (Toronto Butterworths).

Building and engineering standard forms

Adams and Brownsword, 'Contractual indemnity clauses' (1982) JBL 200.

Godwin Ltd, *Building Law Reports*.

Johnston, 'Engineering contracts – some reflections' (1965) JBL 239.

Johnston, *Electrical and Mechanical Engineering Contracts*.

Parris (1982), *The standard form of building contract – JCT 80*.

Government contracts

Daintith, 'Regulation by contract: the new prerogative' (1979) 34 *Current Legal Problems* 41.

Friedmann (1972), *Law in a Changing Society*, 2nd edn pp 389–408, on government contracts.

Harden (1992), *The Contracting State*.

Turpin, 'Government contracts: a study of methods of contracting' (1979) 31 MLR 241.

Turpin (1989), *Government Procurement and Contracts*.

Questions

(1) 'To place an emphasis on negotiated agreement in contract may well be a mistaken emphasis nowadays' (Friedmann). Discuss.

(2) 'A major objective pursued by the drafter of standard form contracts is the elimination of business and juridical risk.' Discuss.

(3) To what extent do the *Waltham Holy Cross* and indemnity clause decisions bear out the contention that, when dealing with building, engineering and similar standard forms, the court's role is primarily interpretative and the general law of contract is of merely secondary significance?

(4) (a) 'The difficulties arise solely because of the amorphous and tortuous provisions of the RIBA contract' (Sachs LJ in *Bickerton & Son Ltd v North West Metropolitan Regional Hospital Board* (1969)).

    (b) 'Paragraph (g) is highly anomalous, and would appear to have been included in this form of contract without any regard to the manifest injustice and, indeed, absurdity implicit in it' (Salmon LJ in *Jarvis & Sons Ltd v Westminster City Council Corpn* (1969)).

Follow up one or more of these statements and relate your findings to the following statement:

    (c) 'I have no doubt that the standard form of RIBA main contract and the standard forms of sub-contract, despite certain obscurities, work well enough in practice' (Lord Salmon in *Gilbert-Ash (Northern) Ltd v Modern Engineering (Bristol) Ltd* (1974)).

(5) (a) In *Farr (AE) Ltd v The Admiralty* (1953), on the basis of the then current government form (since amended), it was held that the government was entitled negligently to knock down what the contractor had put up and then require him, at his own expense, to rebuild it. How did the court manage to come to this startling conclusion?

    (b) Explain the basis of the House of Lords decision in *White (Contractors) Ltd v Tarmac Civil Engineering Ltd* (1967).

(6) Comment on the following statements:

    (a) 'Contracting parties today use those forms with only a hazy idea of their content and of the increasing volume of legal precedent surrounding their words': from a review of a book on international grain contracts.

    (b) 'If buyers choose not to read the documents, they must put up with the consequences': Lord Denning in *Panchaud Frères SA v Et General Grain Co* (1970).

9 Businesses, consumers and unfair terms

It is not the purpose of this chapter to examine the whole body of civil and criminal law, the regulatory mechanisms and voluntary codes of practice which now exist to protect the consumer from unsafe products, qualitatively deficient goods and services, fraudulent trading practices and the other matters which constitute modern consumer protection law and practice. Our main aim is to concentrate on the legal response to unfair and oppressive terms in business contracts made with consumers and others, which has culminated in the passing of the Unfair Contract Terms Act 1977 and the coming into effect (from the end of 1994) of the European Community Directive on Unfair Terms in Consumer Contracts.

We will also consider the gradual emergence of a judicial doctrine of economic duress which gives the courts wider powers to strike down contracts where one party, mindful of their economic power or bargaining position, exerts improper pressure on the other to obtain his 'agreement' to the contract. By putting these topics together, we are able to relate and carry forward such major issues, discussed in earlier chapters, as the decline of freedom of contract, increasing legal awareness of the presence and effect of inequality of bargaining power, the use by businesses of standard-form documents, and the nature and effect of clauses designed to exclude or restrict a seller's or supplier's legal responsibility for defective goods and deficient services.

Exclusion clauses

It will be recalled from Chapter 7 that 60 years ago a Miss L'Estrange bought a cigarette machine under a sales agreement which contained a clause which stated that 'any express or implied condition, statement or warranty, statutory or otherwise not stated herein, is hereby excluded'. Although the machine soon jammed and became unworkable, she lost her action for breach. In 1979 the author purchased a car under a sales agreement which stated that: 'Nothing in these conditions is intended to remove, alter or restrict any rights or obligations of either party arising under the Sale of Goods Act 1893 or the Supply of Goods (Implied Terms) Act 1973.' On the face of it, all or any of Miss L'Estrange's contractual rights or remedies were removed by the exclusion clause. In my transaction, the protection afforded me by virtue of the dealer's implied obligations under ss 12–15 of the Sale of Goods Act (as amended in 1973) was apparently unimpaired. Why the change?

Social concern regarding the exclusion or restriction of their contractual liability for breach of contract by those in business to supply goods and services goes back well into the 19th century. Apart from isolated statutory measures, the legal struggle against such 'unfair terms' was carried on until the 1970s by the judges, who devised a variety of weapons to render such clauses inoperative, particularly where they operated against the interests of consumers. However, successes by the courts merely drove the drafters of exclusion clauses to renewed efforts to produce 'judge-proof' forms of words such as that which defeated the court in Miss L'Estrange's case. The main problem was that the judges felt that they had no general power to strike down unreasonable exclusion clauses as being, for example, against public policy and therefore void. They felt that the concept of freedom of contract overrode such an approach.

Therefore, for example, with contracts for the sale of goods, the position until 1973 was broadly as follows: ss 12–15 of the 1893 Act provided measures of buyer protection by way of the seller's implied obligations concerning fitness for purpose and merchantability, etc. Freedom of contract generally, and s 55 of the 1893 Act specifically (see p 107), allowed sellers to remove the implied terms by the use of exclusion clauses in 'take it or leave it' situations. Buyers of defective goods were deterred from bringing actions or, if they did, it was difficult to be optimistic of their chances of success in the face of tightly worded clauses. The courts, however, developed an increasingly complicated armoury of back door techniques, including the doctrine of fundamental breach (see Chapter 7), to defeat such clauses. Increasing pressure led to the passing of the Supply of Goods (Implied Terms) Act in 1973 which, among other things, banned the exclusion of suppliers' implied obligations in consumer transactions and subjected exclusion clauses used in inter-business dealings to a test of reasonableness.

The Unfair Contract Terms Act 1977 extended statutory protection to, among others, contracts for the provision of services. These two statutes do not apply to a variety of contracts but nevertheless they represent a big step forward in consumer protection. We will examine the present state of the law by reference to the 1977 Act (although we will not consider every matter raised), indicating wherever necessary the changes that have been brought about by reference to the previous position.

The Unfair Contract Terms Act 1977 (re-enacting the 1973 Act's provisions relating to clauses seeking to exclude or limit liability in contracts for the supply of goods) extends statutory control to contracts generally (subject to stated exceptions) and in particular to negligence liability in, as is often the case, contracts for the provision of services. The Act applies mainly to terms and notices which attempt to exclude or restrict liability for things done by a person in the course of a business – 'business liability' as in s 1(3). Section 14 states that 'business' includes a profession and the (business) activities of government departments, local and public authorities. The broad scheme of the Act is to render some exclusion and limitation clauses ineffective and to subject others to a requirement of reasonableness. Although, as stated, it does not apply to a variety of contracts, it places control on a simpler and sounder footing than before. That is not to say, however, that the Act sweeps away all the previous common law rules. While some fall away, others remain intact or find new statutory expression.

To understand the present position, it is necessary to address four main questions:

(1)   Is the clause which seeks to exclude or limit a party's liability incorporated into the contract?

(2)   If so, is it a clause which is rendered ineffective under the 1977 Act?

(3)   If not, as a matter of judicial construction, does the wording of the clause satisfactorily cover the loss or damage at issue?

(4)   If it passes this test, does the clause satisfy the requirement of reasonableness?

Incorporation of the clause

The pre-statutory case law remains to provide the guidelines in this area (see also guideline (c) in Schedule 2 to the 1977 regarding reasonableness):

(a)   *Signed documents: L'Estrange v Graucob Ltd (1934)*

This is authority for the rule that a person who signs a contractual document is bound by its terms even though they have not read them. In this case, the plaintiff was bound by her signature even though the exclusion clause was in 'regrettably small print'. She could not argue that she had no notice of the clause. (This is a case which would now be decided on the basis of the 'reasonableness' of the clause under s 6(3) of the 1977 Act, the plaintiff buying the machine in the course of her business.)

If, however, the true purpose of the signed document has been misrepresented to the party signing, the absolute effect of his or her signature will not be enforced: *Curtis v Chemical Cleaning & Dyeing Co Ltd (1951)* in which the (restricted) scope of an exclusion clause was taken to be as orally represented not as written.

(b)   *Reasonably sufficient notice:*

'In cases in which the contract is contained in a railway ticket or other unsigned document, it is necessary to prove that an alleged party was aware, or ought to have been aware, of its terms and conditions': Scrutton LJ. Thus reasonable notice must be given of a clause set out, or referred to, in such a document, or displayed at the place where the contract is entered into.

Several further questions may be raised: Is the document a 'contractual' document? If not, the clause set out or referred to has no force. In *Chapelton v Barry UDC* (1940), a deck-chair ticket was held to be merely a 'voucher or receipt', but whether a document is one which could reasonably be expected to contain contractual terms is a question of fact which may vary with business practice (ie a 'receipt' may have contractual force in another case).

Second: What is reasonable notice? In 1930 in *Thompson v LMS*, the court was satisfied that reasonable notice had been given to a passenger of an exclusion clause found on p 552 of the company's 6d timetable. (The trail to the clause started with the words 'see back' on her ticket.) Although a similar point would probably be decided differently today, incorporation by reference to a further document or by the use of a clearly exhibited printed notice may, in the nature of things, be the only feasible means of communication for the party relying on a clause.

In *Thornton v Shoe Lane Parking Ltd* (1971), Lord Denning, while stressing the fictional nature of agreement (to the clause) in cases such as *Thompson*, insisted on the need for *special steps* to be taken by a party wishing to incorporate unusual or unexpected protective terms into his contract:

> T parked his car for the first time at SLP's car park. A notice outside the entrance stated: 'All cars parked at owner's risk'. At the entrance, T received a ticket from a machine and an automatic barrier was raised. In small print on the ticket it was stated that: 'This ticket is issued subject to the conditions of issue displayed on the premises.' Inside the building was another notice which purported to exempt SLP from any liability resulting from damage to the car *or personal injury*.
>
> When collecting his car, there was an accident and T was injured, partly as a result of SLP's negligence. The court held that SLP had not taken sufficient steps to draw T's attention to the 'less typical' personal injury disclaimer at the time the contract was made at the entrance (although he was bound by the exterior notice).

The same approach was adopted in a commercial context in *Interfoto Picture Library Ltd v Stiletto Visual Programmes Ltd* (1989). The term in question was not an exclusion clause but referred to holding charges for late return of goods (photographs) loaned to the defendants for promotional purposes. A two-week delay in returning them incurred a charge of £3,783, well above comparable rates elsewhere in the trade. The term was described as 'unreasonable and extortionate'. Given that the plaintiffs had failed to take exceptional steps to bring the defendant's attention to their charges, the term failed for lack of reasonable notice and was disallowed.

Third: Has notice of the clause been brought to the attention of the other party before or at the time of making the contract? If not, it will be ineffective; a key factor in *Thornton*'s case above. In *Olley v Marlborough Court* (1949) the contract was made at the hotel reception desk and the clause, relating to the safe custody of guests' valuables, was to be found in a notice on their bedroom wall.

However, a clause may be incorporated into a particular transaction from a regular previous course of dealing, if it can be established that the clause nonetheless applies despite a failure to incorporate it in the required manner on the occasion in question, eg the Olley's had regularly visited the Marlborough Court before and had seen (or had the opportunity to see) the exclusion clause; see also *Kendall v Lillico* on p 104 and *British Crane Hire Corpn Ltd v Ipswich Plant Hire Ltd* on p 104 as regards a similar method of incorporation from a trade source known and recognised by both parties.

It should finally be noted that a party who might otherwise be entitled to rely on a written exclusion clause will not be allowed to do so if he gives an express oral undertaking which is inconsistent with the written exemption: *Couchman v Hill* (1947) and see also the *Merzario* case on p 101.

Clauses rendered ineffective by the 1977 Act

On the assumption that the exclusion clause *is* a term of the contract, it may nevertheless be rendered ineffective by the 1977 Act (or some other statute).

Negligence liability

Section 2 relates to clauses or notices which purport to exclude business liability for negligence. Under s 1(1) negligence here means not only breach of a contractual duty to take reasonable care or exercise reasonable skill (as, typically, in a contract for services) but also breach of the common law, tortious, duty (in respect, for example, of a notice at a sporting event for which spectators attend free of charge) and the duty of care owed to visitors under the Occupiers' Liability Act 1957.

Under s 2(1) a person *cannot* by any such contract term or notice exclude or restrict his liability for *death or personal injury* resulting from negligence. Prior to the Act, the courts construed clauses seeking to exclude liability for negligence very strictly. As we have seen when discussing indemnity clauses in the last chapter, very clear words are needed to achieve the required result. Nevertheless, the pre-1977 case of *Bennett v Pontin's Ltd* (unreported) is a solemn reminder:

> While on holiday, B died in the swimming pool at P's holiday camp. Mrs B sued P and the court held that P were 50 per cent to blame because: (i) the pool was so dirty that B's body was not found for an hour, and then only by a boy wearing goggles who was swimming underwater; (ii) only one life guard was on duty, although there were more than 200 people in the pool, and despite another death having occurred there only two weeks earlier. However, Mrs B recovered no damages as B had signed a booking form which contained a clause excluding P from any liability in the event of an accident, even if it was entirely their fault.

In the field of public transport, it should be noted that when nationalisation removed the railways from the private sector in 1948, it became somewhat anomalous for British Railways, as a public utility, to exclude liability for death or personal injuries to passengers – as LMS had done in *Thompson v LMS*, see above. Accordingly the law was changed so that any attempt to exclude such liability was void: see s 43(7) of the Transport Act 1962.

The Public Passenger Vehicles Act 1981 contains a similar provision as regards the conveyance of passengers in public service vehicles: see also *Gore v Van der Lann* (1967) where a clause in an old-age pensioner's travel pass, purporting to exempt Liverpool Corporation and its employees from such liability, was held to be void under a previous enactment.

Consumer sale of goods and hire purchase, etc

The most important provision here is s 6(2) to the extent that it establishes that in *consumer* transactions, a business-supplier's liability for breach of the statutorily implied obligations relating to the merchantable (now 'satisfactory') quality and fitness for purpose of his goods cannot be excluded or restricted by any contract term. It would be on this basis that the exclusion clause in the *Karsales (Harrow) Ltd v Wallis* hire purchase case, see p 116 would now be struck down and not on the basis of fundamental breach.

To establish whether a person is contracting as a consumer it is necessary to look to s 12: a party 'deals as consumer' if (a) he neither makes the contract in the course of a business nor holds himself out as doing so; and (b) the other party makes the contract in the course of a business; and (c) in supply of goods cases, the goods are of a type ordinarily supplied for private use or consumption. Section 7 of the Act contains a provision having the same effect as s 6(2) with respect to other contracts for the supply of goods, eg a contract of hire. The implied terms in question are to be found in the Supply of Goods and Services Act 1982.

'Guarantees' of consumer goods

Section 5 of the 1977 Act prevents the use in manufacturers' 'guarantees' or 'warranties' of consumer goods (eg cars or kettles) of clauses designed to exclude or restrict liability for loss or damage that arises from defects in the goods while in 'consumer use' and results from negligence in the manufacture or distribution of the goods. The section is therefore concerned with the manufacturer – consumer relationship (as in *Donoghue v Stevenson*) and not with the supplier – consumer relationship covered by ss 6 and 7. It operates against a manufacturer's guarantee which, for example, states that:

> The company guarantees these goods for a period of 12 months from the date of purchase. Should any defect develop during the guarantee period and the defect be due to faulty materials or workmanship it will be replaced or repaired free of charge. This guarantee is in lieu of, and expressly excludes, all liability to compensate for loss or damage, howsoever caused.

Sections 6 and 7 do operate against a supplier's guarantee (the supplier could be the manufacturer) which, apart from the final sentence, might be drafted in terms similar to the one above but which concludes: 'This guarantee excludes all express and implied conditions and warranties, statutory or otherwise.' The goods must be 'of a type ordinarily supplied for private use or consumption'; they must be 'in consumer use', ie otherwise than exclusively for the purpose of a business; and 'loss or damage' covers death or personal injury (banned in any case under s 2(1)) and economic loss.

Judicial construction of exclusion clauses

If it is settled that an exclusion or limitation of liability clause *is* incorporated into the contract, and it is *not* rendered ineffective by statute, its operation may next rest on judicial interpretation of the meaning and effectiveness of its wording in the face of the loss or damage that has arisen. (This is apart from subjecting the clause to the requirement of reasonableness – as called for by s 11 of the 1977 Act examined below. It may also be the case that the Act does not apply: see Schedule 1 and the insurance case of *Morley v United Friendly Insurance* (1993).)

We have already drawn attention to construction of contractual terms on several occasions, particularly in the last chapter in the context of building and engineering contracts. Questions of construction (from the verb 'to construe') arise where it is necessary to ascertain the true meaning of words and, hence, their legal effect: 'One must consider the meaning of the words used, not what one may guess to be the intention of the parties.' In construing a document, the court must also have regard to its commercial purpose and background: eg see *Prenn v Simmonds* (1971).

It should be appreciated that nowadays a court's 'discovery' of the parties' intentions (see p 16 on 19th century consensual and 'party autonomy' views of contract) must be coloured by the adoption of non-negotiated standard forms. Bearing in mind their purpose and the circumstances giving rise to their presence in the 'agreement', exclusion clauses are strictly construed. They must be expressed clearly and without ambiguity otherwise they will be ineffective. In particular:

(a) A clause must clearly cover the liability which it seeks to exclude. If, therefore, in a non-consumer contract for the sale of goods (as in s 6(3) of the 1977 Act), the clause excludes implied conditions and warranties, it will not exclude an express term: see also *Andrews Bros Ltd v Singer & Co Ltd* (1934).

(b) If there is ambiguity as to the scope or meaning of an exclusion or limitation of liability clause, the doubt will be resolved by construing it *against* the party who seeks to rely on the clause. This is known as the *contra proferentem* rule. In an inter-business contract for the sale of cotton thread (now covered by s 6(3) of the Act), it was stipulated that: 'The goods *delivered* shall be deemed to be in all respects in accordance with the contract' unless the buyer complained within 14 days of their receipt. It was held that this clause was no defence to a claim for damages for *short delivery*; the damages being claimed 'not in respect of goods delivered but in respect of goods which were not delivered'. Courts have been known to 'discover' ambiguity in the interests of justice (and I have been told that in an overseas case the words 'Cars parked at owner's risk' were taken to mean at the risk of the owner of the car park!). However, in the case of *Ailsa Craig Fishing Co Ltd v Malvern Fishing Co Ltd* (1983), the opinion was expressed that the rules of construction would not normally operate as strictly in the case of limitation of liability clauses as for exclusion clauses. (Limitation of liability clauses, eg placing a financial limit on compensation, are generally found in inter-business transactions and are risk-allocation devices to be backed by insurance.)

(c) We saw, when discussing inter-business indemnity clauses in the last chapter and clauses seeking, prior to the 1977 Act, to exclude liability for death or personal injury caused by negligence, that the clearest words are (or were) needed to achieve this result. This principle of construction will still apply to cases under s 2(2) of the Act relating to clauses seeking to exclude liability for 'loss or damage' (*other than* death or personal injury) which are also subject to the requirement of reasonableness.

From the case law, perhaps the best guide was established by the House of Lords in the indemnity case of *Smith v South Wales Switchgear Ltd* (1978) discussed on p 134. A business party seeking to exclude liability for negligence should expressly use the word 'negligence' (or a synonymous expression such as 'any act or omission') in his clause rather than a general phrase such as 'any liability, loss, claim or proceedings whatsoever'. However, see also *Alderslade v Hendon Laundry* (1945).

(d) In the *Photo-Production* case (see the end of Chapter 7), the House of Lords re-affirmed that the efficacy or otherwise of an exclusion clause depends, whether the contract is affirmed or terminated by the injured party, upon its construction. Therefore the doctrine of fundamental breach, operating automatically as a rule of law to deprive a party in default of the benefit of his clause, was in this way laid to rest (and this position was reinforced by s 9 of the 1977 Act, as we will see).

As a *rule of construction* (ie does the wording of the clause cover the fundamental breach?), the doctrine clearly now has no part to play where the Act renders a clause inoperative. Whether it has a role to play prior to the application under the Act of the requirement of reasonableness, or in cases to which the Act does not apply, is open to question. In *Suisse Atlantique* (1967) it was stated that it would be rare for an exclusion clause, as a matter of construction, to protect a party in fundamental breach. Later, in the other major House of Lords decision, *Photo-Production v Securicor*, it was argued that although a breach occasioned dire consequences, this in itself did not bring into play *even harsher* construction of an

149

exclusion clause. In any event, their Lordships tended to steer clear of a fundamental breach basis to this decision, emphasising instead that business parties,
assumed to be of equal bargaining strength, should be left free, through their use
of exclusionary and other devices backed by insurance cover, to apportion risks
of loss as they thought fit without judicial intervention. (In *Photo-Production* the
defendants were protected by the wide-ranging wording of their exclusion
clause in the face of what some of their Lordships termed a fundamental breach.)

The 1977 ACT and the requirement of reasonableness

Other than for cases of negligence liability resulting in death or personal injury under
s 2(1) and supply of goods cases involving consumers, particularly under
s 6(2) but under ss 7 and 5 also, the 1977 Act assesses the effectiveness or otherwise of
exclusion and limitation of liability clauses against a requirement of reasonableness.

The tests of reasonableness: s 11 and Schedule 2

Wherever the Act provides that a contract term or notice must meet the requirement of reasonableness, the *time* for assessing its reasonableness is the time when
the contract was made, set against the background of the circumstances which
were, or ought reasonably to have been, known to the parties at that time: s 11(1).
If a clause is reasonable, then its effectiveness will not be impaired by subsequent
events or conduct (particularly the effect of the breach) – to provide otherwise
would amount to 'changing the rules in the middle of the game'. The burden of
proof regarding reasonableness lies on the party seeking to rely on the clause.

Second, where a term or notice required to be reasonable, places a maximum
financial limit on the amount that may be recovered, s 11(4) lays down that the
court must take account of the resources available to the party seeking the benefit of the clause to meet the liability if it arises and also whether they were in a
position to cover themselves by insurance; for cases, see below.

Third, under s 11(2), in the case of exemptions of implied terms in non-consumer contracts for the sale or supply of goods (see below), the court is referred
to guidelines on reasonableness set out in Schedule 2 to the Act. The following
factors, among others, may be taken as relevant by the court:

- the relative strength of the bargaining positions of the parties;

- whether the plaintiff received an inducement (eg a lower price) to agree to
  the exemption;

- whether the plaintiff knew, or ought reasonably to have known of the existence and extent of the term, having regard to, among other things, any

custom of the trade or any previous course of dealing between the parties (note previous discussion of common law rules on incorporation of terms);

- whether any condition for the enforcement of liability (eg the need to bring a claim within seven days of performance) could practicably be complied with by the plaintiff, see below;

- whether the plaintiff had the opportunity to enter into a similar contract with other persons but without having to accept a similar term;

- whether the goods were specially made to the order of the plaintiff.

These Schedule 2 guidelines are stated to apply only to sale and supply of goods cases but they have influenced courts in other cases. Section 11(1) calls for the 'background of the circumstances' to be taken into consideration.

Negligence liability – 'other loss or damage'

Under s 2(2) a business party cannot 'in the case of other loss or damage' (eg to goods or other property) exclude or restrict his liability for negligence, except in so far as the term or notice satisfies the requirement of reasonableness. In cases under s 2(2), the clause may first be tested against the principles of construction relating to the exclusion or restriction of liability for negligence discussed above, and then, if surviving this test, the party seeking to rely on the clause must show that it is reasonable:

> In *Wight v British Railways Board*, a county court decision in 1982, BR lost W's suitcase but sought to rely on a clause limiting their liability by reference to weight (£1,500 per ton – a limitation which clearly had commercial consignments in mind rather than those of individuals). W's suitcase contained valuable jewellery but according to terms on display and in the consignment note, the case was carried 'at owner's risk'. The clause having been satisfactorily incorporated into the contract, the judge moved to enquire whether the clause was fair and reasonable in the circumstances. It was held that it was easier for the plaintiff to insure than the carriers – in the circumstances there were no real means whereby BRB might ascertain the value of the goods consigned – and the clause was reasonable. (However, see another lost suitcase action, *Waldron-Kelly v British Railways Board* (1981), which produced a quite different result, the judge laying more emphasis on BRB's 'negligence or want of care in a consumer case'.)

In *Photo-Production Ltd v Securicor Transport Ltd* (1980), an inter-business agreement (not decided under the 1977 Act but in conformity with it), although S's employee burnt down P's factory, a factor which influenced the House of Lords when deciding in S's favour was that P was in a better position to insure its factory against such a contingency.

> In *Woodman v Photo Trade Processing Ltd* (1981), another county court decision, a reel of film taken at a wedding was given to PTP for processing. Most of the pictures were lost and the

defendants sought protection on the basis of a clause which read: 'All photographic materials are accepted on the basis that their value does not exceed the cost of the material itself. Responsibility is limited to the replacement of the films. No liability will be accepted, consequential or otherwise, howsoever caused.'

The clause was held to be unreasonable: no insurance cover was offered nor advice on insurance given and the plaintiff's attention was not specifically drawn to the clause. It was noted that the Code of Practice for the Photographic Industry recommended a two-tier system of a normal service with a total exclusion of liability and a special service with full acceptance of liability but a higher charge. PTP had offered no such special service. W recovered £75 damages. (The judgment in this case can be found in Miller and Harvey, *Consumer and Trading Law: Cases and Materials*.)

The following s 2(2) case involved business parties only and damage to property:

In *Phillips Products Ltd v Hyland* (1987), PP hired a JCB excavator and its driver (Hyland) from Hamstead (second defendant). The contract was based on the Contractors' Plant Association model conditions for plant hire. Clause 8 of these conditions stated that the *hirer* was responsible for claims arising from the negligent operation of the plant by the driver. The driver, Hyland, negligently drove the JCB into PP's premises and damaged them. It was argued that Clause 8 merely transferred liability (to the hirer's insurers); it did not act as an exclusion clause and therefore s 2(2) of the 1977 Act did not apply.

The defendants' argument was rejected. It was stated that the owner of the excavator 'does most certainly purport to exclude its liability for negligence by reference to Condition 8'. On the facts, it was found that the hirers did not regularly hire plant and drivers, had no control over the driver, and had little opportunity to arrange insurance.

The question of reasonableness depends on the facts of each individual case and in *Phillips*, the Court of Appeal stated that appellate courts should not readily overturn decisions at first instance on this issue. (The *Phillips* case should be considered in relation to *Thompson v T Lohan (Plant Hire) Ltd*.) Reasonableness was also a central feature of a House of Lords decision involving a private party and economic loss. The clause in this case did not specifically exclude liability for negligence; it was a disclaimer purporting to prevent any obligation from arising in the first place:

In *Smith v Eric S Bush* (1989), a surveyor provided a valuation of a property to the plaintiff via a building society. In the words of Lord Griffiths: 'The report, however, contained in red lettering and in the clearest terms a disclaimer of liability for the accuracy of the report covering both the building society and the valuer.' The report stated that 'no essential repairs [to the house] are required'. S bought the house and 18 months later a chimney collapsed and fell through the bedroom ceiling and floor.

It was held that the disclaimer of liability was caught by s 2(2) as a notice, without contractual force, which purported to exclude liability for negligence. There was no contractual relationship between S and valuer, B, who was instructed by and acting for the building society. B owed a duty of care in tort to S who had relied on the valuation. As liability would exist but for the disclaimer, the clause in question was therefore brought within the scope of the 1977 Act by a combination of s 1(1)(b) concerning the common law duty of care and s 13(1) concerning exclusion of the relevant obligation or duty (see below).

When next considering whether the disclaimer satisfied the requirement of reasonableness, Lord Griffiths stated that, whatever else, the following matters should always be considered:

(1) Were the parties of equal bargaining power? (In this case, 'the purchaser ... has no effective power to object'.)

(2) In the case of advice, would it have been reasonably practicable to obtain the advice from an alternative source taking into account considerations of costs and time? (The house was 'at the bottom end of the market' of a type typically bought by young, first-time buyers who were financially not well placed to pay for a second opinion.)

(3) How difficult is the task being undertaken for which liability is being excluded? (In this case, the work was 'at the lower end of the surveyor's field of professional expertise'.)

(4) What are the practical consequences of the decision on the question of reasonableness? (Is the risk one against which the defendant could easily have insured, but which will have serious consequences for a plaintiff who is required to bear the loss?)

It was held that the clause was not reasonable and S recovered £4,380 damages.

As the disclaimer was a notice not having contractual effect, the test of reasonableness did not have to be, as is normally the case, at the time 'when contract was made' but at the point 'when the liability arose or (but for the notice) would have arisen': s 11(3). Lord Griffiths also stressed that the decision would have been different if the purchase had concerned 'industrial property, large blocks of flats or very expensive houses'.

Non-consumer sale of goods and hire-purchase, etc

As when dealing with s 6(2) relating to consumers (see above), we will concentrate on the most important effect of the Act's provisions in this area. This is that, under s 6(3), a business supplier of goods under a contract of sale or hire-purchase who purports to exclude or restrict his liability for breach of the statutorily implied terms as to, among other things, their merchantable (now 'satisfactory') quality or fitness for a particular purpose will find that his clause is subject to the requirement of reasonableness where the party acquiring the goods deals 'otherwise than as consumer'. Basically we are dealing here with business-to-business transactions, eg *L'Estrange v Graucob Ltd*.

Two cases are instructive here. Although neither was decided on the basis of the 1977 Act and the guidelines in Schedule 2, the relevant prior legislation was of similar effect:

RW Green Ltd v Cade Bros Farms (1978) concerned the reasonableness of a clause in a contract for the sale of 20 tons of seed potatoes which limited claims for compensation to a refund of the price. (As stated, this was a pre-1977 contract but it was caught by a similar test and guidelines in the earlier Supply of Goods (Implied Terms) Act 1973.)

The potatoes were infected by a virus in breach of s 14 of the Sale of Goods Act. However, the limitation clause was found to be reasonable: (a) the contract was concluded on standard terms, based on trade practice and agreed over many years by both merchants and farmers; (b) certified virus free potatoes could be bought at a higher price; (c) the parties were representative of the two sides of the trade and had regularly done business together.

A further clause requiring complaints to be made within three days of delivery (the goods were perishable) was unreasonable in respect of a defect not discoverable on inspection within the time allowed: see now s 13(1) of the 1977 Act.

Reasonableness in the context of a contract for a sale of goods was considered by the House of Lords in *George Mitchell (Chesterhall) Ltd v Finney Lock Seeds Ltd* (1983). This contract was regulated by the Sale of Goods Act 1979 in which reasonableness was to be tested having regard 'to all the circumstances of the case', ie including post-formation circumstances:

FLS supplied cabbage seed to GM at a price of £192. The seed was planted but the crop failed with a loss to the farmers of an estimated £63,000. The contract was on the supplier's standard terms and the parties had dealt with each other for some years. The contract contained a clause limiting liability for defective seeds to the contract price.

On the facts of this particular case, the Court of Appeal and the House of Lords both adopted an interventionist approach to this inter-business transaction. It was held that the clause was unreasonable. In the Court of Appeal, Kerr LJ stated that:

'The balance of fairness and reasonableness appears to me to be overwhelmingly on the side of the plaintiffs ... Farmers do not, and cannot be expected to, insure against this kind of disaster; but suppliers of seeds can ... I am not persuaded that liability for rare events of this kind cannot be adequately insured against. Nor am I persuaded that the cost of such cover would add significantly to the cost of seed. Further, although the present exemption clause has been in existence for many decades, the evidence shows that it was never negotiated. In effect, it was simply imposed by the suppliers, and no seed can in practice be bought otherwise than subject to its terms. To limit the supplier's liability to the price of the seed in all cases, as against the magnitude of the losses which farmers can incur in rare disasters of this kind, appears to me to be a grossly disproportionate and unreasonable allocation of the respective risks.'

Standard forms and further consumer protection

Section 3 of the Act extends control of exclusion clauses and similar devices beyond (but sometimes overlapping with) negligence liability in s 2 and the provisions of ss 6 and 7 concerning the sale and supply of goods, by applying the test of reasonableness to further forms of *contract liability*. This is where one party 'deals as consumer or on the other's written standard terms of business':

s 3(1). The section therefore aims at both unequal bargaining situations and non-negotiated contract situations which may or may not involve a consumer.

A party 'deals as consumer' on the basis of the definition in s 12 (see p 147 above), the burden of proof being on the party claiming that a person is not dealing as a consumer. The case of *R & B Customs Brokers v UDT* (1988), a Court of Appeal decision, lays down that a business party may deal as a consumer as regards a contract which does not form a regular part of its business. As against a consumer or a party dealing on another's standard terms (and see the discussion of standard terms in Chapter 8), the other party cannot by reference to any contract term:

(a) when himself in breach, exclude or restrict his liability in respect of the breach, or

(b) claim to be entitled (i) to render a contractual performance substantially different from that which was reasonably to be expected of him, or (ii) in respect of the whole or any part of his contractual obligation, to render no performance at all,

except in so far as the contract term satisfies the requirement of reasonableness: see s 3(2).

Section 3(2)(a) came into play in a non-consumer context in *St Albans City and District Council v International Computers Ltd* (1994):

ICL supplied the Council with a data base for its community charge register. The contract was on ICL's standard terms and limited its liability for loss to £100,000.

An error in the software resulted in an overstatement of the city and district population of almost 3,000. The community charge was in consequence set too low with a loss to the Council of £1,314,846. Section 3 applied because the contract was made on ICL's 'written standard terms of business' and the court considered that either s 6 or 7 applied, together with their requirement of reasonableness.

Section 11(4) also applied because ICL sought to restrict liability to a specified sum of money. Regard therefore had to be paid to ICL's resources to meet potential liability and the question of insurance cover.

The court held that in this case the determining factors were:

(1) The parties were of unequal bargaining power, ICL dealing on their terms and conditions.

(2) The figure of £100,000 had not been justified in relation to potential risk and actual loss.

(3) ICL were insured to the extent of £50 million worldwide.

(4) In practical terms it was better that the loss should fall on ICL (ie its insurance company) than on the local authority (ie the local population by way of increased charges or reduced services).

ICL failed to establish that the limitation clause was a fair and reasonable one and judgment for the Council was given in the sum of £1,314,846.

Although here the court adopted an interventionary role, it may be argued that, on the basis of the fourth determining factor, this was at bottom a business-consumer issue.

Section 3(2)(b) directs its attack on clauses which do not exclude or limit liability but are phrased to provide a restricted definition of the contractor's obligation, and which deprive the consumer (or other business party) of his reasonable expectations under the contract. A pre-1977 case which would now come to be examined under s 3(2)(b)(i) is the following:

> In *Anglo-Continental Holidays Ltd v Typaldos Lines (London) Ltd* (1967), T substituted an older, inferior vessel and a much less attractive itinerary ten days before a Mediterranean cruise, for which A-C had booked clients, was due to start. When sued for breach, T sought to rely on a clause providing that 'steamers, sailing dates, rates and itineraries are subject to change without prior notice'. It was held that there was a radical departure from the contract and T could not rely on the clause.

Varieties of exemption clause

Section 13 of the Act extends the definition of exclusion clauses and operates in a similar way to s 3(2)(b) above. We have seen how the Act operates (by a ban or the reasonableness test) against terms and notices seeking to *exclude* or *limit liability* – particularly in s 2 (negligence liability) and s 6 (sale and hire purchase implied liability). Section 13 operates in conjunction with ss 2 and 6, as s 3(2)(b) operates in conjunction with s 3(2)(a), and to the same extent against clauses which are differently worded but have the same or an analogous purpose. For example, whereas s 2 relates to the exclusion or restriction of liability for negligence, s 13 prevents, to the same extent, the making of such liability or its enforcement subject to restrictive or onerous conditions: eg 'notice of loss or damage must be delivered in writing to the carrier within seven days'. Such a clause will, by reference to s 2(2), be subject to the test of reasonableness.

Similarly, in accordance with the provisions of s 6, a clause to the effect that the buyer or hirer of goods acknowledges that before signing the agreement he has fully examined the goods and is satisfied with them in every way is controlled to the extent that it seeks to make evidence that the buyer or hirer did not so satisfy himself inadmissible: s 13(1)(c). Section 13 also refers to clauses which exclude or restrict *duties* as opposed to liabilities: eg a car-park ticket states that no duty of care is owed. Such a clause is caught by s 2(2) in the same way as one which states that liability for loss or damage is excluded, see also *Smith v Eric Bush* (1989) on p 152 and *Phillips Products Ltd v Hyland* (1987) on p 152. Likewise a clause stating that 'the seller does not give any warranty or undertaking that the goods are fit for any purpose' is caught by s 6 in the same way as one stating that 'all conditions and warranties are hereby excluded'. A written arbitration clause is not to be treated as excluding or restricting liability: s 13(2); nor is a liquidated damages clause.

156

Unreasonable indemnity clauses in consumer transactions

Under s 4 of the 1977 Act, a consumer cannot be required, under a term of the contract, to indemnify *another person* (eg the business party or his insurers) in respect of liability incurred by that other person for negligence or breach of contract unless the term is reasonable. Section 4 does not apply to inter-business indemnity clauses (discussed in the previous chapter and in the *British Crane Hire case*) but would apply to the following situation:

> A car ferry ticket contains a clause under which a private car owner 'agrees' to indemnify the ferry operator against third party claims arising out of the negligent manoeuvring of the car by the operator's employee. In other words, business party B, while working under contract for consumer C, becomes vicariously liable to X for loss or damage negligently caused by B's employee. In such a situation, an indemnity clause in the contract invoked by B against C must be reasonable before B can recover. It is unlikely that such a clause will be found to be reasonable against a consumer.

Effect of breach

Section 9 of the Act confirms an injured party's right, in the face of a serious breach (or a breach of condition), to elect to terminate or to affirm the contract. The Act thus denies, together with the House of Lords decisions in *Suisse Atlantique* (1967) and *Photo-Production* (1980), that fundamental breach could operate as a rule of law, *automatically* terminating a contract and so expunging any exclusionary term in it (see the section on 'Fundamental Breach' in Chapter 7 and point (d) in the section on 'Judicial Construction' in this chapter).

Section 9(1) makes it clear that if, by election, the contract is justifiably terminated, an exclusion clause survives such termination and it *may*, if not rendered ineffective by the Act, protect the party in breach if, as discussed, it satisfies first the rigours of judicial construction and, second, the requirement of reasonableness.

As discussed earlier on p 117, whether fundamental breach has any role to play as a rule of construction in future cases is doubted but not settled. Treitel feels that 'one can only say that the courts' reluctance to construe a clause so as to apply to a particular breach will, in general, be directly proportioned to the gravity of that breach'. Very serious breaches may or may not be described as 'fundamental'. Statements in *Photo-Production* indicate that in any event where business parties of equal bargaining power are involved, the courts should not strain to defeat clearly expressed exclusionary terms. In Lord Diplock's words:

> In commercial contracts negotiated between business people capable of looking after their own interests and of deciding how risks inherent in the performance of various kinds of contract can most economically be borne (generally by insurance), it is, in my view, wrong to place a strained construction upon words in an exclusion clause which are clear and fairly susceptible to one meaning only.

Section 9(2) of the Act is to the effect that in the less likely event of a party affirming a contract that he is entitled to terminate following its breach, his affirmation does not eliminate the need for a clause to satisfy judicial construction and the reasonableness test.

Other provisions

Section 8 (amending the Misrepresentation Act 1967) subjects terms *excluding or restricting liability for misrepresentation* to the test of reasonableness as at the time the contract was made. This section is more fully discussed in the next chapter.

In Schedule 1 can be found a variety of *contracts which are not covered* by the Act, eg contracts of insurance, for which it was thought better to rely on a code of practice agreed between the government and the insurance industry. Certain contracts relating to the international carriage of goods and persons are governed by statutes implementing internationally agreed 'controlled bargains' allowing for fixed limitations of liability by carriers (eg the Carriage of Goods by Sea Act 1971; the Athens Convention on the Carriage of Passengers and their Luggage by Sea 1974, partly adopted by the Merchant Shipping Act 1974). It should also be noted that, under powers given by the Fair Trading Act 1973, the Director General of Fair Trading in 1976 made it an offence (punishable by a fine or even imprisonment) for a person who sells goods or lets them out on hire purchase in the course of a business to a consumer to apply to the transaction an exemption clause that would be void under s 6 of the 1977 Act. The Director has also worked in co-operation with trade associations to encourage the preparation of 'codes of practice for guidance in safeguarding and promoting the interests of consumers' (see below) and the adoption of fairer, better balanced standard forms for use in consumer transactions.

The European Community Directive on Unfair Terms in Consumer Contracts (Council Directive 93/13)

This EC consumer protection legislation has been implemented in the UK by the Unfair Terms in Consumer Transactions Regulations 1994, which came into force on 1 July 1995. The Directive provides for a *minimum* level of protection throughout the European Union. The Member States are free to provide additional protection on the basis of their own national law, as is already the case with the Unfair Contract Terms Act 1977. The Act and the Regulations therefore operate side by side and overlap to a considerable extent. Consumers will be able to rely on the 1977 Act in cases where it is advantageous for them to do so.

According to Recital 5 of the Directive, the removal of unfair terms from consumer contracts will facilitate the development of the European Single Market by giving consumers the confidence to contract outside their own States, thus increasing choice and facilitating competition. In essence, the Directive, as transposed by the Regulations, applies a fairness test to terms in contracts between 'consumers' and 'sellers or suppliers' which have not been 'individually negotiated' by the parties. A term which is adjudged unfair is not binding on the consumer.

The concept of unfair terms in the Regulations is wider than in the 1977 Act, not being confined to exclusion and limitation of liability clauses and clauses having a similar effect (eg as in s 13 of the Act). Neither do the Regulations apply to inter-business transactions. The Regulations have met with a considerable amount of criticism and speculation, mainly as regards difficulties of interpretation, failures to transpose the Directive's terms correctly into national law and the complexity created by having the Regulations stand alongside the 1977 Act. There is no case law as yet and we will deal only with the main features of the Regulations.

Regulation 2: Definitions

Regulation 2 defines a 'consumer' as 'a natural person who ... is acting for purposes which are outside his business'. The scope of the term 'business' is similar to that in the 1977 Act. It will also be noted that under the Act it is possible for a business to 'deal as consumer': *R & B Customs Brokers v UDT* (1988), see p 155. There is EC case law to the effect that a business cannot be regarded as a consumer.

The 'seller' is defined as 'a person who sells goods and who ... is acting for purposes relating to his business' and a 'supplier' is similarly defined as one 'who supplies goods and services'. 'Person' here clearly covers both natural and legal persons, particularly companies and public authorities. The expression 'relating to' is wide and may be interpreted as such.

Regulation 3: Terms not individually negotiated

The Regulations apply to terms which have 'not been individually negotiated' – essentially (but not exclusively) 'boiler plate' clauses in standard form, non-negotiable contracts. Regulation 3(3) states that 'a term shall always be regarded as not having been individually negotiated where it has been drafted in advance and the consumer has not been able to influence the substance of the term'. (It is for the seller or supplier to overturn this presumption.)

However, under Regulation 3(2) certain 'core' terms, provided they are in 'plain, intelligible language' are not subject to the test of fairness. Thus:

... no assessment shall be made of the fairness of any term which -

(a) defines the main subject matter of the contract, or

(b) concerns the adequacy of the price or remuneration, as against the goods or services sold or supplied.

It will be for the courts to establish, where necessary, the scope of the 'main subject-matter of the contract'. This phrase will probably be interpreted in a restrictive manner. It is doubted that terms such as those caught by s 3(2)(b) of the 1977 Act, and which seek to define a party's *obligations* in a restrictive manner will be regarded as 'core': see the *Anglo-Continental Holidays* case and clause on p 156.

Regulation 4: Unfair terms

Regulation 4 states that '"unfair term" means any term which contrary to *the requirement of good faith* causes a *significant imbalance* in the parties' rights and obligations under the contract *to the detriment of the consumer'*. (Emphasis added.) The test of fairness is to be made against the background of all the circumstances at the time the contract was entered into. A non-exhaustive list of terms which *may* be regarded as unfair is to be found in Schedule 3 to the Regulations. We will examine it shortly. The question of finding 'a significant imbalance ... to the detriment of the consumer' is left to the courts, proceeding on a case by case basis. The term or terms which lead to such significant imbalance must run 'contrary to the requirement of good faith' to qualify as being unfair and so not bind the consumer.

No general principal of good faith is explicitly recognised in English contract law, whereas it can be found in Europe in, for example, the Italian Civil Code and, particularly, the German Standard Form Contracts Act 1976. As regards the negotiation of terms and the carrying out of contracts, English law relies instead on various narrower solutions to problems of unfairness such as misrepresentation, statutory regulation of exclusion clauses, equitable estoppel and economic duress: see Bingham LJ in the *Interfoto Picture Library* case. Collins explains (or complains) that:

> The meaning of the idea is obscure. It tends to function ... as a negative concept in practice, so that various sorts of conduct are labelled as negotiation in bad faith, without any clarity about the positive duty which is envisaged by the concept. But worse than obscurity, the idea of good faith implies a content to the duty which is far too narrow. In its ordinary legal usage, the standard of good faith requires honesty or conduct which does not deliberately deceive or harm another. It does not include negligent or careless behaviour which has the same effect. But many of the pre-contractual obligations arising under English law, such as the duty not to misrepresent facts, require more than honesty. They require carefulness in the giving of information, so that reasonable care must be taken to ensure its accuracy. For this reason, the terminology of good faith proves unsatisfactory as an indication of the reach of pre-contractual obligations.

It may be that Collins' justifiable fears can be allayed at least as regards the incorporation of a good faith requirement in the Regulations. Schedule 2 contains a list of matters to which *particular* (not exclusive) regard is to be had in determining whether a term meets the requirement:

In making an assessment of good faith, regard shall be had in particular to

(a) the strength of the bargaining positions of the parties;

(b) whether the consumer had an inducement to agree to the term;

(c) whether the goods or services were sold or supplied to the special order of the consumer;

(c) the extent to which the seller or supplier has dealt fairly and equitably with the consumer.

Apart from the 'fairly and equitably' issue, these are factors to be found in Schedule 2 to the 1977 Act which may be taken into account (together with others) in assessing reasonableness. The list does reflect the wording of Recital 16 of the Directive but how far (if at all) the English courts will be willing to import the continental concept of good faith on this basis remains to be seen. This is an issue which may ultimately rest with the Court of Justice in Luxembourg.

The Unfair Contracts Terms Act places the burden of proof that a clause is reasonable on the party seeking its protection. The Regulations (in Regulation 4) do not expressly place the burden of proof as to the fairness of a term on the seller or supplier. Although in the interests of consumer protection it would seem best that this were so, it may be that where the burden rests will depend upon the term in question and the circumstances of the case.

The list in Schedule 3 of terms which may be regarded as unfair is indicative and non-exhaustive. The 17 different types of potentially unfair terms are not automatically unfair nor presumed to be unfair. Some such terms, according to object or effect, reflect the 1977 Act: 1(a) corresponds to s 2(1) of the Act concerning negligence liability and death or personal injury. 1(b) covers the exclusion or limitation of the consumer's rights in the event of total or partial non-performance or inadequate performance by the seller or supplier of any of the contractual obligations (cf ss 3, 6 and 7 of the Act).

There are other terms in the list which purport to give a right to the seller or supplier to alter or terminate the contract without any corresponding right for the consumer, and there are other terms which, similarly might lead the court to find a 'significant imbalance' eg 1(o) regarding 'a term obliging the consumer to fulfil all his obligations where the seller or supplier does not perform his'.

Regulation 5: Not binding on the consumer

A term which is found by the court to be unfair will not be binding on the consumer. However, the remainder of the contract will continue to bind the parties, if it is capable of continuing in existence without the unfair term; ie if the unfair term can be satisfactorily severed from the remainder of the contract.

Regulation 6: Plain, intelligible language

As regards the drafting of terms in general (not merely with reference to the 'core' exclusion from the unfairness test: see above), Regulation 6 states that: 'A seller or supplier shall ensure that any written term of a contract is expressed in plain, intelligible language, and if there is any doubt about the meaning of a written term, the interpretation most favourable to the consumer shall prevail.'

'Plain and intelligible' will presumably be tested objectively from the point of view of the reasonable consumer and the outcome in cases of doubt is to be determined on the basis of the *contra proferentem* rule of construction (see p 148). Obscure drafting may be indicative of an absence of fair and equitable dealing and therefore of good faith.

Regulation 8: General use of unfair terms – Member States' duties

Under Article 7(1) of the Directive, Member States are to provide 'effective means to prevent the continued use of unfair terms'. Article 7(2) states that such 'means' should include 'provisions whereby persons or organisations having a legitimate interest under national law in protecting consumers may take action ... before the courts ... for a decision as to whether contractual terms drawn up for general use are unfair'.

Under Regulation 8(1), the Director General of Fair Trading must consider any complaint made to him that a term drawn up for 'general use' is unfair. He cannot act on his own initiative but there is no doubt that he will receive numerous complaints from the Consumers' Association and others. The Director General has a discretion as to whether to seek an injunction 'against any person appearing to him to be using or recommending the use' of unfair terms. (Use of the word 'recommending' suggests that trade associations are 'persons' for this purpose.) The Director General will presumably decide not to seek an injunction if he is satisfied with voluntary undertakings he receives regarding discontinuance of unfair terms in general use. Any injunction sought may relate not only to the particular term but also 'to any similar term, or a term having like effect (so as to forestall evasion by re-drafting). According to Regulation 8(5), the court may grant an injunction on such terms as it thinks fit.

No criminal sanctions are made available. This is in contrast to the position with respect to the continued use of clauses rendered void under s 6 of the 1977 Act and the Director General's powers to fine or imprison offenders (see p 158). Neither does the Regulation allow (as Article 7(2) presumably intended) for a form of representative action to be granted to a body such as the Consumers' Association. It is doubtful if such an organisation has, as required to Article 7(2), a legitimate interest *under national law* in protecting consumers. It has an interest in protecting consumers but the question of *locus standi* before national courts for the purposes of the Directive would need to be tested. At present it is only the Director General who possesses the necessary right of action in this country.

Conclusion

It *may* be the case that the warnings and complaints voiced regarding the Regulations have been overstated. The terms of the Directive were addressed to *all* the Member States with their various regulatory regimes. The national courts and the Court of Justice are available to resolve difficulties as they arise. The wording of the Regulations could no doubt have been improved in certain instances but, as concerns actions brought by consumers, it is possible to fall in with Brownsword and Howells who, according to their preferred reading of the Regulations, state that:

> Generally speaking ... the underlying pattern of the protective regime ushered in by the Directive will closely resemble that under the reasonableness test of UCTA. In both regimes, certain sorts of contractual terms are singled out as potentially unfair. Under UCTA it is terms that exclude or restrict liability (and their cognates); under the Regulations, it is terms that involve a significant imbalance (as elaborated by the indicative examples given in Schedule 3). Under UCTA, once a term is subject to the reasonableness test, attention largely focuses on whether it is plausible to assume that there has been free agreement to the provision; under the Regulations, once a term is seen as involving a significant imbalance, attention turns to whether the dealer has acted contrary to the requirement of good faith – which, we have suggested, is largely a matter (as under UCTA) of satisfying oneself that there has been free agreement to the term.

Whether the 1977 Act and the Regulations will at some future date be welded together to form a more 'user friendly' system of protection for consumers remains to be seen.

Inequality of bargaining power, unconscionable bargains and economic duress

Since the mid-1970s, at the time the struggle against 'unfair' exclusion clauses was culminating in the passing of the 1977 Act, the courts have been slowly and tentatively introducing another element of 'fairness' into some commercial situations. The basic premise is again reasonableness and recognisable points of reference are (or have been) such concepts as 'inequality of bargaining power', 'unconscionability' (unscrupulous conduct) and 'improper pressure'.

As discussed in Chapter 2, the 19th century rules of contract were developed in the context of *laissez-faire* and a free-market economy – free bargaining and (assumed) equality of bargaining power. Fierce competition and commercial pressure were taken for granted and the courts generally declined to recognise a requirement for a legal standard of reasonableness in transactions. The concepts of freedom and sanctity of contract inevitably led the courts to assume a primary role as upholders and enforcers of contracts. The contractual engines of private enterprise were to be kept in motion, and the judges saw themselves as neither the repairers of bad bargains nor the possessors of an absolving power to be used to relieve parties from the normal incidents of business risk-taking.

However, even Sir George Jessel's famous statement of 1875 regarding freedom and sanctity of contract (see p 7) is, if examined at all closely, seen to be qualified. The courts, then as now, would set aside contracts and grant relief to parties where, as in cases of fraud, agreement was clearly not genuine. Similarly some parties, such as infants and persons of unsound mind, were afforded protection against those who would take advantage of their lack of business acumen. The fundamental idea that agreement or consent to a contract must be free and voluntary also let in a number of narrow rules regarding forms of pressure exerted by one party on the other which the law regarded as improper. Such pressures ranged from actual physical violence to the improper use of a position of trust, such as that existing between solicitor and client.

Thus Waddams, writing in 1976, could state that:

> Despite lip service to the notion of absolute freedom of contract, relief is every day given against agreements that are unfair, inequitable, unreasonable or oppressive. Unconscionability, as a word to describe such control, might not be the lexicographer's first choice, but I think it is the most acceptable general word.

Unfairness, protection against improper pressure, and inequality of bargaining power – of the realities of which the courts now have a clearer appreciation – were linked together by Lord Denning in the case of *Lloyds Bank Ltd v Bundy* (1975), where he said:

> English law gives relief to one who, without independent advice, enters into a contract on terms which are very unfair or transfers property for a consideration which is grossly inadequate, when his bargaining power is grievously impaired by reason of his own needs or desires, or by his own ignorance or infirmity, coupled with undue influences or pressures brought to bear on him by or for the benefit of another.

The development indicated by this statement appeared at the time to promise the emergence of a new judicial doctrine operating to provide relief against harsh bargains where there existed a patent inequality of bargaining power between the parties. It was assumed by many commentators that later case law would allow the courts to define more clearly the scope of the emergent principle (whether expressed in terms of unconscionability or inequality of bargaining power). Clarification, however, was not forthcoming beyond statements that the principle would not operate where the bargain was 'the result of the ordinary interplay of market forces'. (In the United States, in cases in which unconscionability has been raised, the court is required to examine the commercial setting of the contract, and it has been said there that the doctrine is 'one of the prevention of oppression and unfair surprise'.)

In any event, judicial support for a new principle based on 'inequality of bargaining power' or 'unfair use of a dominant bargaining position', and to be used for striking down contracts so tainted, has not been forthcoming. Instead it has been overtaken by a related but narrower concept – that of economic duress. The modern beginnings of this development are perhaps to be found in another judgment of Lord Denning's in *D & C Builders Ltd v Rees* (1966). Here, as we have seen in Chapter 6, R, knowing that D & C were in desperate financial straits, put pressure on them to accept £300 in full settlement of a bill for nearly £500. In Lord Denning's view: 'No person can insist on a settlement procured by intimidation.' We have also seen in Chapter 6 the pivotal role accorded to the presence or absence of wrongful pressure in the renegotiation case of *Williams v Roffey Bros* in 1990. In that case, the contract variation having first been suggested by the main contractor, there was no question of economic duress in the form of threats or other wrongful pressure being brought to bear by Williams. We will examine how the concept has developed between those dates.

Economic duress

Duress involves coercion or compulsion as in the case of a contract entered into under a threat of physical violence. The essence of duress is a threat and economic duress arises where a contract is formed – or more likely, a contract is varied – following a threat not to the party himself or to his property but to his economic well-being – his financial standing.

It is only over the last 20 years or so that the courts have established the concept of economic duress based on the idea of *wrongful* commercial pressure involving coercion. Pressure and even threats are a commonplace in the modern business world but the new concept demonstrates, however indistinctly, that there is now a legal limit which must not be exceeded. How then is economic duress, which is actionable and grounds for setting a contract aside, to be distinguished from normal, if fierce, commercial 'cut and thrust' which is not actionable?

Threats and reluctant acquiescence to demands were examined in *The Atlantic Baron (North Ocean Shipping Co Ltd v Hyundai Construction Co Ltd)* (1979):

> H agreed to build a supertanker for N for $30 million. The dollar was devalued during construction and H, without any legal justification, demanded a 10% increase in the remaining instalments of the price – otherwise they would terminate the contract. Being anxious to fulfil a very lucrative charter for the new vessel, N agreed to this demand but under protest. It was held that the shipbuilders threat amounted to economic duress but as the buyers had not taken the matter further, had paid the extra instalments and taken delivery of the ship, they had by implication affirmed the variation in price. They could therefore not recover the extra payments.

The shipbuilder's problems in this case began as a result of a failure in planning (or negotiating) by agreeing to a fixed price (dollar) contract, thereby accepting the risk of adverse currency fluctuations during the construction period. Their transfer of this risk to the shipping company was seen by the court as illegitimate, coercive opportunism founded on a strong bargaining position, and it was only North Ocean's inaction which allowed Hyundai to retain the extra payments.

The doctrine of economic duress was approved by the Judicial Committee of the Privy Council in *Pao On v Lau Yiu Long* (1980), see p 86. Lord Scarman was of the opinion that 'there is nothing contrary in principle in recognising economic duress as a factor which may render a contract voidable, provided always that the basis of such recognition is that it must always amount to a coercion of will, which vitiates consent'. Drawing the line between mere commercial pressure and actionable duress is a question of fact in each case, but Lord Scarman identified four questions to assist the courts in future cases:

1. Did the person alleged to have been coerced protest at the time?

2. Did that person have an alternative course open to him such as an adequate legal remedy?

3. Was that person independently advised?

4. Did he take steps to avoid the contract [as varied]?

Following criticism from academic circles, Lord Scarman, in *The Universe Sentinel* case (see below), conceded that duress does not negate the existence of consent on the part of the person coerced. The victim's decision is intentional; it is not involuntary – he consciously chooses what he sees as the lesser of two evils. As Lord Scarman said in *The Universe Sentinel*, the victim has 'no practical choice but to submit to the duress'. A factor that may influence the court in coming to a conclusion that the victim had no other practical course but to submit to the duress is the extent of the loss he would have suffered if he had not submitted – the coercive effect of the pressure must be 'sufficiently great' in the circumstances:

> In *The Universe Sentinel (Universe Tankships Inc of Monrovia v International Transport Workers' Federation* (1983), UT's vessel, which flew the Liberian flag, was prevented from leaving Milford Haven harbour by ITWF who were engaged in a campaign of blacking 'flag of convenience' vessels in efforts to combat exploitation of their crews. The union had threatened UT that they would induce tug operators not to assist the ship until various union demands were met. The ship was in fact delayed, at great expense to the owners, for eleven days; tugs not being made available (in breach of the operators' contracts) until the demands were acceded to. Shortly afterwards UT themselves demanded the return of payments made to ITWF as money paid under duress.

> The union did not dispute that their demands amounted to economic duress. (In Lord Diplock's words: 'it is conceded that the financial consequences to the shipowners of the Universe Sentinel continuing to be off hire ... while the blacking continued, were so catastrophic as to amount to a coercion of this shipowner's will'.) However, ITWF argued that their threat had been made in contemplation or furtherance of a trade dispute and that they were therefore protected by the immunity against actions in tort conferred by the Trade Union and Labour Relations Act 1974.

A majority of the House of Lords held that there was no trade dispute (within the meaning of the Act) and the pressure exerted by the union was illegitimate. The agreement regarding the payments in question was voidable and UT could recover the payments made.

Neither this nor subsequent cases have really made clear the meaning of 'illegitimate' in this context. Treitel states that 'the threat must be illegitimate either because what is threatened is a legal wrong ... or because the threat itself is wrongful'. In *The Universe Sentinel* there would appear to have been intimidation by threats to induce, which actually did induce, breaches of contract by third parties upon whom the victim heavily relied. Cartwright has explained the position as follows:

> So we have only limited guidance on the circumstances in which economic pressure will be illegitimate for the purposes of duress. If the thing threatened, or the circumstances in which the pressure is exerted, amount to a crime or a tort, it appears from *The Universe Sentinel* that the coercion will be illegitimate; if the pressure was overwhelming, so as to give the coerced party no choice but to submit, then economic duress is likely to be held to have been established. Moreover, the threat of a breach of contract may be 'illegitimate', and so the question will be whether the threat was sufficiently overwhelming to constitute duress.

Where one party to the contract exerts pressure on the other by threatening breach of the contract, it has been suggested that such a threat is only illegitimate if 'accompanied by bad faith or malice – the deliberate exploitation of difficulties of the other party'. Again, it has been said that the party threatening must be exploiting a 'situational monopoly', which gives the victim no realistic alternative but to comply:

> In *Atlas Express Ltd v Kafco (Importers and Distributors) Ltd* (1989), A discovered that they had badly underpriced a contract to transport K's goods to retailers throughout the country, particularly to Woolworths, with whom K had a valuable, long-term contract. Shortly before Christmas, A demanded an increase in the carriage charges. Unless a new agreement, drawn up by A, was signed by K, no deliveries would be made. Fearing being in breach of their contract with Woolworths and with no alternative transport being available, K signed but only under protest.
>
> When A sued to recover the increased charges, K pleaded economic duress. It was held that K were not obliged to pay the additional charges.

An application of Lord Scarman's four questions in *Pao On v Lau Yiu Long* (see above; in that case economic duress was not established), readily substantiates the decision in *Atlas Express*. The possibility of losing the Woolworths contract presented K with the gravest financial consequences and an action against A for breach of the original contract would not have compensated them for the loss of their lucrative business relationship with Woolworths. For a similar outcome see *B & S Contracts and Design Ltd v Victor Green Publications Ltd* (1984), where the Court of Appeal stated that the plaintiffs had the defendants 'over a barrel'.

References and further reading

Exclusion clauses and unfair terms

Adams and Brownsword, 'The Unfair Contract Terms Act: a decade of discretion' (1988) 104 LQR 94.

Adams and Brownsword, 'Double indemnity – contractual indemnity clauses revisited' (1988) JBL 146.

Beale, 'Unfair Contract Terms Act 1977' (1978) 5 *British Journal of Law and Society* 114.

Brownsword and Howells, 'The implementation of the EC Directive on unfair terms in consumer contracts – some unresolved questions' (1995) JBL 243.

Clarke, 'Notice of contract terms' (1976) CLJ 51.

Collins, 'Good faith in European contract law' (1994) 14 OJLS 229.

Dean, 'Unfair contract terms: the European approach' (1993) 56 MLR 581.

EC Council of Ministers, Council Directive on Unfair Terms in Consumer Contracts: 93/13/EEC, (1993) Official Journal L95/29, 21 April.

Harvey and Parry (1992), *The Law of Consumer Protection and Fair Trading*, 4th edn.

Macdonald, 'Mapping the Unfair Contract Terms Act 1977 and the Directive on Unfair Terms in Consumer Contracts' (1994) JBL 441.

Nichols and Rawlings, 'Note on *Photo-Production v Securicor*' (1980) 43 MLR 567, also Guest (1980) 96 LQR 324.

Peel, 'Making more use of the Unfair Contract Terms Act 1977: *Stewart Gill Ltd v Horatio Myer and Co Ltd*' (1993) 56 MLR 98.

Statutory Instruments Unfair Terms in Consumer Contracts Regulations 1994: SI 1994/3159

Wheeler and Shaw (1994), *Contract Law: Cases, Materials and Commentary*, ch 11 'Exclusion Clauses'.

Yates and Hawkins (1986), *Standard Business Contracts: Exclusions and Related Devices*.

Unconscionability and economic duress

Birks, 'The travails of duress' (1990) LMCLQ 324.

Cartwright (1991), *Unequal Bargaining*, particularly pp 158–169.

Carty and Evans, 'Economic duress' (1983) JBL 218.

Coote, 'Duress by threatened breach of contract' (1980) CLJ 40.

Halson, 'Opportunism, economic duress and contractual modifications' (1991) 107 LQR 649.

Macdonald, 'Duress by threatened breach of contract' (1989) JBL 640.

Phang, 'Whither Economic Duress?' (1990) 53 MLR 115.

Waddams, 'Unconscionability in Contracts' (1976) 39 MLR 369.

Specimen exclusion clauses, related terms and documents

The following pages contain extracts from standard form agreements and other documents relating to both consumer and inter-business transactions. In some instances, in order to show the practical effect (or otherwise) of recent legal developments, particularly the legislation discussed in this chapter (but not the 1995 Regulations), both 'old' and 'new' versions are reproduced.

A Contracts for the sale and supply of goods

'OLD' MOTOR VEHICLE RETAIL ORDER FORM

I/We (The Purchaser) hereby offer to purchase from you (The Seller) a vehicle of the type described in Column 'A' below together with the extras listed in Column 'B' below (which vehicle, extras and accessories shall hereinafter be called 'The Goods') UPON AND SUBJECT TO THE TERMS AND CONDITIONS HEREOF INCLUDING THOSE PRINTED OVERLEAF.

PURCHASER'S DECLARATION

I/We agree that I/We have not been induced to make this offer by any representation as to the quality, fitness for any purpose, performance, or otherwise of the Goods and subject to the Seller's acceptance of this offer I/We agree to be bound by the terms and conditions hereof in all respects including the conditions of sale printed overleaf. In making this offer I/We have not relied on the skill, judgment or opinion of the Seller, his servants or his agents in relation to the Goods. I/We certify that the details and description of the part exchange vehicle.

SELLER'S ACCEPTANCE

I/We accept and confirm this offer subject to its terms and conditions.

.... Date ....

(Signature of Director or other authorised person for and on behalf of the Seller)

CONDITIONS OF SALE

Owner's service statement

1. (i) Service facilities are available to the purchaser of new Goods in accordance with the Owner's Service Statement, copies of which are available at the office of the Seller.

    (ii) Used Goods are not sold subject to any Warranty or other benefit whatsoever unless expressly agreed in writing between the parties.

Capacity of Seller

2. The Seller contracts as a principal and not as an agent of the Manufacturer of the Goods and has no authority to make any representation or otherwise act on behalf of the Manufacturer of the Goods .

'NEW' MOTOR VEHICLE RETAIL ORDER FORM
PURCHASER'S DECLARATION

I/We (The Purchaser) hereby offer to purchase from you (The Seller) a vehicle of the type shown in Column 'A' below together with the extras listed in Column 'B' below (which vehicle, extras and accessories shall be called 'The Goods'). The Purchaser agrees that any contract formed by The Seller's acceptance of this offer shall be governed by the Terms and Conditions of Sale overleaf and that this order form shall represent the agreed contract between The Purchaser and The Seller. The Purchaser certifies that the details and description of the part-exchange vehicle, given in Column 'C' below are true and accurate in all respects.

SELLER'S ACCEPTANCE

I/We accept and confirm this offer subject to its terms and conditions.

.... Date ....

(Signature of Director or other authorized person for and on behalf of the Seller)

CONDITIONS OF SALE

Acceptance

1. Any offer to purchase the Goods and (where applicable) to sell a part exchange vehicle is subject to acceptance and confirmation in writing by the Seller. Once such acceptance has been given the Purchaser shall be legally bound to buy the Goods and the Seller to sell them.

Capacity of Seller

2. The Seller contracts as principal and not as agent of the manufacturer of the Goods and has no authority to make any representation or otherwise act on behalf of the manufacturer of the Goods.

Nothing in these conditions is intended to remove, alter or restrict any rights or obligations of either party arising under the Sale of Goods Act 1893 or the Supply of Goods (Implied Terms) Act 1973.

USED VEHICLE WARRANTY (GUARANTEE) (issued by the Motor Agents Association to members only)

CONSUMER TRANSACTIONS

Nothing herein contained is intended to affect, nor will it affect, a consumer's statutory rights under the Sale of Goods Act 1979 or the Unfair Contract Terms Act 1977 or any amendment thereof.

Specific Warranty

(1) In this warranty the expression 'the warranty period' shall mean a period of .... months from the date of sale as shown in the Schedule or until the vehicle shall have covered .... miles in addition to the recorded mileage shown in the Schedule whichever shall first happen.

(2) We undertake to examine any alleged defect which appears during the warranty period provided that the alleged defect is brought to our attention by notice in writing as soon as practicable after the defect becomes known to the purchaser.

(3) Having examined the vehicle and established to our satisfaction that:

   (i) the defect (not being a defect subject to which the vehicle was expressly sold, or which should have been revealed by an examination) was present when the vehicle was sold we will rectify any such defect free of charge; or

   (ii) the defect was not present when the vehicle was sold but has materialised in a manner inconsistent with the age, mileage and general condition and price of the vehicle and provided that the owner can show to our satisfaction that the vehicle has been serviced since the date of sale in accordance with the manufacturer's schedule (we reserve the right to request proof of such service), we undertake to contribute to the total retail cost of rectification as follows:

(4) Our liability under this warranty is limited as set out above, and save insofar as the Sale of Goods Act 1893 (as amended) may be applicable, we will not be responsible for any loss, damage or liability actual or contingent howsoever caused arising out of the operation of this warranty.

(5) This warranty will not come into operation unless the Schedule to this document is completed and signed by the Purchaser. No work will be carried out under the terms of this warranty until this document completed and signed as aforesaid is presented in advance to our service reception.

(6) The rights under this document or the warranty above referred to are not transferable without our written consent.

(7) This warranty shall be of no effect if the vehicle has at any time been used after the date of sale for the purposes of racing, rallying or for any competitive event, for hiring or for driving tuition ...

MANUFACTURER'S GUARANTEE (portable electrical appliances)

Continental

The Ultimate range of iron

Morphy Richards have specifically designed this range of irons to cope with all kinds of ironing situations, giving you the chance to own one of our 'Continentals' which is just right for you.

MORPHY RICHARDS

G U A R A N T E E

From the moment your product is purchased, Morphy Richards guarantee it for TWELVE MONTHS. During this time if your product has a defect, we will at our option repair or replace it free of charge.

This guarantee, which does not limit your rights, excludes accidents or misuse of the appliance and only applies in the United Kingdom.

After the first year your product will be repaired at a fair price.

In the packaging you will find a Service Information Leaflet listing our conveniently situated service agents.

A better name –

A better product.

RENTAL AGREEMENT (television equipment)

'Old' (1972)

The Owners shall be under no liability for any injury or damage to any person or property whomsoever or whatsoever whether direct or consequential arising out of the use of the equipment howsoever such injury or damage was caused and the Renter agrees to indemnify the Owners in respect of any liability for damage and/or costs incurred to any person whatsoever arising out of the possession and/or use of the equipment howsoever such liability may have arisen.

'New'

IMPORTANT – YOU SHOULD READ THIS CAREFULLY.

YOUR RIGHTS

The Consumer Credit Act 1974 covers this agreement and lays down certain requirements for your protection which must be satisfied when the agreement is made. If they are not, the owner cannot enforce the agreement against you without a court order.

If you would like to know more about the protection and remedies under the Act, you should contact either your local Trading Standards Department or your nearest Citizens' Advice Bureau.

(4)   TERM OF HIRE

We shall supply and You shall rent the Equipment for the minimum period of hire shown on the Form and after that upon the terms and conditions set out in this Agreement until terminated in accordance with clause 6(j) of these Conditions.

(5)   OUR RESPONSIBILITIES/RIGHTS/LIABILITIES

(d) We shall not be responsible for any direct or indirect or consequential injury, damage or loss to any person or any property arising out of the installation, possession, use or condition of the Equipment. We shall only be responsible for personal injury caused directly by Our negligence.

(e) We shall in no circumstances be responsible for loss of business or profit arising from a breakdown of the Equipment.

(f) We shall not be responsible for faults or damage caused by British Telecom equipment to any property or the Equipment where Prestel viewdata facilities are included in the Equipment.

(g) We shall not be responsible for any breach of copyright resulting from the use of Equipment rented under this Agreement.

(6)   YOUR RESPONSIBILITIES/RIGHTS/LIABILITIES

(g) You shall indemnify Us against all liability arising out of the possession or use of the Equipment except liability for personal injury caused directly by Our negligence.

(h) From the date of delivery of the Equipment to You the Equipment shall be at Your risk and You shall insure the same:

(i) with the Insurers in respect of Equipment Failure on the terms of Group Policy ... a summary of which is set out below in the ... Insurance Certificate.

(1)   PROPERTY INSURED

The Insurers insure the Equipment which you have hired under the Agreement, while you maintain it at the Premises.

(2)   BENEFIT

The Insurers will indemnify you against the cost of Failure. The cover is limited to the lowest of the current market value of the Equipment, or its replacement cost, or £2,000. The Insurance can either meet the cost of repairs which have already been carried out or they can send in repairers at their own expense. Repairs can only be carried out by Authorised Repairers. Such payments will be made to the Rental Company for the benefit of the insured customer.

(3)   EXCLUSIONS

Failure does not include failures caused by such things as defects in the electrical supply, misuse, neglect, wilful act, theft or accidental damage, or any other extraneous cause, or interference by any third party or use of the Equipment anywhere except at the Premises or for any unauthorised use. The benefit is limited to that described at 2. above, and will not cover any other loss (such as consequential loss, damage to other property, or death or bodily injury).

(5)   HOW TO CLAIM

Claims should be made by telephone to the Service centre shown in your Welcome Pack, or to your local Rental Company shop within a reasonable time of the Failure. Failure to make a claim within a reasonable time will invalidate any claim.

POST-1977 NON-CONSUMER SALE (engineering products)

Orders placed with the Company will only be accepted on the following terms and conditions. No variation or modification of or substitution for any such terms and conditions shall be binding unless expressly agreed by the Company in writing. No buyer's conditions of order or purchase and no other conditions, particulars, standards, specifications, statements or other matters whether printed, written or verbal shall form part of or be deemed to be incorporated into any contract with the Company unless specifically referred to in the Company's acceptance ...

The Company's liability under any order is limited to replacement or remedial work under these conditions of sale, to the entire exclusion of any other remedy which, but for this condition, the buyer might have. Any representation, condition, warranty or other undertaking in relation to the contract whether express or implied by statute, common law, custom or otherwise and whether made or given before or after the date of the order or acceptance thereof, is hereby excluded for all purposes. Save as provided in these conditions, the Company shall be under no liability of any sort (howsoever arising) and shall not in any circumstances be liable for any damage, injury, direct consequential or other loss or loss of profits or costs, charges and expenses, howsoever arising.

B   CONTRACTS FOR THE PROVISION OF SERVICES

LAUNDERERS AND CLEANERS: Extract from the Textile Services Association Code of Practice for Domestic Laundry and Cleaning Services

STATEMENT PREAMBLE

As a Member of the Textile Services Association Ltd., we undertake not to restrict our liability under the General Law.

(3)   The Preamble sets the tone for the whole Code of Practice. By virtue of these words, TSA Members undertake not to seek to contract out of liability imposed on them by the law of the land (see paras 15 and 16). The Code of Practice Statement then sets out the series of undertakings with which TSA Members will, so far as is reasonably practicable, comply.

Legal Liability

(4)   In law, a launderer or cleaner who loses or destroys a customer's article through his or his employees' negligence is liable for the market value of the article at the time it is lost or destroyed ie allowing for depreciation but reflecting to some extent the cost of replacement at current costs. If the article is only damaged and is capable of adequate repair the launderer/cleaner is only liable for the cost of that repair save that if this

174

exceeds the market value of the article at that time, the launderer/cleaner is only liable for the latter (see para 14).

(5) The liability of the launderer/cleaner is a liability for negligence, that is to say for a breach of a duty or obligation, whether imposed by law or by an express or implied term in a contract, to take reasonable care or exercise reasonable skill in relation to the articles left with him. In considering negligence it must be remembered that the launderer/cleaner holds himself out as possessing specialised knowledge and might be held to be negligent if he uses an unsuitable process or fails to realise that a particular article would be damaged, at any rate where such a risk would be generally recognised by others in the industry.

(6) It must be emphasised that because the launder's/cleaner's liability is based on negligence, any damage which cannot be attributed to negligence cannot be the responsibility of the launderer/cleaner. Among the possible causes of damage for which neither the law nor commonsense expects the launderer/cleaner to be responsible (unless, and to the extent that, the launderer/cleaner adds to the damage by his negligence) are:

faulty manufacture (eg fugitive colours. relaxation of stretch imparted during manufacture, inadequate seaming, incorrect care labelling, etc), (see para 12). prior misuse by the customer (eg drying of razor blades on towels, excessive use of bleach, spillage of acids or other corrosive liquids on fabrics etc), normal but unrecognised wear (eg weakening of curtains by exposure to light).

STATEMENT THREE

Pay fair compensation for loss or damage due to negligence on our part.

(14) TSA members undertake to pay fair compensation in the above circumstances, and what is fair is a matter which has to be determined according to the facts of each case. The launderer/cleaner is not obliged at law to replace a lost or damaged article with a new article, nor to reimburse the customer the complete cost of buying a new article. Both parties should take into account the depreciation, wear and tear which had occurred to the article prior to the loss or damage as this may affect the article's value in respect of which compensation is assessed.

Exclusion clauses

(15) Any clause which is intended to exclude, limit or restrict the launderer's/cleaner's legal liability is contrary to the Code and may in certain cases be unenforceable at law. Members of the Association will therefore not attempt to restrict either their liability for certain types of damage caused by their negligence, or the amount of fair compensation which they will pay. They may however wish to ask the customer at the time the article is accepted, for an indication of the value which the customer places on the article; this may be done when the article is clearly of exceptional value or of unusual manufacture (see para 20).

Owner's risk clauses

(16) These clauses are only inconsistent with the Code if their effect may be to exclude, limit or restrict legal liability; in such cases they may also be unenforceable at law. There

may be certain articles however, such as curtains, where the Member can foresee that some damage may be an inevitable consequence of the application of the laundering, dry cleaning or dyeing process even though that process will be expertly applied. In such cases therefore the Member may ask the customer to acknowledge (in writing) his acceptance of the risk of such damage occurring. Acceptance of this risk by the customer will not relieve the Member from liability if he is negligent and so this procedure is in complete accordance with the Code.

Fire and burglary

(17) Naturally if a customers's article is lost or damaged by fire or burglary while in a TSA Member's custody, the customer will look to the Member for compensation. In law the customer is entitled to compensation only where the fire or burglary in question was caused by the launderer's/cleaner's negligence. To eliminate this potential source of dissatisfaction and hardship and in the interest of good customer relations, TSA Members undertake to pay fair compensation for loss or damage caused by fire or burglary – in cases where the article in question is not covered by the customer's own insurance policy – even though no negligence can be attributed the Member.

PACKAGE HOLIDAY BOOKING CONDITIONS (Extracts)

(7) AMENDMENTS BY THE COMPANY

We try never to change our clients' holidays but we must reserve the right to change your holiday arrangements if necessary. A change may be 'significant' or 'minor'. A 'significant' change will be a change of your place of departure to a less convenient airport or seaport, a change of departure time by more than 12 hours or a change of accommodation to a lower grade than that booked. Any other change will be 'minor'.

We reserve the right to make minor changes at any time, although we will, if practicable, notify you of a minor change before you leave. We are not obliged to notify you in advance of a minor change, nor are we obliged to pay you compensation for the change.

If there is a significant change, we will tell you about it as soon as practicable and, in this case, you will have three options. The first option is to accept our suggested alteration. The second option is to change your booking to another holiday operated by us and available. If the replacement you choose is more expensive, you will have to pay the difference, but if it is cheaper we will give you the appropriate refund. The third option is to cancel your holiday altogether and to receive a full refund.

Occasionally, significant changes after departure are unavoidable. If this happens, or if we become unable to provide a significant proportion of the services you have booked, we will either arrange for you to return to the UK (if you wish) and give you a refund in proportion to the cost of the services you did not receive, or we will make alternative holiday arrangements for you.

If we make a significant change to your holiday arrangements for any reason other than 'force majeure' or low bookings (see below), we will also pay you compensation on the following scale:

Time Before Departure When You Are Told of a Significant Change	Compensation per person
More than 60 days	nil
Between 45-60 days	£20
Between 30-45 days	£35
Between 15-30 days	£50
Less than 15 days	£65

'Force Majeure' means unusual and unforeseeable circumstances beyond our control, the consequences of which neither we nor our suppliers could avoid, for example, war, threat of war, riots, civil strife, terrorist activity, industrial disputes, natural or nuclear disaster, fire, adverse weather conditions, level of water in rivers or similar events beyond our control.

'Low Bookings' refers to the fact that we may require a minimum number of bookings before being able to operate the holidays described in this brochure at the prices shown. No changes will be made because of low bookings less than 21 days before you depart.

(10) COMPANY LIABILITY

We accept responsibility if any of the services we are contractually obliged to provide proves deficient or if you suffer personal injury or death as a result of any of the services or facilities we arrange for you UNLESS the deficiency, personal injury or death is not attributable to our fault, nor to the fault of our suppliers, but is attributable to your fault, to the actions of someone unconnected with your holiday or to an unusual and unforeseeable circumstance beyond our control which neither we nor our suppliers could have anticipated or avoided even exercising all due care.

Except in cases of personal injury or death, the amount of compensation we will pay you will be limited to a reasonable amount having regard to the cost of the holiday. Our assessment of the reasonable compensation to which you are entitled will depend upon the circumstances of your particular case.

In cases of death or personal injury arising in the course of international air or sea travel or in connection with hotel accommodation, the amount of compensation you will receive is limited by certain international Conventions, namely the Warsaw Convention, the Athens Convention and the Paris Convention. Copies of these Conventions should be available at your local reference library or can be borrowed from us on written request accompanied by an A4 £1 stamped envelope.

(15) COMPLAINTS

Any deficiency in your accommodation or its contents should be reported immediately to the owner or manager, or his representative, to allow an opportunity for immediate remedial action to be taken. Failure to do this may reduce or completely extinguish your legal right to claim compensation.

Further, if the deficiency threatens seriously to affect your enjoyment of your holiday, you must report it to us by phone or fax within 48 hours. Again, failure to do so may reduce or even extinguish your legal rights.

The relevant telephone and fax numbers are set out in our ticket wallet. In the unlikely event that, having taken the action outlined above, any problem cannot be resolved to your satisfaction while you are on holiday and you wish to take the matter up with us after your return you should write to us within 28 days of the end of your holiday. If, subsequently, your complaint cannot be resolved amicably, the Independent Dispute Settlement Service of the Association of Independent Tour Operators may be called upon by either side to bring the matter to a speedy and acceptable conclusion. Claims which exceed £1,500 per person or £7,500 per booking form, or claims which apply principally or exclusively in respect of (or as a consequence of) illness or physical injury, are not admissible for settlement under the service.

Note: In relation to holiday contracts, see the Package Travel, Package Holidays and Package Tours Regulations 1992, SI 1992/3288. The Association of British Travel Agents (ABTA) operates two Codes of Conduct, one for Travel Agents and the other for Tour Operators.

Questions

(1) (a) Under the Unfair Contract Terms Act 1977, what is meant by (i) 'business', (ii) 'business liability', (iii) 'dealing as consumer', (iv) 'negligence'?

(b) Does Schedule 2 to the 1977 Act in any way affect the rule in *L'Estrange v Graucob Ltd*?

(c) In what way, if at all, would the 1977 Act apply to the bank's disclaimer in *Hedley Byrne & Co Ltd v Heller & Partners Ltd* (1964)?

(d) What is meant by an 'unfair term' in the Unfair Terms in Consumer Transactions Regulations 1994?

(2) On what basis did the House of Lords in *Photo-Production Ltd v Securicor Transport Ltd* (1980) overrule the Court of Appeal decision in *Harbutt's 'Plasticine' Ltd v Wayne Tank and Pump Co Ltd* (1970)? See case notes by Sealy (1980), Guest (1980) and Nicol and Rawlings (1980).

(3) Comment on the validity or otherwise of the following clauses or notices:

(i) 'Any faults or short weight or any other complaint about these goods will be made good but only if the seller is notified within seven days of the articles being received by the buyer.'

(ii) 'This written agreement contains all the terms thereof and no other document or statement is to be referred to in construing its contents.'

(iii) 'The manager may – at his absolute discretion – refuse admission to any person.'

(iv) 'In accepting this guarantee given by us (the manufacturer), the buyer agrees that he will make no claim whatsoever relating to a fault in the goods against the retailer.'

(v) 'Passengers accepting a free ride in this car do so entirely at their own risk.'

(vi) 'Since our advice is given without charge we will accept no liability for any loss howsoever caused' (Notice in Citizens Advice Bureau).

(vii) 'No money refunded.'

(viii) 'No condition or warranty that the vehicle is roadworthy or as to its age, condition or fitness for any purpose is given by the owner or implied herein.'

(ix) 'All luggage is carried at owner's risk. We recommend insurance if you intend to carry valuables.' (Long distance coach timetable and leaflet.)

(x) 'Provided always that our total liability for loss, damage or injury shall not exceed the total value of the contract.'

(4) Douglas goes to Brightpool for a week's holiday. While there he decides to visit the swimming baths. A notice at the turnstile says: 'The Management accept no responsibility for loss or damage to valuables unless left at the office.' Douglas ignores this notice. In his cubicle there is another notice which reads: 'No liability for personal injury.' Douglas ignores this notice and places his watch on the ledge above it. As he runs to dive into the water, he trips over a brush negligently left on the floor by the attendant and breaks his arm. He later finds that his watch was stolen while he was at the hospital having his arm set. Discuss whether Douglas has any claim against the management in respect of his watch or his injury.

(5) (a) Mrs X, on leaving her fur coat valued £10,000 with Y Ltd for cleaning, signed an order form which stated that: 'All garments are expressly accepted at the owner's risk.' Three weeks later, having not heard from Y Ltd, Mrs X telephoned and discovered that the coat had been irreparably damaged by a fault in the cleaning process. Advise Mrs X.

(b) Explain the position if Y Ltd had told Mrs X that they did not do cleaning themselves and Mrs X had authorised them to send the fur to Z Ltd, a reputable firm of specialist cleaners. The fur had been stolen by an employee of Z Ltd. There is no exclusion clause in the contract between Mrs X and Y Ltd but there is a wide and well-worded clause in the contract between Y Ltd and Z Ltd. Advise Mrs X.

(6) 'The doctrine of privity was never a satisfactory instrument for controlling undesirable exemption clauses, and should no longer be used for this purpose now that such clauses are directly controlled under the Unfair Contract Terms Act 1977.' (Treitel, *Law of Contract*) Discuss this statement in relation to *Adler v Dickson* (1955). What would be the position today if it was Mrs A's luggage that was damaged? (See s 28 of the 1977 Act.)

(7) (a) In *Lloyds Bank Ltd v Bundy* (1975), a farmer guaranteed the bank account of his son's company and charged his farm to the bank as security. The Court of Appeal set aside the guarantee and dismissed the bank's claim against the farm. Why?

(8) (a) Discuss the basis on which the court (JCPC) rejected a claim of economic duress in *Pao On v Lau Yiu Long* (1980).

(b) Examine the question of economic duress in the context of *The Atlantic Baron* (1979) and *Williams v Roffey Brothers* (1990).

(9) 'In sum, for both market-individualists and consumer-welfarists, the doctrine of economic duress rightly shields contractors against unacceptable pressure for renegotiation, but ... it is unclear how adherents of either approach will apply this central idea in individual cases': Adams and Brownsword, *Understanding Contract*. Discuss.

10   Misrepresentation and mistake

Misrepresentation

As a general rule, a party must not make any false and misleading statements to the other party thereby inducing him to enter into the contract. Thus, although there is no general duty to *disclose* material facts, 'a single word or ... a nod or a wink, or a shake of the head or a smile' may amount to a misrepresentation of fact allowing for the rescission (avoidance or setting aside) of the contract and the payment of damages. Where such is the case, consent is said to be vitiated and agreement not to be 'genuine' – in many cases the value of the contract's subject-matter being significantly less than what it has been represented to be.

Atiyah, in *The Rise and Fall of Freedom of Contract*, has sketched out the background to developments in this area:

> The older notion that a man could say what he liked to a prospective contracting party, so long only as he refrained from positively dishonest assertions of fact, seems to have come up against a new morality in the late nineteenth century. The courts began to insist on the duty of a party not to mislead the other party by extravagant or unjustified assertions ... in their determination to stamp out the laxer business morality.

Nevertheless, the law of misrepresentation became 'bogged down in a mass of technicalities' and it was not until 1967 that an attempt was made at reform with the Misrepresentation Act. Although the law is still somewhat complicated, the general effect of developments in the last 20 years has been to improve the position of the injured representee, whose remedies are now more in line with those of the party who suffers loss through breach. As with promissory estoppel, the essence of misrepresentation is reliance – reliance on truth and reasonable conduct in pre-contractual dealings.

The law relating to misrepresentation is now a mixture of common law, equity and statute law, and analysis also quickly reveals an intertwining of tort and contract law principles. Three types of misrepresentation are recognised, classified according to the state of mind of the representor: (i) fraudulent misrepresentation (a dishonest assertion); (ii) negligent misrepresentation (not dishonest but careless); and (iii) wholly innocent misrepresentation (not dishonest, not careless but nevertheless incorrect). All are capable of causing loss and are actionable; the remedies of the representee (so one might expect, but see below) generally being widest in the case of fraud and successively narrowing in availability for negligent and innocent misrepresentations. (When looking at the cases it should be borne in mind that prior to 1967 only two types of misrepresentation were recognised: fraudulent and non-fraudulent, ie innocent.)

There is a further important dimension to the study of misrepresentation. On the basis that a representation is a pre-contractual inducement, it is clear that such a statement does not amount to a term of the contract. Although it affects agreement, it is not an integral part of the contract and, if untrue, its untruth does not amount to a breach of the contract. It is usually in this sense that what used to be called a 'mere' representation is actionable (or can be set up as a defence to an action on the contract) with remedies available which are akin to but not the same as the remedies for breach.

A difficulty to be found in some situations concerns the question of whether a statement (usually oral) made by one party to the other during negotiations is a representation or a term. Conflicting case law on this matter can be found, but now that the remedies are similar the problem is lessened. (This is a problem we have referred to before, in Chapter 7, regarding the 'scope' or 'map' of the contract and the parties' obligations.) Further, there is case law which shows that a representation may be 'promoted' to a contractual status by *the court*, so making breach remedies available.

Yet again, the effect of a fraudulent misrepresentation may be such as to lead to a claim by the representee that he was not merely misled about the subject matter of the agreement, but that he was induced into acting under a fundamental mistake which negatived agreement altogether. As we shall see, a contract vitiated in this way is not merely voidable at the representee's option but is void with quite different results. Thus a misrepresentation may be actionable in itself, it may become a term, or it may lead to a claim in mistake.

Statements of fact, opinions, promises and terms

We have established that a misrepresentation is an untrue statement of existing fact made by one party to the other which, while not forming part of the contract, is nevertheless one of the reasons that induces the representee to enter into it. In this context, such statements of fact, which are actionable, are normally distinguishable from extravagant and unverifiable sales talk, statements of opinion, statements of intention and statements of law – which are not actionable. However, in some situations the distinction is a rather subtle one. For example, in *Bissett v Wilkinson* (1927) the vendor of land, which to the knowledge of both parties had not previously been used for sheep farming, stated that it would support 2,000 sheep. It was held that this was merely a statement of opinion which, when it proved to be unfounded, was not actionable. However, in a later case an expert's inaccurate estimate of the future annual petrol sales of a filling station, resting upon negligently prepared data, was, having been heavily relied upon by the defendant, found to be a considered judgment that was actionable: *Esso Petroleum Co Ltd v Mardon* (1976), see p 189 below.

It has been argued that the distinctions between facts, opinions, intentions and other statements as to the future that can be found in the cases over many years have now reached a state of over-subtle complexity. For example, it is a misrepresentation of fact for a person to say that he holds an opinion which he does not hold, or 'There must be a misstatement of an existing fact; but the state of a man's mind [which does not accord with his stated intentions] is as much a fact as the state of his digestion.' (Both are difficult to prove.) An alternative test would be to ask whether, in the circumstances, it was reasonable for the representee to rely on the statement rather than on his own judgment. For example: 'Reliance on statements of fact is usually more easily justifiable than reliance on the other party's opinion, but in particular circumstances even this may be justifiable.'

It might appear that a pre-contractual statement as to future conduct made by one party to the other which is later not borne out by the facts is neither a misrepresentation nor a contractual promise. However, in *Quickmaid Rental Services Ltd v Reece* (1970) the company's representative, shortly before concluding a written rental agreement for a coffee machine with R, told him that they would not be installing another machine on the same road. Later another machine was installed and the representative's statement was held to be a promise in a contract partly written and partly oral. See also *Evans & Son (Portsmouth) Ltd v Merzario Ltd* (1976) on p 101.

More generally, the test of whether a representation has become a term of the contract (a promise) depends on an *objective* (ie judicial) test of intention: Can the representor be held to have intended to be bound to the truth of the statement so as to render himself liable to an action for breach? The courts have laid down certain guidelines available for use when seeking an answer to this question, but the essential criterion would seem to be that of fairness in the particular circumstances presented to the court.

The cases must be seen in their historical and legal context. The claim that a pre-contractual statement is a term has been made for a variety of reasons: to secure a remedy where none otherwise existed at the time, to secure a more advantageous remedy, or to provide a defence to the plaintiff's claim. The guidelines include the following (see the judgment of Denning LJ in the *Oscar Chess* case, below):

(a) the more important a statement made during negotiations, the more likely it is a term: see *Couchman v Hill* (1947) in which an oral statement was held to be a warranty which over-rode written exclusionary terms.

(b) the longer the time between the making of the statement and the agreement being concluded, the more likely that it is not a term: the defendant's statement in *Couchman* was elicited from him by the plaintiff the same day, shortly before the agreement was made. Point (d) below also applied in this case.

(c)   if an oral statement is not recorded in a written contract, it is evidence against a warranty being intended.

(d)   the statement is more likely to be a term if made by a person possessing special skill or knowledge regarding its truth.

In *Chess (Oscar) Ltd v Williams* (1957) a statement made to a motor dealer by a private seller of a car, based on an earlier alteration of the logbook by an unknown person, that the vehicle was 'a 1948 model' (worth £290), whereas in fact it had been registered in 1939 (and worth only £175), was held to be an innocent misrepresentation for which, at that time, no damages could be awarded. Neither, through lapse of time (see below), could the contract be rescinded, ie set aside with the parties restored to their original positions. However, in *Bentley v Harold Smith (Motors) Ltd* (1965), where the positions were reversed, a pre-contractual statement made by a dealer to a private purchaser, based on a reading of the mileometer, that a car had done 20,000 when it had in fact done almost 100,000, was held to be a warranty – for the breach of which damages were awarded.

It is clear that several or all these guidelines may apply in a particular case and they may pull in different directions. The court must weigh their individual significance, bearing in mind such factors as consumer protection, and should ultimately achieve a fair result.

Silence and partial non-disclosure

There is no general duty for parties to disclose material facts to each other except, most notably, if the contract is one 'of the utmost good faith', in which knowledge of the material facts generally lies with one party alone. Thus it is contrary to good faith for a party seeking insurance to withhold material facts from the insurer; such facts are generally known only to the assured and if he does not disclose them, the contract is voidable, ie may be set aside at the insurer's option.

Although silence does not otherwise amount to misrepresentation, a partial non-disclosure may do so. For example, a statement may omit facts which render what is actually said false or misleading: see *Curtis v Chemical Cleaning and Dyeing Co Ltd* in the last chapter. Also a statement may be made which is true at the time, but which subsequently ceases to be true to the representor's knowledge before the contract is entered into. Here a failure to inform the representee of the change in circumstances will amount to misrepresentation. In *With v O'Flanagan* (1936) a medical practice was stated to be worth £2,000 during negotiations for its sale. By the time the contract was entered into some months later, the practice had become worthless owing to the illness of the vendor. The contract was set aside as the changed circumstances had not been revealed.

Inducement and reliance

The representee must, in order to rescind or claim damages, be able to show that he relied on the statement and that it induced the contract; although it need not be the sole inducement: see *Edgington v Fitzmaurice* (1885). Thus once it is established that the misrepresentation was calculated to induce entry into the contract, and that the representee has in fact entered, it is a fair inference that he was influenced by it – and it is no defence that the representee might have discovered its untruth by the exercise of reasonable care. In *Redgrave v Hurd* (1881), H was induced to buy a share in a solicitor's practice by an innocent (non-fraudulent) misrepresentation as to its annual value. He was allowed to rescind the contract and recover a deposit paid, even though he had been given the opportunity of examining the accounts and so discovering the true position. R's action for specific performance of the contract failed.

It has been argued that this rule is most likely now only to prevail in cases of fraud and *Alliance & Leicester Building Society v Edgestop Ltd* (1994) confirms that contributory negligence on the representee's part is irrelevant in cases of fraud. What is the position in the case of negligent misrepresentation? In *Gran Gelato Ltd v Richcliffe (Group) Ltd* (1992), involving a claim for damages under s 2(1) of the 1967 Act (see below), no reduction in damages for contributory negligence was made. Nicholls VC stated that 'In principle, carelessness in not making other inquiries provides no answer to a claim when the plaintiff has done that which the representor intended he should do', ie act in reliance on the misrepresentation.

Fraudulent misrepresentation

Lord Herschell in *Derry v Peek* (1889) stated that 'fraud is proved when it is shown that a false representation has been made (1) knowingly, or (2) without belief in its truth, or (3) recklessly, careless whether it be true or false': see also *Reese River Silver Mining Co Ltd v Smith* (1869). A person, however, who honestly believes his statement to be true, cannot be liable for fraud, however careless he might be. The plaintiff who alleges fraud must prove the absence of an honest belief, and although this burden is the same as in other civil proceedings, ie proof on the balance of probabilities, it is not easily discharged in practice.

Damages are recoverable for loss resulting from reliance on a fraudulent misrepresentation in a common law action for the tort of deceit: *Derry v Peek*. The representee *may* also rescind the contract, a right which was unaffected by the Misrepresentation Act 1967. It is as convenient to say something more of rescission as a *general* remedy for misrepresentation at this point as elsewhere.

Rescission involves setting the contract aside so as to restore *both* the parties, where this is at least substantially possible, to their positions before the contract was made. A party who wishes to rescind should, if possible, do so by taking active steps against the representor himself, eg by seeking a cancellation of the contract, but legal proceedings will be necessary if, say, money paid by the representee is claimed and the representor refuses to pay it back. Alternatively, as seen in *Redgrave v Hurd*, the representee may rely on the misrepresentation as a defence and as the basis for a counterclaim in an action brought on the contract by the representor.

A good illustration of fraudulent misrepresentation is *Doyle v Olby (Ironmongers) Ltd* (1969):

> D bought the defendant's business for £4,500 plus stock at valuation, having been shown accounts for the preceding three years and told that all the trade was over the counter. He soon found that the turnover had been misrepresented and that half the trade had been obtained by a traveller paid £555 pa. D began an action for damages for fraud whilst attempting to keep the business going. After three years he was forced to sell it, incurring a considerable loss. The Court of Appeal held that the proper measure of damages for the tort of deceit, as distinct from damages for breach of contract, was 'all the actual damages flowing directly from the fraudulent inducement ... it does not lie in the mouth of the fraudulent person to say that [the damage] could not reasonably have been foreseen.' D was awarded £5,500 for his overall, out of pocket loss up to selling the business. (This final point is examined more closely shortly.)

It will be noticed that Doyle chose not to rescind the contract. By attempting to keep the business going, he impliedly affirmed the contract (ie it remained valid and binding) and he, as seen, later sold the business to a third party.

Nevertheless, as stated above, rescission, an equitable remedy, is available in *all* cases of misrepresentation – subject to certain limitations. If the representee chooses to rescind the contract, and the court so orders, it is avoided *ab initio* and treated as if it never existed. However, the limitations, or bars, to rescission are as follows:

(1) Affirmation of the contract (as in *Doyle*), whereby the representee continues with the contract in the knowledge of the other party's misrepresentation: see also *Long v Lloyd* (1958), which is not a fraud case.

(2) The impossibility of restitution – putting the parties back into their original positions before the contract was made means that the representee is required to restore any benefits obtained to the other party. If he cannot do this, the impossibility of restitution will probably bar the right to rescind. The representee may have made changes to the subject-matter causing its value to decline or it may be a wasting asset, eg a mine. However, the equitable influence comes into play in that a representee who can make substantial, though not precise, restitution can rescind if he returns the subject- matter, albeit altered, and makes allowance for its deterioration.

(3) The intervention of third party rights – the right to rescind will be lost through the intervention of third party rights. Thus, for example, a person who has been induced by fraud to sell goods on credit cannot rescind the contract after the goods have been bought by an innocent third party: see *Lewis v Averay* (1972) below.

(4) Lapse of time – if, in cases of *non*-fraudulent misrepresentation, the representee delays in taking action to rescind, his right can be barred: *Leaf v International Galleries* (1950) in which a five-year delay in a case of innocent misrepresentation was held to bar the plaintiff's claim. (A reasonably diligent buyer would have discovered the truth earlier.) In fraud cases, lapse of time is merely evidence of affirmation, time running from the discovery of the truth.

Finally, as regards the measure of damages in fraud cases, it will be recalled from *Doyle* above, that the action is tortious (for deceit) and the object is to put the misrepresentee into the pre-contractual financial position he would have been in had the tort not been committed – to compensate him for his out-of-pocket or 'reliance' loss. (The measure of damages for breach of contract is normally assessed on a different basis, see also Chapter 13.) *Doyle* shows that for fraud the court will award damages for all loss including consequential loss such as expenses incurred as a result of entering the contract. *East v Maurer* (1991) reconsidered whether 'all the actual damages flowing directly from the fraudulent inducement' covered loss of profits, an 'expectation' loss found only in breach cases and so, on that basis, excluded from consideration in *Doyle*:

> E bought one of M's two hair salons in Bournemouth for £20,000 in 1979. Although during negotiations, M said that he did not intend to work in the other salon except in emergencies, he in fact continued to work full-time in that salon. The effect was that the plaintiffs' business was never profitable. They sold it in 1989 for £5,000 and sued M for fraudulent misrepresentation.
>
> At first instance, damages were awarded to cover the difference in value of the business between the purchase price and its true market value, for trading losses, and also included an award of £15,000 for loss of profits based on the profit the defendant would have made in the salon had he not sold it, less 25% because the plaintiffs were inexperienced. On appeal, it was held that 'all the actual damage' did include loss of profits.
>
> However, using tortious principles, this loss was to be calculated so as to compensate the plaintiffs for the profit they might have made had the fraud not been committed. This meant assessing the profit they might have expected to make in another salon bought for a similar sum, and not on the contractual basis of the profits that the salon might have made if M had *promised* that he would not work in the other salon. Somewhat surprisingly nevertheless, the loss of profits award was reduced to £10,000.

It will be appreciated that in this case M did not contractually bind himself not to work in the other salon. The statement he made was a pre-contractual statement of intention which was held to be a statement of *fact* because it was proved that he did not have this intention when he made the statement, see *Edgington v Fitzmaurice* and the quote on p 183 above. The outcome was virtually the same as if he had bound himself.

Negligent misrepresentation

Until relatively recently, the common law provided no remedy for a non-fraudulent misrepresentation. Such a misrepresentation was classed as 'innocent', ie the maker believed it to be true (whether reasonably or not). In equity, however, the representee might be allowed to rescind (within the limits outlined above, plus others now abolished) and in a few cases an indemnity was allowed against certain losses. Broadly speaking, the absence of the availability of damages placed the innocent misrepresentee in a poor position *vis-à-vis* a party suffering loss through breach.

In 1962 the Law Reform Committee recommended that damages should be given for negligent misrepresentation – that is, where the maker honestly believed his statement to be true but he did not have reasonable grounds for his belief. Before this recommendation was enacted in 1967, other developments took place in the common law which complicated the position.

First it became clear from the House of Lords landmark negligence decision in *Hedley Byrne* (1964) that where a 'special' professional or business relationship, short of contract, existed between parties a duty of care could be owed as regards statements made and relied upon (and which caused financial loss). In *Bentley v Smith Motors* (1965), noted earlier, Lord Denning in particular canvassed the view that a pre-contractual statement made by a party possessing special knowledge, and made carelessly, gave rise to a claim for damages for breach of 'incorporated' warranty:

> S, a motor dealer, negligently told B that a custom-built Bentley motor car had done only 20,000 miles since having a replacement engine fitted, when in fact it had covered 100,000 miles. In the circumstances (before the passing of the Misrepresentation Act), no action for damages would have succeeded unless the statement could be regarded as a contractual warranty. This the Court of Appeal was willing to do. In Lord Denning's words:

> If a representation is made in the course of dealings for a contract for the very purpose of inducing the other party to act on it, and it actually induces him to act on it by entering into the contract, that is *prima facie* ground for inferring that the representation was intended as a warranty ... But the maker of the representation can rebut this inference if he can show that ... he was in fact innocent of fault in making it ... but here we have a dealer, Mr Smith, who was in a position to know, or at least to find out, the history of the car. He could get it by writing to the makers. He did not do so. Indeed it was done later. When the history of this car was examined, his statement turned out to be quite wrong. He ought to have known better. There was no reasonable foundation for it.

These developments led up to the decision in *Esso Petroleum Co Ltd v Mardon* (1976), noted above, another case involving a contract which was entered into before the Misrepresentation Act 1967 took effect. Here it was held that not only could a pre-contractual inducement be construed as a warranty – in this case an over-optimistic forecast of the sales potential of a filling station made to its prospective tenant by E's senior sales representative – but also that the relationship between the negotiating parties could be regarded as 'special' in the sense of giving rise to a duty of care as in the negligence case of *Hedley Byrne*. Although the estimated throughput of 200,000 gallons a year was only a forecast, it was based on special knowledge and expertise, and it was to be treated not as an expression of opinion but as a warranty that the forecast was reasonably reliable – which it was not, and E was liable in damages.

Lord Denning made it clear that damages, as seen above, were tortious:

> Whether it be called breach of warranty or negligent misrepresentation, its effect was *not* to warrant [guarantee] the throughput, but only to induce him to enter the contract. So the damages in either case are to be measured by the loss he suffered. Just as in *Doyle v Olby (Ironmongers) Ltd* ... he can say: 'I would not have entered into this contract at all but for your representation. Owing to it, I have lost all the capital I put into it. I also incurred a large overdraft. I have spent four years of my life in wasted endeavour without reward: and it will take some time to re-establish myself.'

> For all such loss he is entitled to recover damagers ... [It] can only be a rough-and-ready estimate. But it must be done in estimating the loss.

Bearing in mind the decision in the later fraud case of *East v Maurer* (above), it would appear that Mardon recovered damages not for loss of profits that would have been made if the filling station in question had produced a turnover of 20,000 gallons, but on a *tort* basis of putting him back into the position he would have been in had he not taken the lease of the filling station. He recovered capital expenditure and operating losses (his overdraft incurred in his unsuccessful attempt to make the business profitable) *plus* 'the return he would have made from investment and work in another comparable business': see Lord Denning's analysis and Collins, *The Law of Contract*. (We will see that these measure of damages issues also arise in relation to s 2(1) of the Misrepresentation Act, below.)

Section 2(1) of the Misrepresentation Act 1967

Under s 2(1) of the 1967 Act a statutory liability for negligent misrepresentation was created. It does not rest on any 'special relationship' and, reversing the normal burden of proof, requires the *representor* to prove 'that he had reasonable grounds to believe and did believe up to the time the contract was made that the facts represented were true'. The subsection also creates a liability in damages which is in addition to the right to rescind subject to the limitations or bars discussed.

In *Howard Marine & Dredging Co Ltd v Ogden & Sons (Excavations) Ltd* (1978), O wished to hire two sea-going barges to carry earth. HM quoted a price and stated that the carrying capacity of each barge was about 1,600 tonnes. This statement, based on a recollection of an incorrect figure in Lloyd's Register, was made honestly but was wrong – the true figure, given in other shipping documents available to HM, was 1,195 tonnes. O later refused to pay hire charges when the barges' limited carrying capacity delayed progress in their work. HM withdrew the barges and sued for charges unpaid; O counterclaimed for damages, *inter alia*, under s 2(1).

Although Lord Denning thought it reasonable for HM to rely on the Lloyd's Register, the majority held that it was not reasonable not to refer to the shipping documents on this matter.

There has been considerable confusion concerning the measure of damages under s 2(1). Assessment is on the tort basis (not on a contractual loss of bargain footing) and until recently the weight of academic opinion was in line with Treitel's analysis in 1987:

> Where the action is brought under s 2(1) of the Misrepresentation Act, one possible view is that the deceit rule will be applied by virtue of the fiction of fraud. But the preferable view is that the severity of the deceit rule can only be justified in cases of actual fraud and that remoteness under s 2(1) should depend, as in actions based on negligence, on the test of foreseeability.

The 'deceit rule' (as in *Doyle v Olby Ironmongers Ltd*, above), it will be recalled, means that a representee can recover all loss flowing directly from the fraud even if the loss was not foreseeable. The 'fiction of fraud' is an allusion to the wording of s 2(1) itself where it states that the liability for damages should arise *as if* the statement had been made fraudulently. In the case of *Royscot Trust Ltd v Rogerson* (1991), the Court of Appeal held that s 2(1) liability gave rise to liability under the 'deceit rule':

> A car dealer misrepresented to the plaintiff finance company both the price of a car and the amount of deposit paid by a customer who wished to take the vehicle on hire purchase terms. This was done in order to meet the company's 20% deposit requirement.
>
> The company financed the deal but the customer (first defendant) sold the car in breach of the HP agreement and defaulted on his payments. The finance company brought proceedings against both customer and dealer for loss suffered.
>
> It was accepted on all sides that the dealer's misrepresentation was not fraudulent. It was held that the measure of damages under s 2(1) of the 1967 Act is tortious, not contractual, and that the dealer's liability was such that, in the judgment of Balcombe LJ, 'the finance company is entitled to recover from the dealer all the losses which it suffered as a result of entering into the agreements with the dealer and the customer, even if those losses were unforeseeable.' The finance company was awarded £3,625 plus interest and accepted that it would have to give credit for any sums received from its judgment against the customer.

The literal interpretation of s 2(1) in this case means that as regards the measure of damages a negligent misrepresentor is in the same position as the fraudulent – the more generous award applies in either case (cf *East v Maurer* and, arguably, *Esso Petroleum v Mardon*). However, it is difficult to appreciate why the traditional tort law distinction between intentional and negligent conduct should be disregarded in this way, so making the negligent misrepresentor liable beyond the bounds of forseeability (but see also *Naughton v O'Callagham* (1990) in which the 'fiction of fraud' was also followed as regards the measure of damages).

Innocent misrepresentation

As we have seen, before the advent of negligent misrepresentation, damages could not be awarded for non-fraudulent (innocent) misrepresentation, and rescission, if not barred, was not necessarily an appropriate remedy – involving as it does the setting aside of the whole contract. There is still no *right* to damages for a wholly innocent misrepresentation – one proved to have been made honestly and upon reasonable grounds – although rescission, within the limits discussed earlier, remains. Although there is no *right* to damages for innocent misrepresentation under s 2(2) of the 1967 Act, the court is given a *discretionary* power to declare the contract subsisting and to award damages in lieu of rescission if it would be equitable to do so. The court must bear in mind the nature of the misrepresentation and the loss caused (a) to the representee if the contract were upheld and (b) the loss caused to the representor if the contract were set aside.

This discretionary power extends to negligent misrepresentation so making available the remedies of rescission *and* damages under s 2(1) or, if appropriate, rescission or damages under s 2(2) in cases of this kind. However, the court's power to award damages in lieu of rescission (so long as this remedy is not barred) is more likely to be used where the representor is not at fault and compensation is an adequate remedy.

The assessment of damages under s 2(2), where the representation is wholly innocent, may well be on the basis of making the representor only liable for the amount by which the actual value of what he has transferred under the contract is less than the price paid by the representee. This is the normal tortious measure which excludes consequential loss.

Exclusion of liability for misrepresentation

A clause in a contract excluding or restricting liability for misrepresentation is subject to the rules already discussed in Chapter 9 regarding incorporation and construction. It is also subject to s 3 of the 1967 Act, as amended by s 8 of the Unfair Contract Terms Act 1977, which applies the requirement of reasonableness, as laid down by s 11(1) of the latter Act, to the clause.

In *South Western General Property Co Ltd v Marton* (1982), M, an experienced builder, bought land at auction. It was described in the particulars of sale as building land for which planning permission had previously been refused because the proposed house was out of character. The sale was subject to a clause which stated that 'any intending purchaser must satisfy himself by inspection or otherwise as to the correctness of each statement contained in the particulars'.

M, who had bought the land as a site for his own residence later discovered that planning permission had been refused in terms that made any further application futile.

The court held that the description in the particulars was misleading; it implied that the land could be used for building if the house was in character, and this was untrue. The defendant had relied on the description, which 'failed to tell more than a part of the facts which were material to the whole contract of sale'.

M had been within his rights to rescind the contract and the company's action failed. The exclusion was held to be unreasonable.

As seen in the previous chapter, reasonableness or otherwise can only be determined in the circumstances of the particular case. In a case involving dealers and an individual, as above, an exclusion may be found to be unreasonable, whereas the same clause might be regarded as reasonable if found in a contract with a property speculator.

Fraud and mistake

As stated at the beginning of this chapter, fraudulent misrepresentation may in certain circumstances lead to a claim that it has induced a fundamental mistake which renders the contract void. In the cases discussed so far, the misrepresentation related to the attributes of the contractual subject matter (a filling station's annual turnover of petrol or the earth-carrying capacity of barges, etc). However, what is the position if, instead, the misrepresentation relates to the question of who a party is? In some cases it has been held that the party misled has made a fundamental mistake as to the person or identity of the other party with the result that the contract is not merely voidable for fraud but void for mistake. (It should be pointed out, however, that the identity of the person with whom one is dealing is often of no consequence.).

Although the courts are probably moving away from finding that a contract can be void in such circumstances, and the whole area is rife with decisions that are difficult to reconcile (not to mention the availability of a great deal of 'explanatory' academic theory and counter-theory on the question), the cases do raise interesting points of analysis and policy within seemingly intractable problems involving deception and intention, identity and attributes, and contract, tort and property.

Nevertheless, a disproportionate amount of time can be spent on mistake – which can arise or be claimed for reasons other than fraud. It is a confused area

of no pressing social or business significance and only a few general introductory points will be made.

Mistake in contract

The idea of mistake rendering a contract void came into the law from continental
jurisprudence in the second part of the 19th century. It grew out of strict 'consensus' or 'will' theory (now out of favour) which insisted that, obligations being self-
imposed, if there were any factor present which vitiated consent, then this was fatal
to the binding nature of the parties' agreement. There was a need for 'real', subjective concurrence of minds or intention (see Chapter 2). This subjective approach to
agreement has now been almost entirely superseded by an objective view of agreement based on what the parties say and do (see Chapter 5 on Agreement).

Nevertheless, House of Lords decisions remain – such as *Cundy v Lindsay*
(1878) discussed below – which rest on absence of consensus. In *Bell v Lever Bros
Ltd* (1932) Lord Atkin said that: 'If mistake operates at all, it operates to negative
or nullify consent.' Although it is difficult to formulate a doctrine of mistake
which keeps it within reasonable bounds, we should understand that the courts,
seeing themselves primarily as upholders of agreements and expectations, placed
strict limits on pleas of mistake just as they do on pleas of frustration: 'The law
does not take the simple line of ruling that a contract is void merely because one
or both of the parties would not have made it had the true facts been realised.'
(Mistake, as said, can arise in a variety of ways not merely through fraud.)

Mistake when shared by both parties *nullifies* consent, in Lord Atkin's terms,
if it goes to some fact that lies at the very root of the contract: known as 'common' mistake by some writers, 'mutual' mistake by others. Here agreement has
been reached but it is to no purpose because it has been reached on the basis of
a particular and fundamental assumption which is not true. The main problem
lies in deciding when an incorrect assumption is sufficiently fundamental. The
weight of opinion is that a contract will only be void in such circumstances
where there is in fact *nothing* to contract about (eg specific goods, which are the
subject matter of the agreement, have already, unknown to the parties, ceased to
exist). An agreement devoid of all content does not require a doctrine of mistake
to render it a nullity, but there is a close analogy between the questions of
whether a contract is void owing to some *pre-existing* shared mistake, or
whether it is frustrated (and void) as a result of some *subsequent* event which
displaces the basis of the contract (see Chapter 12 on Frustration).

It is doubtful if a shared mistake regarding the quality or attributes of contractual subject matter such as goods will have this effect: see *Harrison and Jones
Ltd v Bunten and Lancaster Ltd* (1953). In *Bell v Lever Bros Ltd*, Lord Atkin said
that mistake as to quality, in a case where a shared mistake allegedly nullified
consent, 'will not affect consent unless it is the mistake of both parties, and is as
to the existence of some quality which makes the thing without the quality

essentially different from the thing as it was believed to be'. Such cases will be rare – and would probably be decided on some other basis such as misdescription. However, the question of mistaken attributes reappears in cases where the *fraud* of one party induces, so it is claimed, a (unilateral) mistake rendering the contract void rather than merely voidable.

Fraud and mistake which negatives consent

In general terms, in the cases which follow only one party (A) is mistaken – it is an (alleged) mistake as to the other party's (B's) identity, brought about by B's fraudulent deception when in some way representing himself to A as C. C is a person of actual, or apparent, financial standing whose name is assumed by B in order to inspire confidence in A. The purpose of B's deception is usually to obtain valuable goods from A on credit – often against a worthless cheque. B then disposes of the goods to D, an innocent third party, for cash. The action is usually brought by A against D; B no longer being available. It is an action in tort (conversion) for recovery of the goods or their value on the basis that D has no title to them. As the law stands, it is a question of which of two 'innocent' parties (A or D) should suffer for the fraud of a third (B).

If A can prove mistaken identity, his contract with B is void and B obtains no title to the goods. Hence D obtains no title from B, and A succeeds. If there is only fraud, A's contract with B is merely voidable and, usually, B passes a good title to D *before* A avoids the contract. In such a case A will fail.

An early leading case is the House of Lords decision in *Cundy v Lindsay* (1878) in which a mistake of identity was found. Professor Simpson urges us to see this decision as an example of a case decided under the influence of a then 'full blown' (but 'now repudiated') *consensus* theory of contract: 'If contract requires *consensus ad idem*, there must be a real subjective concurrence of minds ... whatever the outward appearance if the parties were not in fact in agreement there is no contract.'

> The plaintiffs (Lindsay) received an order for goods from a fraudulent person, Blenkarn, who gave his address as 37 Wood Street, Cheapside. He signed his letter in such a way as to make it appear that the offer came from Blenkiron & Co, a firm known by reputation to the plaintiffs, and whose address was 123 Wood Street. The goods were despatched to Blenkiron and Co, 37 Wood Street. Blenkarn took possession of them but, without paying the plaintiffs, sold them to the defendants, who were sued by the plaintiffs for conversion. It was held that there was no contract between the plaintiffs and Blenkarn, therefore no title to the goods passed to Blenkarn or consequently to the defendants who were accordingly liable.

The court inferred that the plaintiffs intended to sell to Blenkiron & Co and not to the person who traded at 37 Wood Street. They accepted Blenkiron & Co's 'offer' – as Blenkarn knew full well – therefore there was no 'concurrence of minds', consent was negatived and no agreement arose between the plaintiffs and Blenkarn. Lord Cairns stated that: 'The principal parties concerned ... never came into contact personally' and later: 'how is it possible to imagine that ... any contract could have arisen between the respondent Lindsay and Blenkarn, the dishonest man? Of him they knew nothing, and of him they never thought. With him they never intended to deal. Their minds never, even for an instant of time rested upon him, and as between him and them there was no consensus of mind which could lead to any agreement.'

If, alternatively, the court had inferred that the plaintiffs, though misled by Blenkarn's fraud, had intended or at least were content to deal with the person at 37 Wood Street (from which address the offer had come and to which the goods were sent), then there would have been a contract between the plaintiffs and Blenkarn. It would have been voidable for fraud but the defendants' title to the goods would have been secure, since they would have acquired a good but voidable title from Blenkarn before the plaintiffs had avoided their contract with Blenkarn and so defeated any transfer of title.

By highlighting the 'subjective concurrence of minds' basis of the decision in *Cundy v Lindsay*, it is not suggested that the 'no contract' ruling was wrong. (A three-judge QBD court did however prefer the second inference above – on the basis of which the contract was only voidable.) From an *objective* viewpoint, we must ask if the plaintiffs, Lindsay, had clearly shown that their intention was only to deal with Blenkiron & Co, who were known to them. Thus, in line with what is now the basic test for establishing agreement, we must answer the following questions: Did Lindsay (the offerees) so conduct themselves that a reasonable man would think that they were accepting an offer from Blenkiron & Co, and did Blenkiron (the rogue) know – or ought he reasonably to have realised – that Lindsay were prepared only to contract with Blenkiron & Co. Put in this alternative way, in order to agree with the decision in the case, both questions must be answered in the affirmative. There is no difficulty in doing so with the second question. Further, as other cases show, the *identity* of the person the rogue passes himself off to be must be crucial. In the circumstances (eg where the parties are at a distance), the party defrauded must show that he intended only to contract with that person.

Since this case, and particularly in recent years, there has been a trend *against* finding an operative mistake in similar cases – in finding instead that there *is* a contract between the plaintiff and the rogue which is only voidable for fraud. The following points are relevant: .

(1)   The courts are now primarily concerned with the 'outward and visible signs' of agreement and not with the presence of an inward and mental assent', ie they adopt the objective and not a subjective approach.

(2)   In the significant 'mistake' cases since *Cundy v Lindsay*, the plaintiff and the rogue have dealt with each other face to face and, in line with the objective view of agreement, a strong *presumption* has been developed to the effect that the plaintiff intended to contract with the person physically present before him and identified by sight and hearing. (The plaintiff, as we will see, has a difficult task in overcoming this presumption.) Whether 'at a distance' cases like *Cundy v Lindsay* and 'face to face' cases are different in kind or in degree is debatable.

In *Citibank NA v Brown Shipley & Co Ltd* (1991), Waller J stated that: 'The no contract situation, as opposed to a voidable contract, only arises if it is fundamental to the contract that one party to the contract should be who he says that he is. That is easier to establish where contracts are made entirely by documents and is less easy to establish in an *inter praesentes* position.' (In this interesting fraud case, it was held that the mistake, such as it was, was not that of the identity of a party to the contract.)

(3)   Cheshire and Fifoot, for example, felt that 'it is permissible to regret the inference which their Lordships drew from the facts' in *Cundy v Lindsay*. They, and others, are concerned that a finding of mistaken identity 'prejudices third parties who later deal in good faith with the fraudulent person'.

(4)   A Law Reform Committee Report of 1966 recommended 'that contracts which are at present void because the owner of the goods was deceived or mistaken as to the identity of the person with whom he dealt should in future be treated as voidable so far as third parties are concerned'. This recommendation has, however, never taken legislative effect.

(5)   That the plaintiff has been careless in his dealings with the rogue is, it would appear, a factor which in recent years has influenced decisions in favour of third party rights. One should get a cheque cleared before parting with property worth several hundred pounds: see *Lewis v Averay* (below), and also the mistakenly signed document case of *Gallie v Lee* (1971).

Taking these considerations into account, the main stumbling block in the plaintiff's (A's) path is his need to overcome the legal presumption (based on an objective view of agreement) that despite *a* mistake, A and B entered into a binding, though voidable, contract. In order to rebut the presumption A must prove the following points:

(1)   First of all it must be shown that C is a definite and identifiable person. In other words, A must show that he intended to deal with some person (C) *other than* the person (the rogue B) with whom he has apparently made a contract. If there is no confusion between two distinct entities, there is no fundamental mistake:.

In *King's Norton Metal Co Ltd v Edridge, Merrett & Co Ltd* (1897), B ordered goods from A by business letter using the alias 'Hallam & Co'. Since B and 'Hallam & Co' were the same person, A made no mistake of identity. A did mistakenly believe that 'Hallam & Co' existed but was unable to show that they meant to contract with 'Hallam & Co' and not with the letter writer, B. A had taken a risk as to the credit-worthiness of the letter writer, with whom they had made a voidable contract. A's action against D failed as this contract had not been avoided (for fraud) at the time of the sale of the goods by B to the defendants.

(2) A must also prove that B *was aware of his intention* to deal with some person (C) other than himself. This requirement is easily met where it is B's fraud that has induced the alleged mistake – it is the crux of B's scheme.

(3) A must further prove that, during negotiations and before entering into the contract, *he regarded the 'identity' of the other contracting party as being of vital importance* and he indicated as such.

(4) Finally, A must prove that he took *all reasonable steps to verify* that 'identity'.

An interesting question which has arisen here is: What is meant by identity? It has been said that a mistake as to identity renders the contract void; a mistake as regards attributes does not. However, this is not a meaningful distinction because, as Professor Glanville Williams points out, there are no things (or persons) apart from their qualities (or attributes). A person is a bundle of attributes and the so-called distinction only arises as a 'matter of linguistic convenience'. In the cases, what has actually happened is that A 'has constructed in his mind a sort of composite person, who does not correspond to any real person'. Where the parties are face to face, this is a person possessing the bodily characteristics of B plus certain other attributes, actual (name) or presumed (financial standing), of C. A means to contract with a person who has *all* these attributes – but who does not exist.

The outcome of this analysis is 'that a mistake of identity occurs where the victim confuses the attributes of two particular persons'. There are two further important findings: (i) A must be independently aware (ie have knowledge other than that imparted by B) of some of C's attributes, and (ii) 'an error of identity is an error as to important attributes'. Therefore, according to Glanville Williams, if it is an 'important' attribute of C, and not of the fraudulent B, which induces A to enter into the apparent bargain, there is no contract.

Applying this analysis, at least to the cases discussed below, we find that A identifies the person present (B) by sight and hearing, except so far as B assumes C's name and hence (presumed) financial standing. What the cases below seem to show is that A's mistake as regards the attribute of credit-worthiness is not one which can be relied upon to negative consent. The credit-worthiness of a party can be established but, in the circumstances of the cases, A relies on his own personal (and mistaken) judgment and so takes a deliberate business risk – with the result that he, and not an innocent third party must bear the loss.

When we come to the *actual* decisions and the reasoning of the various courts in the mistaken identity cases, there are problems of reconciling one decision with another and of establishing the principles upon which the courts are proceeding. It may be advisable to work backwards from the most recent important decision, *Lewis v Averay*, decided by the Court of Appeal in 1972:

> Lewis advertised his car for sale and was approached by B who falsely claimed to be Richard Greene, a film and television actor. When B wrote a cheque for £450, Lewis, on asking for proof that he was Greene, was shown a film studio pass with the name 'Richard A Green' and B's photograph. Lewis took the cheque (signed 'RA Green') which was later dishonoured; and B took the car, which he sold to Averay who bought in good faith. It was held that the contract was not void for mistake and that title in the car had passed to Averay.

The following points are of particular importance:

(1) The presumption that the plaintiff intended to contract with the person physically present had not been overcome: the contract was good though voidable for fraud: see also *Phillips v Brooks Ltd* below, and the dissenting judgment of Devlin LJ in *Ingram v Little*, another Court of Appeal decision of 1961 in which, on very similar facts, the contract was held to be void. In *Lewis*, disagreement with the majority decision in *Ingram*, and its basis 'either in logic or practical considerations' was expressed.

(2) Lord Denning rejected the distinction between mistaken identity and attributes; the former making the contract void, the latter not. He said it was 'a distinction without a difference ... These fine distinctions do no good to the law'.

(3) Lord Denning also contrasted the position of the innocent purchaser, who knew nothing of what had passed between Lewis and B, and Lewis himself 'who let the rogue have the goods and thus enabled him to commit the fraud'. (Both parties were students.)

(4) Lord Denning expressed agreement with the Law Reform Committee's recommendation of 1966 to the effect that contracts entered into in these circumstances should be voidable so far as the acquisition of title by innocent third parties was concerned.

(5) Lewis's mistake was as to credit-worthiness and it is clear that he did less than was reasonable to establish that B was Greene, and, even if he was, that was no guarantee that the cheque would be honoured.

> In *Phillips v Brooks Ltd* (1919), B (the rogue) entered the plaintiff's shop and selected pearls worth £2,550 and a ring worth £450. He wrote a cheque for £3,000, stating that he was Sir George Bullough of St James' Square (a wealthy man known by name to the plaintiff). Phillips checked the address in a directory and, at B's request, allowed him to take away the ring. B pawned the ring with Brooks Ltd and the cheque was dishonoured. Horridge J held that Phillips had 'con-

tracted to sell and deliver [the ring] to the person who came into his shop ... who obtained the sale and delivery by means of the false pretence that he was Sir George Bullough'.

Although the judge stated that the plaintiff's intention was 'to sell to the person present and identified by sight and hearing' (the *prima facie* legal presumption), it may be opportune to recall the 'composite person' analysis and concentrate on the jeweller's failure to prove that he intended to contract with Bullough and with nobody else. His looking up the address was scarcely sufficient to verify B's claim. The plaintiff took a risk as regards credit-worthiness and his case failed.

The Court of Appeal in *Lewis v Averay* applied the decision in *Phillips v Brooks Ltd* that the contract was merely voidable and had not been avoided in time to defeat the defendant's title.

A final point: in *Ingram v Little*, Devlin LJ expressed the view that 'the relevant question in this sort of case is not whether the contract was void or voidable, but which of two innocent parties shall suffer for the fraud of a third. The plain answer is that the loss should be divided between them in such proportion as is just in all the circumstances ... if the fault or imprudence of either party has caused or contributed to the loss, it should be borne by that party in the whole or in the greater part'. This suggestion, with its comparisons to apportionment where there is contributory negligence or, following frustration, under the Law Reform (Frustrated Contracts) Act 1943 (see Chapter 12), was found to be 'plainly attractive at first sight' by the Law Reform Committee in 1966 but was rejected as leading, in some cases, to 'uncertainty' consequent upon 'a wide and virtually unrestrained judicial discretion'. Problems were seen in particular where the goods passed from the rogue to an innocent purchaser and then on to E and F – all innocent parties.

In conclusion, our experience of mistake in this chapter shows that in Adams and Brownsword's 'market-individualist' terms: 'Mistake is not to be used as an excuse for bad bargains, and nor is it to be allowed to jeopardise the security of market transactions.'

References and further reading

Atiyah and Treitel, 'Misrepresentation Act 1967' (1967) 30 MLR 369.

Bishop, 'Negligent misrepresentation through economists' eyes' (1980) 96 LQR 360.

Brownsword, Case note on *Howard Marine* decision (1978) 41 MLR 735.

Cartwright (1991), *Unequal Bargaining* (on both Misrepresentation and Mistake).

Fairest, 'Misrepresentation and the Act of 1967' (1967) CLJ 239.

Hooley, 'Damages and Misrepresentation Act 1967' (1991) 107 LQR 547.

Taylor, 'Expectation, reliance and misrepresentation' (1982) 45 MLR 138.

Glanville Williams, 'Mistake as to party in the law of contract' (1945) *Canadian Bar Review* 271 and 380.

Greig, 'The passing of property and the misidentified buyer' (1972) 35 MLR 306.

Sutton, 'Reform of the Law of Mistake in Contract' (1976) *New Zealand Universities Law Review* 40.

Jackson (1988), *'Law, Fact and Narrative Coherence'*, pp 102–106.

Questions

(1)   Over a year ago, Greene bought Powell's dental practice in the village of Hotwell. At the beginning of negotiations in October 1993. Powell assured Greene that there was no other practice within a 40-mile radius of the village and told him that the practice grossed about £30,000 per annum. He said Greene could examine the accounts for the last six years if he wished but Greene declined. Whilst he was thinking about the purchase, he met his brother-in-law, a dentist in Moorside (a town about 50 miles from Hotwell) and made casual enquiries as to whether he thought the practice would be a good buy.

In fact, the practice had never grossed over £25,000 per annum. Furthermore, two months after the negotiations started (but before the sale was completed in mid-1994) a new practice opened up two miles away, taking many of Powell's patients. Powell did not tell Greene about this.

Greene raised a loan of £40,000 on which interest of £250 per month was payable, in order to finance the transaction (along with capital of his own which he had available).

Later in 1994, Greene found out that the rival practice had been set up and that Powell's practice could never have grossed £30,000. Nevertheless, he continued with the practice in the hope that he would be able to build it up. He has failed to do so despite considerable further injections of capital to buy new equipment. He wishes to take action against Powell. Advise Greene.

(2)   In *Howard Marine Ltd v Ogden (Excavations) Ltd* (1978), it was claimed that a statement (i) amounted to a collateral warranty, (ii) gave rise to a claim for damages under the Misrepresentation Act, and similarly (iii) for damages in negligence. There was little unanimity between the members of the Court of Appeal on these three claims. Where do you stand on these points?

(3) In what manner, if at all, does the measure of damages differ in cases of (a) fraudulent misrepresentation, (b) negligent misrepresentation, and (c) breach of contract?.

(4) (a) In an action in tort for negligent advice, it is not necessary to show that the statement complained of was a representation in the sense in which this term is understood in contract law. Discuss.

     (b) A makes an offer to B in the belief that B is *not* B. (i) Can B accept this offer so as to create a binding contract? (ii) Why was there no contract in *Said v Butt* (1920)?

(5) B, a rogue, has recently taken the name of C, an Italian millionaire, whose exploits are widely publicised in the press. Miss A is the owner of an antique shop. She is delighted when B, elegantly dressed, enters her shop and introduces himself as C. He persuades Miss A to part with a £5000 painting in exchange for his cheque, explaining that he would like the painting delivered to a suite at the Savoy (which he has specially taken for the day). The cheque is dishonoured, and B sells the painting to D, an innocent third party. What remedies, if any, has Miss A against D?

(6) (a) Following the decision in *Johnson v Agnew* (1980), what is the difference between 'rescission for misrepresentation' and 'rescission for breach'?

     (b) To what extent, if at all, have recent developments in the 'documents mistakenly signed' field followed trends discernible in other areas of mistake?

11   Contract and competition

Restraint of trade: restrictive trading agreements

By the mid-19th century, contract law was firmly established as the legal corollary of a free market economy. A significant reason for acceptance of the doctrine of freedom of contract was its links with the principle of free trade. However, it by no means follows that freedom of contract necessarily promotes freedom of trade and competitive markets. In fact it can be shown that in this respect there is an internal contradiction in the freedom of contract concept. For example, if distributor D agrees to take 50% of his requirements of goods from supplier S^1, he restricts his freedom to contract with S^2. If D agrees to take all his requirements from S^1 and no one else, he precludes himself from trading with S^2. If S 'ties' all national distributors in this way, foreign exporters will be prevented from gaining access to the market unless they can secure new outlets for their goods.

Contracts of this type are said to fall within the area of restraint of trade – they restrict or prevent trade and competition. Somewhat paradoxically, therefore, it is possible for the courts, in upholding freedom of contract, to uphold contracts containing a significant element of restraint. This was recognised by Lord Atkinson in *Herbert Morris Ltd v Saxelby* in 1916 when he said that: 'Two principles or views of public policy come into conflict in such cases as these, namely, freedom of trade and freedom of contract. While the community is vitally interested in trade being free, it is also vitally interested in people being free to contract and being held to their contracts.'

Unencumbered by conflicting policies, it was clear to business entrepreneurs long before the end of the 19th century that economic (profit-making) advantages might be gained by entering into restrictive agreements among themselves so as to create the economic power necessary to influence and perhaps control markets:

> It is plain that contracts in restraint of trade may be used in attempts to destroy the market mechanism itself, to destroy its diversity and multiplicity of decision making, and to centralise it in the hands of those who enter the contracts in restraint of trade. This fact is but one facet of potential or actual monopoly control of an economy. The extent to which there is or is not monopolistic control of a given market economy, the extent to which monopoly is not an inevitable accompaniment and outgrowth of a capitalist system, and related problems, are subjects of great dispute among economists and political theorists. For the contract student it is enough to note that contracts in restraint of trade are intimately connected with those political and economic problems, as are the attempts of legislatures and courts to control such contracts (Macneil, *Contracts-Instruments for Social Co-operation*).

Assuming that competition and freedom of trade are 'good' things, what efforts did the courts make at the turn of the century to control such contracts? As regards cartel agreements between formerly competing suppliers of goods and services, they invariably came down on the side of freedom of contract at the expense of freedom of trade. At a time, in 1875, when the then Master of the Rolls was declaring that businessmen and others must have 'the utmost liberty of contracting', restrictive trading agreements of all kinds – market-sharing, price-fixing and resale price maintenance, etc – were beginning to permeate business. These agreements the courts normally upheld and so assisted in the destruction of freedom of trade by their pursuit of freedom of contract. Later, in an important case in 1914, it was said that 'the onus of showing that any contract is calculated to produce a monopoly or enhance prices to an unreasonable extent will lie on the party alleging it, and ... if once the court is satisfied that the restraint is reasonable as between the parties this onus will be no light one'. Naturally the parties to a successful agreement to 'enhance prices' would themselves consider it more than reasonable and would be extremely unlikely to bring an action on it: 'In combine cases the parties may be on velvet while the public is looted.'

The failure of the courts to look beyond the interests of the parties, although in line with freedom of contract, was a major reason for their inability to stem this rise, continuing into the first part of the 20th century, of restrictive business agreements and monopoly positions. The restraint of trade doctrine remained under the shadow of the *laissez-faire* school of economics and the judges followed the government's lead in adopting a basically non-interventionary role in such business matters. (They did however do much to prevent workers combining in the early days of the struggle for legal recognition of trade unions.)

In 1913 the Judicial Committee of the Privy Council was 'not aware of any case in which a restraint though reasonable in the interests of the parties has been held to be unenforceable because it involved some injury to the public'. If an agreement was reasonable in the interests of the parties, it was presumed to be in the interests of the public in the absence of proof to the contrary, and since the public was not represented in any litigation, there was no one to argue the case from the public interest point of view. In any event neither judges nor juries (regularly used up to 1934) were economists and so there was no pressure to bring 'competition versus monopoly' arguments into the courts. The following case is a prime illustration of the attitude of the courts at this time as regards cartel agreements:

> In *Mogul SS Co Ltd v McGregor, Gow & Co Ltd and Others* (1892), the defendants were ship owners who formed an association or conference to monopolise the tea-carrying trade from the Far East. On the basis of the conference agreement, it was possible to regulate the ships that were to call at each port, divide the cargoes between them and fix the freight to be charged for shipment to England. The members allowed a rebate of 5% to cargo-owners who had shipped exclusively on members' vessels during the previous six months, and shipping agents were warned that they would not be given business if they dealt with non-members.

When Mogul, who was not a member, sent vessels to pick up a cargo of tea, the conference, acting on the basis of the agreement, arranged that member vessels were in port first. These vessels offered to carry tea so cheaply that the Mogul ships could find alternative cargoes only at unprofitable rates.

In this action brought by Mogul, claiming an injunction to prevent the conference from operating this agreement in restraint of trade, the House of Lords upheld the conference agreement and the plaintiff's case failed. Although the agreement – regulating routes to be used, rates to be charged and ports to be served – was probably in unreasonable restraint of trade, the members could not be sued upon it by a company that was not a party to it. The agreement was clearly in the interests of the parties, but was it against public policy and void? There was no evidence on this wider issue but Lord Bramwell was 'by no means sure that the conference did not prevent a waste and was not good for the public'.

Further light on judicial attitudes towards such restrictive trading agreements is to be found in Bowen LJ's judgment in the Court of Appeal in the same case:

> I myself should deem it to be misfortune if we were to attempt to prescribe to the business world how honest and peaceable trade was to be carried on in a case where no such illegal elements as I have mentioned exist, or were to adopt some standard of judicial 'reasonableness', or of 'normal' prices, or 'fair freights', to which commercial adventures, otherwise innocent, were bound to conform.

The *Mogul* case concerned a horizontal restrictive agreement, ie one between suppliers only. *Dunlop Pneumatic Tyre Co Ltd v Selfridge & Co Ltd* (1915) offers an early illustration of the attempted enforcement by a supplier of vertical restrictions, ie those which he seeks to impose on others, such as retailers, further up the chain of distribution. Resale price maintenance is, or was, a common form of restriction of price competition and is designed to ensure that, whatever the channels of distribution through which goods pass, they shall be sold to the retail customer at a price which has been fixed, usually by the manufacturer. In the *Dunlop* case, an attempt by the manufacturer to enforce his RPM conditions against a price-cutting retailer fell foul (as seen in Chapter 6) of the privity of contract doctrine:

> D sold tyres to a distributor on condition that he would not resell below D's list price and would only resell to a trade customer on condition that the latter would observe D's resale price. S bought tyres from the distributor, accepting that condition and agreeing to pay D £5 for each tyre sold by them in breach of it. S resold tyres at less than D's stipulated price but it was held that, there being no privity of contract between D and S, the action failed.

Manufacturers who turned from individual to collective enforcement of resale price maintenance, usually through their trade association, met with more success before the courts. (Such arrangements demonstrate both horizontal and vertical restrictive elements.)

> In *Ware and De Freville v Motor Trade Association* (1921), the defendant association of car manufacturers adopted a scheme and rules for maintaining fixed prices for their goods. Dealers

who departed from these prices had their names put on a 'stop list' and no member of the association was to supply them. An offender could, however, plead his case before a domestic tribunal and be allowed to pay a fine instead. The plaintiffs, who had been placed on the 'stop list', complained that all they wanted was to exercise their lawful freedom to deal in cars as they wished. The Court of Appeal held that the MTA arrangements were not unlawful.

Decisions such as this one and *Thorne v Motor Trade Association* (1937) were by now in line, in a new time of depression and difficult trading conditions, with an increasingly prevalent, *generally held* view – in government and business circles – that business people, bent on eliminating or minimising competition throughout British industry, knew their own interests best and should be free to pursue them. The courts, who earlier had failed to see the implications of their freedom of contract decisions, now actively supported the suppression of competition and encouraged the fixing of prices at artificially high levels by continuing adherence to the outworn legal concept. 'A principle which had originally been justified by the political economists was pursued by the courts to an extent which had no economic justification': Atiyah. (Resale price maintenance agreements are now almost entirely prohibited by competition policy legislation.)

Of the period discussed so far, Lord Diplock has written:

> By the end of the 19th century the common law had finally given its blessing to the cartel provided that its members were actuated by self-interest, and such legislation as was passed between the first and second World Wars was directed to encouraging the amalgamation of undertakings and the enforcement of restrictive trade practices in the depressed industries of agriculture and coal-mining. The economic theories upon which this legislation was based were reflected in the voluntary adoption of similar restrictions in a whole variety of other trades and industries ... by the beginning of World War II there were few domestic markets in goods and services in which free competition survived.

He continues:

> The change of economic theory in favour of unrestricted competition [not, however, in the public sector, vastly enlarged by the post-war nationalisation programme] which followed upon World War II was not something to which effect could have been given by the development of the common law. Judges are not economists and the judicial process is not suited to determining where the balance of economic advantage lies. This was a field in which if changes were to be brought about the only method was by legislation.

And so, on the basis of the presumption that 'the benefits of competition are no longer disputed, at least in the Western world', the regulation of monopolies, mergers and restrictive trade practices (both horizontal and vertical) has become an important part of government policy for the private sector of the economy, and the 1980s and 1990s privatisation programmes now follow the same path. So important is this trend that, in this and other countries, the courts have to a large extent been removed from the front line as law-makers and law-enforcers in this field. The common law doctrine of restraint of trade has largely given way to a statutory competition policy, the enforcement of which is the function of administrative bodies and a specially created Restrictive Practices Court. Competition policy and consumer protection are related areas in modern economic thinking.

Competition and consumer law are relatively new and growing subjects, each taking up ground previously occupied by contract law, whilst growing away from it as successive statutory measures seek to serve *the public interest* better than was the case under the old régime.

The statutory basis of competition policy was laid down in 1948 and 1956 and at the present time the Office of Fair Trading possesses wide regulatory powers under such statutes as the Restrictive Trade Practices Act 1976 (as amended) and the Competition Act 1980. Examination of these statutes is beyond our scope, except to say that under the 1976 Act, a variety of restrictive trading agreements (eg price-fixing agreements between suppliers of goods and most services) are, as regards proceedings before the Restrictive Practices Court, deemed to be *against the public interest* unless the parties can show that benefits flowing from the agreement (relating to price stability, quality, employment, public health, etc) outweigh the detriment to consumers.

Instead, we will move to a brief study of a particular form of restrictive business practice, exclusive dealing agreements, which will allow us to take note of their position in the UK, both under statute and in relation to a development in the common law restraint of trade doctrine, and under the competition law of the European Union.

Distribution systems

Although manufacturers (suppliers) of goods employ a variety of methods for distributing their products, we are here concerned with the regularly found method whereby a supplier sells his goods to intermediary distributors on the basis of a distribution agreement under which restrictions upon their trading activities are accepted by one or both parties.

Under a typical *exclusive* distribution agreement a supplier agrees to sell his products, for a fixed period and in relation to a defined area, only to the (exclusive) distributor. The distributor accepts that he will not sell any competing products and he will not sell the contract goods outside his territory (ie in the territory of another of the supplier's exclusive distributors). Such an agreement, it will be recalled, is of a vertical nature and it is restrictive not only as regards the trading activities of the parties but also of third parties (other distributors).

In the UK, such an exclusive dealing agreement is generally exempted from the provisions of the Restrictive Trade Practices Act 1976, so long as it is merely of a bilateral (two-party) nature, ie not based on a horizontal, collective arrangement between the suppliers in question. This was not a decision which met with general approval when originally taken in 1956, and in the European Union where the authorities are seeking to secure a single, common market for goods and services, exclusive distribution agreements which operate to partition that market along national frontiers are not allowed under European Community law. Exclusive national distributors in the Common Market cannot secure absolute territorial protection from competition by means of an agreement with their supplier.

At the international (European) level, Article 85 of the EC Treaty, which is directly effective law in this country, 'prohibits as incompatible with the common market all agreements between undertakings ... which may affect trade between member states and which have as their object or effect the ... distortion of competition'. Exemptions are allowed where the effect on competition is insignificant and where there are off-setting economic and other advantages. In the following case, the supplier (as is commonly found) had established a network of distribution agreements:

> In *Consten and Grundig v Commission* (1966), G, a German manufacturer of TV sets and tape recorders, etc., established an exclusive dealing network for the distribution of its products throughout the Common Market. In 1957 G appointed C as exclusive distributor in France. G agreed not to sell directly or indirectly to anyone else in France; G's other national distributors were bound not to sell outside their allotted territories – so they could not sell in France; and C agreed not to deal in competing products nor to sell outside France.

> UNEF and other French firms managed to import G's products through a 'back-door' into France and undercut C's prices. C sued these 'parallel importers' in French law for 'unfair competition' and the question of the exclusive distribution agreement's validity under Article 85 was raised.

> The European Court in Luxembourg decided against the agreement to the extent that its aim of securing absolute territorial protection for C against parallel imports partitioned the Common Market along national frontiers. The agreement adversely affected the free movement of goods between members states and distorted competition within the Common Market by giving rise to different prices for the same goods in the different member states.

As EC competition law has developed, it has become clear that exclusive distribution agreements concluded between a supplier (but not an association of suppliers) and a distributor in another member state are exempt from Article 85 so long as, in general terms, they do not provide for absolute territorial protection for the distributor; ie a distributor must be allowed (within limits) to sell outside his area. The supplier-distributor relationship is now controlled by EC Regulation 1983/83 which enables the parties to draft their agreements in such a way as to allow them in effect to self-certify exemption through compliance with the list of permitted clauses set out in the Regulation. (The exclusive distribution agreement is, in practical business terms, probably the most effective way for a supplier to get his goods on to a large market.)

The EC Commission and Court of Justice have also been called upon to rule on the position under Article 85 of a similar business operation designed, however, to facilitate the distribution of a supplier's products not across frontiers but merely *within a single Member State*. As such, these agreements would appear not to meet the requirement under Article 85 that trade *between* Member States may be affected. Several cases have concerned Belgian 'brewery contracts' and a further distinction between the agreements involved and ones such as that found in *Consten* and *Grundig* is that only the distributor is burdened with restrictions on his trading activities.

In the UK, a parallel development has occurred as the courts, in a number of cases since 1966, have applied the common law doctrine of restraint of trade to similar agreements operating as regards national distribution of petrol by oil companies through 'tied' distributional outlets. The common law doctrine was resorted to because, as we have seen, these agreements were exempted from the provisions of the Restrictive Trade Practices Act 1956. Section 8(3) of that Act stated, among other things, that agreements for the supply of goods between two persons in which the only restrictions accepted are those accepted by the party acquiring the goods in respect of the sale of other goods of the same description are exempt from registration and scrutiny by the Restrictive Practices Court (and see now the 1976 Act).

'Solus' petrol agreements fit this description, the garage or filling station operator agreeing not to sell the products of competing oil companies. There are clear economic advantages for both parties under such agreements. In a market dominated by a handful of suppliers, 'tying' contracts of a fixed duration enable oil companies to achieve continuity of sales through their established outlets; distributors gain access to loans for site development offered at favourable rates by their suppliers and they receive rebates on the wholesale price of petrol. Although from the nature of the business it is obvious that garage proprietors will not sell petrol outside their 'territory', a network of 'solus' agreements must give oil companies absolute territorial protection as regards their individual percentages of tied national market outlets at any particular time. In addition if, as was the case for UK retail petrol, over 90% of the outlets were tied in the 1960s and it was difficult to obtain planning permission for new sites, it could be argued that these barriers to entry into the market had an anti-competitive effect and, in EC terms, tended to separate the UK market (or any other member state market where similar conditions prevailed) from the rest of the Community. This point, however, has not been tested specifically in the courts, although guidance on the matter has been gradually forthcoming from Europe; particularly from the Belgian brewery cases and from an EC regulation of 1983, both of which are discussed below.

The leading national case on 'solus' petrol agreements was decided before we joined the Common Market:

In *Esso Petroleum Co Ltd v Harper's Garage (Stourport) Ltd* (1968), H owned two garages, A and B, both subject to 'solus' agreements with E. Under the garage A agreement, H agreed to purchase his total requirements of petrol from E and from no other source for four years and five months. He received 1¼ per gallon rebate from E on all petrol purchased. For garage B a similar undertaking was accepted, but the agreement was for 21 years. This was because the tie was part of a package deal under which, in return for a loan of £7,000, H mortgaged garage B to E, and the loan was to be repaid over 21 years and not earlier. After a time H began selling another type of petrol and when sued by E he pleaded that both agreements were in unreasonable restraint of trade and therefore void.

The House of Lords held that the 'solus' agreements were caught by the restraint of trade doctrine. (This particular question had not been addressed by the House of Lords previously.) They were therefore both *prima facie* void and required to be justified on the basis of their reasonableness (i) as between the parties and (ii) as regards the public interest. The four year tie on garage A was found to be reasonable and therefore binding; the 21-year tie on garage B was unreasonable and therefore void.

It was felt that the restrictions placed on distributors by such agreements should be no wider than was reasonably necessary to protect the legitimate interests of suppliers in facilitating distribution and ensuring continuity of sales over a number of years. However, there was no added advantage – except protection from competition – in a 21-year tie as opposed to a five-year tie. Whether the restraint is reasonable depends on the circumstances of each case, in particular upon the length of the tie. (The maximum, renewable, period was generally felt at the time to be no more than five years, as recommended by the Monopolies Commission in its Report on the Supply of Petrol in 1965, and no UK case law, statutory revision or administrative action since then has disturbed this assumption. However for 1983 EC developments, see below.)

It has rightly been said, however, that the public interest protected in such cases is narrowly conceived. No attempt is made to ensure that petrol suppliers compete with each other; the effect is merely to allow a particular distributor to opt out of his bargain where the length of tie exceeds five years. The court was fortunate in having the Monopolies Commission's analysis of the market in question to hand, although as regards a similar market (reported upon later by the Commission: Supply of Beer 1973), the House of Lords apparently felt that brewers' tied-house agreements were not subject to the restraint of trade doctrine for reasons that have not been squarely before the English courts in modern times.

'Brewery contracts' have, however, been the object of the attention of the European Court of Justice in the context of Article 85 EC and the case law makes an interesting comparison with that of the English courts in the petrol cases:

In *Brasserie de Haecht v Wilken Janssen* (1967), the plaintiff brewery made business loans to the defendant café proprietors, who agreed to obtain their requirements of beer and other beverages exclusively from the plaintiffs. When the café began selling another brewery's products, de Haecht sought to stop this breach of the agreement. In the Belgian court the defendants claimed that the 'brewery contract' was prohibited under Article 85 and was therefore unenforceable against them.

Although the agreement was between two Belgian undertakings, and any effect on inter-member state trade would appear to be insignificant and excusable, it was argued that such agreements must be viewed in their overall context. Approximately half such Belgian distributors were bound by exclusive purchasing contracts and the cumulative effect, it was argued for W, was to present a substantial barrier to foreign undertakings seeking to penetrate the Belgian market. (For example German brewers would be restricted or prevented from selling in Belgium in the same way as the Italian oil company AGIP was prevented from establishing itself in the UK petrol market where 90% of outlets were tied. However, it is easier to open a new café in Belgium than a new filling station in the UK.) In *de Haecht* this general argument was the basis of the contention that the individual agreement was, as a consequence of its economic and legal context, caught by Article 85 and therefore unenforceable against W.

The Belgian court requested a preliminary ruling from the European Court of Justice as to whether this argument was applicable. The court in Luxembourg ruled that while exclusive purchasing contracts do not *per se* infringe Article 85, they may do so: 'The existence of similar contracts is a circumstance which, together with other circumstances, can as a whole create the economic and legal context within which the contract must be weighed.' The Belgian court was saved from the need, following the ECJ's ruling, to conduct a depth inquiry into the national brewery sector by the EC Commission, which carried out its own investigation, and a later case, *Concordia Brewery* (1977), made it clear that national 'solus' contracts of the tied-house variety would normally be exempt from Article 85.

In 1983 the Commission issued a Regulation – binding and to apply uniformly throughout the Common Market – relating to both 'service-station agreements' and 'beer supply agreements'. It applies to agreements made after 1983; 'old' agreements coming gradually into line. Briefly, such agreements are exempt from Article 85 unless (a) in the case of petrol, the tie is for more than 10 years (although if the distributor is the supplier's tenant, the tie may be imposed for the duration of the period in which the distributor 'operates the premises'); (b) in the case of beer, the tie is again for more than 10 years. If the tie covers beer and other drinks, the maximum allowable tie is five years, and in either case the tenancy proviso similarly applies. Thus, the *Harper's Garage* decision should now be read in the light of this development from Brussels. The petrol Regulation provides that *stricter* provisions of national law than those found in the Regulation itself may be applied.

Although there are many other national and international factors that have a bearing on the level of competition and the pricing structure in the UK retail petrol trade and brewing sector, an examination of 'solus' agreements brings together consideration of the common law doctrine of restraint of trade and the competition policy of the EC. For decades the English courts, preoccupied with entrepreneurial freedom of contract and the right therefore of parties to restrain trade in the furtherance of their own particular interests, effectively disqualified themselves from examining the economic, social and political complexities of the public's interest in outlawing business practices of the kind discussed in this section. Or perhaps the judges believed that Adam Smith's 'invisible hand' was busy converting the parties' interests into the interests of the public at large.

Consideration of the public interest in the context of monopolies and restrictive business practices is now almost entirely in the hands of such bodies as the EC Commission, the Office of Fair Trading and the Monopolies and Mergers Commission. Regulation cannot ensure competition but it does attempt to secure the required preconditions.

Restraint of trade: sale of a business and employment contracts

The common law doctrine of restraint of trade, while failing to meet the challenge of restrictive trading agreements (noting, however, its relatively recently acquired jurisdiction as regards 'solus' petrol agreements), nevertheless continues to operate, as it has done since the 16th century, in other fields. Although, as seen, all contracts are to some extent in restraint of trade, there is somewhere a dividing line between normal commercial relations between parties (not covered by the doctrine) and situations (which are covered) where one party agrees with another that he will 'restrict his liberty in the future to carry on trade with other persons ... in such manner as he chooses'.

Most of the cases in these 'other fields' concern a contractual clause (covenant or promise) which prevents a person from working in a certain line of business or profession – subject usually to limitations of time and geographical area. The cases also usually concern one of two types of contract:

(i) *contracts for the sale of a business or practice* (including intangible assets such as goodwill), in which the *buyer* restrains the seller from setting up in immediate competition with him so drawing away customers or clients from the business sold;

(ii) *contracts of employment,* in which an *employer* similarly restrains his employee from competing with him (by setting up his own business or moving to a rival firm) on leaving his present job. These clauses and cases are not as economically significant as those discussed earlier (in the employment cases there is probably no strong union presence) but they are worthy of consideration.

Such clauses are presumed to be void and unenforceable (against a defaulting seller or employee) at common law. They are only enforceable if the court considers them to be *reasonable,* and (as seen in *Harper's Garage* above) the reasonableness of a clause is, according to Lord Macnaghten's re-statement of the law in *Nordenfelt v Maxim Nordenfelt Guns and Ammunition Co Ltd* (1894), to be assessed by reference to both the interests of the parties concerned and the public interest. As concerns the parties, the question is essentially one of personal freedom and fairness. In an employment case it was said that: 'it is difficult to see how any restraint in itself can ever be advantageous to [the employee]. The true meaning of the proposition that the restraint must be in the interests of both parties is [that the clause] is not a covenant against mere competition but is a covenant directed to securing a reasonable protection of the business interest of the employer, and in the circumstances is not unjust to the employee.'

As regards the *public interest* in the enforceability or otherwise of such restraints, the courts, as we have already observed, have usually concentrated on fairness between the parties. If the party imposing the restraint has proved it to be reasonable in that way, the second leg of Lord Macnaghten's test has tended to fall away. (Strong *statutory* competition policies, embracing social, economic and legal issues, are more capable of dealing with the public interest in 'an effective working of the economic system' or in 'effective competition', eg United States, EC and statutory UK policy.)

The inquiry into reasonableness therefore proceeds along the following lines (and working from the quotation above):

(a) The party imposing the restraint must not be seeking *merely* to protect himself from ordinary business competition, but must additionally be aiming to safeguard, in a manner which is no more than reasonably necessary, a legitimate *business interest* of a proprietary nature (eg the goodwill of the business bought – its standing, reputation and established custom; or trade secrets, confidential information and customer connections in the case of employees who leave their jobs; or, in the 'solus' agreement cases, the oil company's commercial interest in the maintenance of its network of outlets and continuity of petrol sales).

In ex-employee cases, the employer can protect his trade secrets and confidential information, to which the employee had access and knowledge, even though this to some extent prevents the ex-employee from using skill and knowledge of his own which he utilised during his former employment. The employer can also protect his customers or clientèle to the extent that the employee's former position, say as a representative, enabled him to gain sufficient influence over them to attract them later to his new firm.

(b) As between the parties, reasonable protection of the business interest involved usually raises questions relating to the *scope* of the restraint, its *geographical area* and its *duration*. First, a restraint must remain within the scope of, and the activities relating to, the interest which merits protection. For example, it cannot cover those who become customers of the firm *after* the employee leaves; a restraint in a tailor's contract against working as a milliner or hatter is unenforceable: *Attwood v Lamont* (1920); and a covenant by an employee of a company framed with the intention of protecting not only that company's business but also that of a subsidiary company, with which the employee had no connection, is again an unreasonable restraint.

An employer can restrain his employee from working in competition in the *area* from which his customers or clients come, but in some cases a more precise and selective 'solicitation covenant' (against soliciting the employer's customers or clients) is all that is reasonably required: *Gledhow Autoparts Ltd v Delaney* (1965). In any event an 'area covenant' must not be drawn wider than is necessary to protect the employer's interest (nor, as previously stated, cover products or processes with which the employer has no real connection or interest: see *Commercial Plastics Ltd v Vincent* (1965) below).

(c) The question of what is reasonable in terms of the length of time of a restraint depends very much, as in all these matters, on the facts of the individual case. Generally speaking, long restraints are only appropriate where a business's custom or clientèle is of a long standing, stable nature (eg a solicitor's) – but not where it is more of a fluctuating or passing nature.

(d) The relative bargaining strength of the parties has often been a factor in assessing fairness or reasonableness as between the parties (eg employer and employee with no union backing), as has, in some cases, the adequacy of the consideration flowing from the party imposing the restraint: *Schroeder Music Publishing Co Ltd v Macaulay* (1974).

(e) As already stated, judicial inquiries into the relationship between the operation of a restraint and the public interest have rarely played a part in the cases. If, as Lord Atkinson said in 1916 (see p 202), a balance is to be struck between liberty to trade and freedom of contract, it is probable that the nearer the parties are to equality of bargaining strength, the more likely the court will take them to be the best judges of their interest and, on this basis at least, will refrain from interfering with the restraint. The public's interest is taken to be in securing the liberty of the subject, not in general economic utility or 'effective competition' as it is under the statutory scheme of regulation. However: 'The difficulty with this view is that the requirement of public interest adds nothing to the requirement that the restraint be reasonable in the interests of the parties ... The two limbs of the traditional formula for assessing restraints [as laid down by Lord

Macnaghten] are then simply tautologous': Prentice. In *Harper's Garage*, the House of Lords did reassert (in a 'solus' agreement case) the need to inquire into the public interest.

Case law illustrations

(1)   Business transfer restraints

In *Nordenfelt v Maxim Nordenfelt Guns and Ammunition Co Ltd* (1894), N, an armaments manufacturer, sold his business to a company for £287,500 under a contract which restrained his future business activities. Later this company became M N Ltd and it engaged N as managing director. Under this contract, which contained a similar restraint, N agreed not to compete in the armaments business or in 'any business competing or liable to compete in any way with that for the time being carried on by the company' anywhere in the world for a period of 25 years.

The House of Lords held that, apart from the words quoted above, the restraint was valid. The business sold by N was an armaments firm with worldwide interests, but the part referring to 'any business competing or liable to compete' was clearly wider than reasonably necessary to protect the proprietary interest that the company had bought. The court was able to sever these words from the restraint and enforce the remainder (for 'severance' see below).

This decision reflects that the parties had relatively equal bargaining strength (buyer and seller dealt 'at arm's length'), and that a buyer of goodwill (lost if subject to unrestrained competition) can more easily restrain a seller's future activities than can an employer restrain an employee's future use of his skill and knowledge – which is partly his own and partly acquired. An employer must also show 'an exceptional proprietary interest' such as trade secrets.

In *British Reinforced Concrete Engineering Co Ltd v Schelff* (1921), BRC manufactured and sold BRC road reinforcements throughout the UK. S sold (but did not manufacture) 'Loop' reinforcements in part of the UK. S sold his business to BRC and covenanted that, for a certain period, he would not carry on a business or act as employee 'of any person concerned or interested in' the manufacture or sale of road reinforcements anywhere in the UK. S entered the employment of a road reinforcement company and BRC sued. It was held that the clause was too wide. It would have prevented S from becoming an employee of a company holding shares in a road reinforcement company. It was also too wide in *area* and as regards *activities* covered, S's firm not having manufactured reinforcements.

It should be recognised that contracts for the sale of a business which contain a 'non-competition' clause extending beyond the UK are also subject to scrutiny under Article 85 EC. In the German *Reuter/BASF* case (1976), the EC Commission adopted a similar approach to that taken by the common law. R, the seller, complained about an eight-year restraint which restricted him from engaging in research and manufacturing, etc in the relevant field and from divulging know-how to any third party The Commission decided that where a sale involves goodwill and know-how, a 'non-competition' clause is allowable provided it is necessary 'to secure to the buyer the transfer of the *full* value of the transferred undertaking' and does not 'exceed what is necessary for such preservation'. However, the restraint would be caught and declared void under Article 85(2), if it was excessive as regards (a) the *interest* to be protected (eg goodwill and know-how); (b) the *area* covered (the undertaking's actual or potential markets at the time of the sale); (c) its *duration* (being limited 'to the period required by an active competitive purchaser ... to take over undiminished the undertaking's market position as it was at the time of transfer'). The *Reuter* restraint was too wide; it extended to non-commercial research and was too long (more than five years). It restricted competition and reduced inter-Member State trade.

In the later Dutch case, *Nutricia* (1984), the following additional *guidelines* emerged: If only goodwill is sold, the period of the restraint should not normally exceed two years; if know-how is also transferred, the maximum period is likely to be four years. As regards territorial scope, potential markets (see above) are probably now to be excluded from the restraint.

(2) Employer-employee restraints

In *Commercial Plastics Ltd v Vincent* (1965), CP manufactured thin PVC calendered plastic sheeting for adhesive tape. Technical difficulties had been met and £200,000 spent on research, with precautions being taken to ensure the secrecy of new discoveries in this rapidly expanding field. CP's main competitors were all UK firms and the vast bulk of their sales were in the UK. V was employed as research and development co-ordinator and his contract contained a clause stating that he was 'not to seek employment with any of our competitors in the PVC calendering field for at least one year after leaving'. V left and joined a UK competitor. CP sued for an injunction to restrain V from taking up this employment. It was held that (i) CP had an interest, which could be protected, in confidential coded information to which V had regularly had access (even if it was impossible for him to remember its detailed nature); however (ii) the clause was too wide, extending to the whole calendering field, not merely to adhesive tape, and, being worldwide, was wider than necessary to protect CP against their actual competitors. The clause was unreasonable and therefore unenforceable.

Kores Mftg Co Ltd v Kolok Mftg Co Ltd (1959) raised the question of an indirect restraint by which K and K, who manufactured similar products, agreed that neither would employ any employee who had been employed by the other over the preceding five years. In this action against Kolok for breach of the agreement, it was held that (i) there were trade secrets which merited protection but (ii) the covenant was too wide, covering all employees whether they knew trade secrets or not, and it was too long in its duration. (It has since been said, in the House of Lords, that this agreement should have been attacked on public interest grounds.) A so-called attempt to 'protect labour supplies' was in fact an indiscriminate attempt to prevent workers moving to higher paid jobs, and to do indirectly what could not be done by direct covenant with individual employees. Public policy cannot allow third parties to restrict by contract a person's freedom to work for whom he will.

(3)　　Restraints on professional sportsmen and women and entertainers

In *Eastham v Newcastle United Football Club Ltd and Others* (1964), E, a top-class footballer, had a contract with the first defendants, but wished to move to another club. However, under the then current rules of the Football Association and the Football League, a 'retain and transfer' system operated under which a player 'retained' by his club at the end of the football season was prevented from joining another club unless he obtained the consent of the retaining club.

E sought a declaration (the only remedy available) against the Newcastle club, the Football Association and the Football League that the 'retain and transfer' system was in unreasonable restraint of trade. He had no contract with the second and third defendants (cf the position in the *Mogul Steamship* case above).

Wilberforce J could find no legitimate interest worthy of protection in this case (the system was, it was claimed, designed to prevent rich clubs poaching the best players from small clubs) and in any event the system was in restraint of trade: 'the court has jurisdiction to grant a declaratory judgment, not only against the employer who is in contractual relationship with the employee, but also against the association of employers whose rules or regulations place an unjustifiable restraint on his liberty of employment.' (Cf the *Kolok* case.)

Although the declaration in *Eastham* did not require the defendants to take any action, the Football Association and the Football League did alter the transfer system as a result; see also the cricket case of *Greig v Insole* (1978). At the time of writing, the European Court of Justice has been asked for a preliminary ruling by a Belgian court in Case C–415/93 *Bosman* regarding the Belgian FA transfer rules and national and UEFA (European) regulations which restrict the access of foreign players from EC countries to their football competitions. The action has been brought under Article 48 of the Treaty (free movement of workers across frontiers) and Articles 85 and 86 (competition rules applying to companies and associations of companies).

The final case is important as regards the application of the restraint doctrine to a contract in which there was a patent inequality of bargaining power. The House of Lords also laid emphasis on the 'public interest' element of the doctrine:

In *Schroeder Music Publishing Co Ltd v Macaulay* (1974), M, a young and unknown writer of pop songs, signed SMP's standard form contract, under the terms of which he assigned to SMP the world copyright in any compositions produced by him for five years. SMP did not undertake to use his work to advantage but if they did they would pay him royalties on the returns. If the royalties reached a total of £5,000, the contract was automatically extended for a further five years. SMP could terminate the agreement by giving a month's notice but there was no provision for determination by M.

Their Lordships held that such an agreement was covered by the restraint of trade doctrine and the agreement in question was unreasonable since its terms combined a total commitment by M with an almost complete lack of obligation on the part of SMP. As a result M, who had achieved considerable success, was able to escape from the contract.

Severance

As a general rule, the presence of an unreasonable, void and unenforceable restraint within a contract does not affect the validity of the rest of the agreement. In addition, as we have seen in the *Nordenfelt* case, the court has the power to sever 'bad' parts of a restraint clause from the 'good', enforcing only the latter: 'the promise remains in the contract shorn of its offending parts and so reduced in extent.' For *severance* to operate therefore, it would seem that it must be possible to construe the restraint (or promise) as being divisible into a number of separate and independent parts. Cutting out, or putting a 'blue pencil' through, the unreasonable parts must leave the promise, it is argued, substantially the same in character as when originally framed by the parties – though now reduced to reasonable proportions.

Alternatively, where the restraint cannot properly be seen as falling into distinct parts, its 'indivisibility' means that it can only be rendered reasonable by amendment rather than severance. This is a task – rewriting the parties' agreement – that the courts say they will not undertake. However, it is not difficult to find cases where these tests or principles of construction have produced decisions that are difficult to reconcile, eg *Attwood v Lamont* (1920), with severance not applied to a seemingly divisible clause, and *Goldsoll v Goldman* (1915) where, with a similar type of clause, severance was undertaken. Several sources suggest that in these situations the courts are mainly influenced by other factors: eg a very oppressive clause will not be reduced in its extent but merely declared void; severance will not be readily applied to employee restraints where bargaining strength does not approximate to equality (*Attwood v Lamont*); with business sale restraints, the courts, conscious that the purchaser should get what he has paid for, ie material *and* intangible assets (goodwill), are more ready to tailor a restraint and enforce it against the seller.

References and further reading

Bryan, 'Restraint of trade: back to a basic analysis' (1980) JBL 326.

Davies, 'Post-employment restraints: some recent developments' (1982) JBL 490.

Furmston, *Cheshire, Fifoot and Furmston's Law of Contract*, ch 12(1)(3) 'Contracts in restraint of trade'.

Hacker, 'Exclusive distribution agreements and EEC Law I and II' (1978) NLJ 14 September at 907, and 12 October at 1005.

Heydon (1971), *The Restraint of Trade Doctrine*.

Wyatt, 'Restraint of trade, tied houses and 'Solus' agreements' (1974) NLJ 14 March at 243.

Whish (1993), *Competition Law*, ch 2 'Common Law' (and see also the coverage of exclusive distribution agreements and 'solus' agreements).

Questions

(1) 'By far the most serious failure of the classical model of contract was its inability to offer any contribution to the problems raised by monopolies and restrictive agreements': Atiyah. Discuss.

(2) In order to ensure that its petrol and allied products will be sold exclusively in certain garages and filling stations, Finesse Petroleum Co Ltd includes 'ties' to that effect for a period of six years in the mortgages, leases and supply agreements it has with these retail outlets. A competing oil company, NIOC Ltd, offers Brown, the owner of one of the garages, an interest-free loan of £30,000 if he will break his 'tie' with Finesse and commence exclusive selling of its products. Brown, who urgently needs money for site development, is keen to accept NIOC's offer. Explain to Brown the legal developments in this field since 1968 as they relate to his position.

(3) Carefully examine the decision in *Shell (UK) Ltd v Lostock Garage Ltd* (1977) and be prepared to discuss the issues raised and the answers provided by the Court of Appeal.

(4) (a) What are the main points which, for a contract lawyer, distinguish exclusive distributorship agreements from exclusive agency agreements?

(b) *Consten and Grundig* is an example of a 'closed' exclusive distributorship agreement; in *LTM v MBU* (1966), the European Court examined the effects on competition of 'open' agreements.

What are 'closed' and 'open' agreements? (See article by Hacker in References and further reading.)

(5) (a) What was the nature of the 'public interest' in the *Nordenfelt* case?

(b) Edward purchased the Royal Hotel from George in August 1994. As a condition of purchase George covenanted that he would not 'for a period of two years from the date of transfer of ownership engage, either directly or indirectly, in the business of hotelier or restaurateur within ten miles of the Royal Hotel'. Edward has now heard a rumour that George is going to put his money into a guest house eight miles from the hotel.

Six months ago Edward engaged Charles as a trainee barman to work in the cocktail bar of the hotel. This bar, which serves a wide range of unusual cocktails, is very popular with members of the general public as well as the hotel guests and those dining at the hotel's restaurant. On entering Edward's employ, Charles agreed that he would not 'work as a barman in any hotel, restaurant, club or public house within two miles for a period of one year' after the termination of his employment. Charles' cousin, who owns a local public house, has offered him a job.

Advise Edward as to whether he can enforce the restraints against George and Charles.

(6) In *Littlewoods Organisation Ltd v Harris* (1978), Megaw LJ, when examining a restraint clause, said that its reasonableness was 'not a question of severance but it is a question of construction'.

(a) In what way did he construe the clause?

(b) What was Browne LJ's reaction to this approach?

(c) Does the majority's 'construction' approach accord with principles laid down in *Liverpool City Council v Irwin* (1977)?

(d) What was the nature of the protected interest in this case?

(e) As a result of this decision Mr Harris was not allowed to work for GUS for 12 months. Was this fair?

12 Frustration of contract and 'force majeure' clauses

Although the vast majority of business agreements proceed to satisfactory completion, some commercial ventures may be thwarted, not by breach of contract, but by events beyond the parties' control which overtake their agreement and render its performance impossible or illegal or, although physically possible, futile in the sense that its object has been wholly defeated. As Friedmann has pointed out (see Chapter 4): 'The economic security aspect of contract ... is increasingly affected by the spread of such political, economic and social upheavals as war, revolution or inflation. Its legal result is the doctrine of frustration of contract, with its consequent extension of the legal excuses for the non-performance of contract.' By 'legal excuse', Friedmann means that both parties, where the contract is frustrated, are no longer bound from the moment of frustration, ie from that moment the contract is void.

Frustration cases usually come before the courts in situations where, despite a party's plea that events occurring subsequent to agreement, and over which he had no control, have defeated the venture, the other party contests that claim and, in the face of non-performance, he sues for breach.

Litigation is, expensive and time-consuming and prudent business people, particularly those operating in international markets susceptible to 'upheavals', have long appreciated the wisdom of 'drafting out' frustration by means of an appropriate clause in the contract itself. Such clauses are, as we have already noted (see clause 12 of the Ruritanian Bus Contract in Chapter 3), known, among other things, as 'force majeure' clauses. In general terms such clauses stipulate what is to be the effect of certain contingencies which affect performance. For example, in export sales contracts, delay through strikes may be a problem. An appropriate clause will allow for the suspension of performance for a reasonable period of time followed by a right to bring the contract to an end if the delay persists.

Whether the contract is terminated by frustration or by agreement – through the operation of a 'force majeure' clause – a question often remains as regards a fair adjustment of the financial position that then exists between the parties to a partially performed but now abortive venture. This and other relevant matters will now be examined more closely.

The doctrine of frustration of contract

In line with their role as upholders of contracts, and so as not to allow parties to escape from their obligations without good cause, the courts have said that: 'Frustration is a doctrine only too often invoked by a party to a contract who finds performance difficult or unprofitable, but it is very rarely relied on with success. It is, in fact, a kind of last ditch, and ... is a conclusion which should be reached rarely and with reluctance'. The judges have therefore kept the doctrine within strict limits since it was first introduced over 100 years ago, just as they have similarly curtailed the doctrine of mistake in so far as it relates to a pre-existing impossibility of performing a contract, see p 193 and the case of *Amalgamated Investment & Property Co Ltd v John Walker & Sons Ltd* (1977).

In 1956 in the *Davis Contractors* case (see below), Lord Radcliffe said that:

> ... frustration occurs whenever the law recognizes that without default of either party a contractual obligation has become incapable of being performed because the circumstances in which performance is called would render it a thing radically different from that which was undertaken by the contract ... The court must act upon a general impression of what its rule requires ... But, even so, it is not hardship or inconvenience or material loss itself which calls the principle of frustration into play. There must be as well such a change in the significance of the obligation that the thing undertaken would, if performed, be a different thing from that contracted for.

In 1981, in *National Carriers Ltd v Panalpina (Northern) Ltd*, the House of Lords upheld Lord Radcliffe's 'radical change in the obligation' test, which was restated by Lord Simon as follows:

> Frustration of a contract takes place when there supervenes an event (without default of either party and for which the contract makes no sufficient provision) which so significantly changes the nature (not merely the expense or onerousness) of the outstanding contractual rights and/or obligations from what the parties could reasonably have contemplated at the time of its execution that it would be unjust to hold them to the literal sense of its stipulations in the new circumstances; in such a case the law declares both parties to be discharged from further performance.

The cases can generally be explained by establishing what, in a Gurvitch 'rapprochement' sense, is the basic obligation underlying the common venture. Only if this basic obligation is displaced has the contract been frustrated. In the words of Lord Sumner in 1926: 'It is the common object that has to be frustrated, not merely the individual advantage that one party or the other might have gained from the contract.' It is clear therefore that, in large part, the judiciary take a hard line (in Adams and Brownsword terms, a market-individualist line) when it comes to frustration pleas and relief from an unfavourable bargain. Frustration as a defence was first to be found in the following case:

In *Taylor v Caldwell* (1863), C agreed on 27 May to let T have the use of the Surrey Music Hall at £100 per day for four concerts, the first to be held on 17 June. On 11 June the hall was accidentally burnt down and the parties had made no provision in the contract for such a contingency. T claimed damages in respect of wasted advertising expenses. It was held that the contract was discharged by frustration and C was not liable.

In this case, which, as stated, saw the introduction of the general principle, Blackburn J said:

> Where, from the nature of the contract, it appears that the parties must from the beginning have known that it could not be fulfilled unless ... some particular specified thing continued to exist, so that, when entering into the contract, they must have contemplated such continuing existence as the foundation of what was to be done; there ... the parties shall be excused in case, before breach, performance becomes impossible from the perishing of the thing without the fault of the contractor.

The vast majority of frustration cases are not as clear-cut as the one involving the Surrey Music Hall. They frequently concern not physical impossibility, but pleas of commercial futility brought about by a wide variety of political, economic or other disabling factors. In one of the 'coronation cases', *Krell v Henry* (1903), H hired rooms in Pall Mall at a high price for the purpose of viewing the coronation procession of Edward VII. The procession was cancelled owing to the King's illness but K sued for the hire charge. The court held that the contract had been frustrated; it was therefore void and the claim failed: 'It is the coronation procession and the relative position of the rooms which is the basis of the contract.'

However, in another 'coronation case', *Herne Bay Steam Boat Co v Hutton* (1903), the hire of a boat by H for the purpose of carrying passengers at high prices to see the royal naval review and for a day's cruise round the fleet at Spithead was held not to be frustrated when the review was cancelled, because the royal review was not the basis of the contract. As Sir Frederick Pollock said: 'In point of fact the fleet was still there and it was very well worth seeing without the review.'

Alternatively, Brownsword argues that Hutton's problem was merely that insufficient people were willing to pay high prices for the trip: 'following *Davis Contractors Ltd v Fareham UDC*, it is now settled that a plea of frustration cannot succeed on grounds of purely economic loss; and, with the benefit of hindsight, it is clear that this was the sole basis for Hutton's argument.' It should also be noted that *Krell v Henry*, although itself justifiable, has not in any way established a firm 'frustration of purpose' principle. For example, in *Amalgamated Investment & Property Co Ltd v John Walker & Sons Ltd* (1977), it was held that a contract for the purchase of property for redevelopment at a cost of £1,710,000 was not frustrated when, shortly after the contract was made, the building in question, an old whisky warehouse, was listed by the Department of Environment as being of special architectural or historic interest. The effect of the listing was to make the redevelopment more difficult or impossible and the market value of the property was cut to £210,000.

It is now clear that the doctrine of frustration will not be invoked to allow a party to escape from a contract, the basic obligation of which has not been displaced but which has merely become a bad bargain for him:

> In *Davis Contractors Ltd v Fareham UDC* (1956), D in effect agreed to build F 78 houses in eight months for £92,000. Serious shortages of labour and materials resulted in the contract taking 22 months to complete and costing D £18,000 more than estimated. D (the plaintiff) contended that the contract had been frustrated and consequently he was not bound by the agreed price. He claimed a larger sum on a fair reward for services rendered ('quantum meruit') basis. The House of Lords held that (i) a letter stating that D's tender was subject to adequate supplies of labour and materials was not part of the contract; (ii) the delay caused did not mean that the basis of the contract was displaced. Lord Radcliffe stated that: 'There must be as well [as mere hardship or inconvenience to one of the parties] such a change in the significance of the obligation that the thing undertaken would ... be a different thing from that contracted for.' The thing contracted for was 78 houses; these had been built. In the circumstances, the risk fell upon the builder.

In a number of export sales cases arising out of the closure of the Suez Canal in 1956, it was held that the basis of the contract was the continuing possibility of sale and delivery of the goods and not merely *the way* in which the seller was to carry out this basic obligation:

> In *Tsakiroglou & Co Ltd v Noblee Thorl GmbH* (1962), T in Port Sudan agreed to ship groundnuts to N in Hamburg under a cif contract. Shipment was to be made during November/December 1956 but no delivery date was named. Following the closure of the Suez Canal in early November, T made no effort to ship the goods and, when sued for damages, pleaded frustration. It was held that the closure of the canal did not fundamentally transmute the contractual obligation into one of a different character. The thing undertaken was still the same, ie the shipment of goods from Port Sudan to Hamburg, albeit under the changed circumstances, by a lengthier and more expensive voyage round the Cape of Good Hope. T was liable to pay £5,600 damages to N for breach of contract. It has been said that it would require 'very strong facts (such as, perhaps, a contract to carry perishable goods from Port Sudan to Alexandria and the subsequent closure of the Canal)' to bring about frustration in such a case.

Delay is frequently a factor in frustration cases; for example goods cannot be shipped on time because flooding prevents them reaching the port of loading, a strike holds up their movement, or the government requisitions vessels suitable for their carriage. Delay frustrates a contract when, but only when, it defeats the commercial venture: 'Whether or not the delay is such as to bring about frustration must be a question to be determined by an informed judgment based upon all the evidence of what has occurred and what is likely thereafter to occur': Lord Roskill in *The Nema* (1981).

In *Tamplin SS Co Ltd v Anglo-Mexican Petroleum Co Ltd* (1916), a five-year charter signed in December 1912 was disrupted when the government requisitioned the vessel for war service in February 1915. The majority of the court felt that it seemed likely *at that point* that the vessel would be released in time to render further substantial services under the contract – which, on that basis, was not frustrated. (The war did not end until 1918 so the court's 'informed judgment' as to the probable length of the requisition was wide of the mark. This situation may be compared to that in *Hong Kong Fir*, a case of alleged 'frustration through breach'. In that case, as well as delay already occasioned, the court had to speculate on the period of further unseaworthiness (after the contract had been brought to an end by the charterers), steps having been taken by the owners to repair the vessel and secure new engine-room staff.)

However, in *Metropolitan Water Board v Dick, Kerr & Co Ltd* (1918), DK agreed in 1914 to build a reservoir at Staines for M. The work was to be completed in six years, subject to an extension of time for 'difficulties, impediments or obstructions howsoever occasioned'. In 1916 the Ministry of Munitions ordered the work to stop and DK to sell all disposable plant. It was held that the interruption created by the statutory order was of such a character and probable duration as to make the contract, if resumed, a different contract from that entered into. The extension of time clause was interpreted as covering only non-frustrating delays and the contract was discharged.

Thus, where indefinite delay, as opposed to temporary interruption, is all that can be envisaged for the parties from the time of the intervening act then the contract is discharged by frustration. It is not a case that the contract is definitely impossible to perform some time in the future (eg when peace is restored) but that, in the circumstances, it is not reasonable to hold the parties to their obligations.

The discharge of a contract through supervening *illegality* is explained by public policy and not by physical impossibility or even a radical change from the original obligation: 'There cannot be default in not doing what the law forbids to be done.' In *Fibrosa Spolka v Fairbairn etc Ltd* (1943) the export of textile machinery to Lithuania via the port of Gdynia was held to be frustrated by the occupation of that port by German troops in September 1939. It is also to be borne in mind that parties cannot 'contract out' of the operation of the doctrine of frustration in cases of illegality.

It was decided by the *House of Lords in National Carriers Ltd v Panalpina (Northern) Ltd* (1981) that the doctrine of frustration could apply to leases. There has been controversy on this point for many years. It will, however, be a 'rare event', applying most probably where the lease is short-term: to give Treitel's example (quoted with approval by Lord Hailsham), 'where a holiday cottage which has been rented for a month is burnt down' (cf *Taylor v Caldwell* where the property was taken under a licence not a lease). A tenant is more interested in the use and occupation of the land than the legal estate that the contract creates, which, it is sometimes argued, cannot be frustrated. However, a long-term lease is more speculative, the parties taking the risk of supervening events which, although interrupting the commercial purpose for a time (say, when building on the land is prevented by government order or premises are 'sealed off' by road closures on local authority orders) will, when they come to an end, allow that purpose to be resumed for the substantial portion of the lease.

Limitations on the doctrine

(1) The doctrine does not apply in situations where (as seen) the alleged frustrating event does not displace the basic obligation of the contract but merely makes its performance more onerous or expensive (less profitable) for one party.

It is generally a supplier of goods or services, as opposed to the party paying for them, who pleads frustration. The 'displacement' rule strictly limits a debtor's rights under the doctrine – it would seem that parties with an obligation to pay, and who have not guarded against the contingency, cannot plead inflationary effects as a frustrating event, although it may be that hyper-inflation or 'market fracture' could bring about this result: see *Staffordshire Area Health Authority v South Staffordshire Waterworks Co* (1978), a fixed-price contract not frustrated by inflation. The contract was of indefinite duration and over a period of 76 years the price had risen to 18 times the contract price. It was held that the contract could be terminated by the implication of a term regarding reasonable notice.

(2) The doctrine does not apply where the alleged frustrating event is the result of a party's own voluntary act or negligence. In *The Eugenia* (1964) it was stated that a charterer who ordered the vessel into a war zone, with the result that she was detained, could not rely on the detention as the basis for frustration – the detention was due to the charterer's prior action, which was a breach of contract and an instance of 'self-induced frustration'.

The leading case on 'self-induced frustration' is *Maritime National Fish Ltd v Ocean Trawlers Ltd* (1935), a Privy Council decision:

> OT operated five trawlers for fishing with otter trawls. Three of the trawlers were owned by OT and of the other two, one was chartered from the plaintiffs MNF. In order to use the otter trawls a licence was required from the Canadian government and as a result of a change in government policy, OT was granted only three licences. They allocated two to their own vessels and one to the chartered vessel *not* owned by MNF. OT argued that the charter of MNF's vessel was frustrated.

> This claim was rejected; the frustration was 'self-induced': 'it was this act and election of [OT] which prevented the *St Cuthbert* from being licensed for fishing with an otter trawl' – rather than the action of the government. OT could have allocated one of the three licences to the *St Cuthbert* rather than to one of their own vessels. The supervening event was not beyond their control and so did not frustrate the contract.

In this case, OT need not have broken any contract (charterparty); in *The Super Servant Two (Lauritzen AS v Wijsmuller BV)* (1990) a shipowner lost one of his two vessels capable of transporting oil drilling rigs. This meant that a contract for the transportation of the plaintiff's rig from Japan to Rotterdam could not be

225

performed because the defendant's other vessel had been contracted to other duties. The defendants claimed that the contract was frustrated but the plaintiffs argued that the impossibility sprang from the defendant's own decision regarding their 'election' to use their remaining vessel on other work. The Court of Appeal held that although the defendants were neither negligent nor in breach of contract as regards their allocation of duties, there was no frustration.

It would appear to be generally agreed that this was a harsh decision and Treitel, a leading critic, has argued that 'where a party has entered into a number of contracts, supervening events may deprive him of the power of performing them all, without depriving him of the power of performing some of them ... It is submitted that frustration should not be excluded by a party's "election" where his only choice was which of two contracts to frustrate'. The court, however, also ruled that a 'force majeure' clause in the contract applied to exclude frustration, provided the vessel had not been lost as a result of the defendant's negligence.

In *Constantine (Joseph) SS Line Ltd v Imperial Smelting Corpn Ltd* (1942), an explosion in a ship's boiler made completion of a charterparty impossible. However, as the charterers were unable to prove that the explosion was caused by the owner's negligence, but could have been caused by some other reasons not the fault of the owners, the defence of frustration was successful to relieve the owners from liability.

(3) The doctrine will not apply where the parties have clearly foreseen the precise risk but have nevertheless gambled on its non-occurrence: for an inadvertent example of this, see *Davis Contractors* above. This limitation appears to operate between narrow bounds: for example, the fact that the parties foresee and provide for a possible delay does not prevent frustration if the delay which actually occurs is of a totally different order of magnitude which was not foreseen: see the *Metropolitan Water Board* case. Also, where the contract is discharged through illegality as a matter of public policy, foreseeability, say of war, does not prevent frustration if to allow continuance of the contract would, as seen in the *Fibrosa Spolka* case, involve giving assistance to an enemy economy.

(4) The doctrine does not apply (except to the extent noted above) where the parties have made express provision for the event which occurs. Here the contract will govern the position, and this situation will be discussed below.

Contracts, allocation of risk and frustration

In this section we will view some of the points already made from a different perspective: 'One who makes a contract never can be absolutely certain that he will be able to perform it when the time comes, and the very essence of it is that he takes the risk within the limits of his undertaking ... when the scope of the undertaking is fixed, that is merely another way of saying that the contractor takes the risk of the obstacles to that extent': Holmes J. For example, a seller who needs an export licence in order to ship goods assumes a greater risk if he agrees to 'deliver as soon as licence granted' (interpreted as an absolute undertaking) than if he agrees to 'deliver subject to licence' (a conditional obligation). In the first instance if he fails to get a licence he will be liable in damages for the buyer's lost expectations; in the second if he fails after reasonable efforts to obtain a licence he will not be liable.

Where the parties expressly allocate risk (and therefore loss) in this way to one or the other of them, or apportion it between them, their agreed terms will govern the situation if the contingency arises: the doctrine of frustration is properly limited to contingencies not specifically provided for in the contract. In a similar vein, Lord Wilberforce, outlining the policy behind the Unfair Contract Terms Act, said that 'in commercial matters generally, where the parties are not of unequal bargaining power, and where risks are normally borne by insurance, not only is the case for judicial intervention undemonstrated, but there is everything to be said ... for leaving the parties free to apportion the risks as they think fit and for respecting their decision'.

A party is generally taken to assume the risks consequent upon 'normal' (eg the seller in *Tsakiroglou*) or 'foreseeable' (eg the builder in *Davis Contractors*) changes in circumstances (the need to send the goods by a different route in the first case and the shortages of labour and materials in the second). The onset of such risks does not frustrate the contract and excuse the party concerned. What is 'normal' or 'foreseeable' is a question of degree. A party can protect himself from such contingencies: as we saw in Chapter 3 a cif seller agrees to arrange freight and marine insurance cover for the buyer; he pays for these services and builds their cost into his selling price. An increase in freight charges is at his risk. After the 1956 closure of the Suez Canal, sellers began to stipulate for a 'Cape Surcharge' to be paid by the buyer if the Canal was closed again – as it was in 1967, see *Henry Ltd v Clasen* (1973). Similarly, Davis Contractors were in a position to (and had tried to) protect themselves by their letter stating that their tender was subject to adequate supplies of labour and materials being available, or by the use of price fluctuation and extension of time clauses.

If the change in circumstances does make performance fundamentally different in a commercial sense (ie sufficient to allow the doctrine of frustration to apply), but the parties have nevertheless properly provided for the contingency (supervening event) which has arisen, then, again, their agreed terms will govern the situation: see s 2(3) of the Law Reform (Frustrated Contracts) Act 1943 and the discussion of 'force majeure' and 'hardship' clauses below.

It is apparent, therefore, that a 'force majeure' clause, which generally operates on the basis of first suspending performance for an agreed period of time, followed by, if necessary, a right to exercise an option to cancel the contract, can be invoked on the occurrence of a contingency which might or might not call for frustration in the legal sense. The risk, or loss contingent upon invoking the clause, may again be allocated by the parties under the terms of the clause, whether the contract is cancelled or not: eg 'Buyers shall have no claim against Sellers for delay or non-shipment under this clause.' (A discussion of the nature and range of insurance available to contractors from commercial companies and government sources as cover against loss in respect of risks of a commercial, political and economic nature is beyond the scope of this book: see, for example, for the insurance facilities offered to exporters by the Export Credits Guarantee Department, *Schmitthoff's Export Trade*, Chapter 25.)

A 'hardship' clause serves a different purpose from a 'force majeure' clause and operates in the context of long-term contracts (eg the construction of works, or crude oil or natural gas supply). In the face of fundamental changes in circumstances not foreseen – at least to the degree encountered – and, not wishing to bring the contract to an end either by invoking a 'force majeure' clause or by litigation involving a plea of frustration, the parties on the contrary wish to continue with the contract. The most effective way of doing this, English courts having no power to adapt the terms of long-term contracts in such situations, is for the parties to re-negotiate their contract under the terms of the 'hardship' clause so as to minimise losses and avoid undue hardship. 'Businessmen often prefer to modify rather than to terminate their arrangements in the face of disruptions of trade. They choose to increase or decrease their contract price ... or alter the quality of their performance because part-performance is usually better than non-performance. They modify their promises because salvaging segments of a contract is preferable to salvaging no segments at all': Trakman.

Even where the contract is brought to an end by the operation of the doctrine of frustration, the aim of the law is to allocate or distribute the loss brought about by the supervening event. The Law Reform (Frustrated Contracts) Act 1943, improving on earlier common law rules, now governs the position. The court's decision that a frustrating event took place means that *from the time of frustration* the contract is automatically brought to an end. What was a binding contract has become void and the parties are excused from further performance by operation of law. However, in the period during which the contract subsisted, ie between agreement and the time of the frustrating event, work may have been undertaken, expenses incurred, and advance payments made. The Act seeks to achieve a just settlement between the parties in the circumstances; it does not apply to all contracts and, as stated above, it can be excluded by contrary agreement: s 2(3).

The Act covers four main points:

(a) Money *paid* before the frustrating event is recoverable, whether the failure of consideration (performance) is total or partial.

(b) Money *payable* before the frustrating event, but not in fact paid, ceases to be payable.

(c)   A party who has incurred *expenses* in performance of the contract prior to its discharge may, at the court's discretion, be awarded those expenses up to a maximum of *sums paid or payable to him* under the contract before the frustrating event. In exercising this discretion, the court (or, more likely in practice, an arbitrator) can split the loss in such proportion as it thinks just. The court will be influenced by the extent to which the expenses have been rendered useless following frustration; very little will be awarded if the expenses have been incurred in manufacturing machinery for X which can readily be sold to Y.

These points are governed by s 1(2), and under s 1(3):

(d)   A party who has gained a *valuable benefit* (not money) under the contract before the frustrating event may be required to pay a just sum for it: see the decision of Robert Goff J in *BP Exploration Co (Libya) Ltd v Hunt* (1979), affirmed on appeal, in which it was stated that 'the fundamental principle underlying the Act itself is prevention of the unjust enrichment of either party to the contract at the other's expense'.

The Act does not apply to voyage charterparties and other contracts for the carriage of goods by sea, contracts of insurance and certain contracts for the sale of goods where the goods have perished. In this way, well-established applicable common law or statutory rules are preserved, eg freight paid in advance cannot be recovered if the goods are lost, and the Sale of Goods Act provides that an agreement to sell *specific* goods is avoided if the goods perish without any fault on the part of the seller or buyer *before* the risk has passed to the latter.

'Force majeure' clauses

In *The Eugenia* (1964), Lord Denning said: 'To see if the doctrine [of frustration] applies, you have first to construe the contract and see whether the parties have themselves provided for the situation that has arisen. If they have provided for it, the contract must govern. There is no frustration.' (We have already noted that a 'force majeure' clause will not take effect in cases of supervening illegality, or, as Lord Denning implies, where it is incomplete or narrowly construed as in the *Metropolitan Water Board* case. Also the parties may, as we shall see, fail to implement terms within the clause, say as to notice, in the correct manner.)

The application of the doctrine of frustration to an event which has occurred and which is now the subject matter of litigation rests, of course, in the hands of the courts and it is often a difficult question as to whether the doctrine does or does not apply. Therefore the prudent business person may well consider it wiser to introduce into his contracts a clause defining *in advance* the rights and duties of the parties if certain events beyond their control occur, *whether or not* such events would result, in legal terms, in frustration of the contract. Such a clause is generally known as a 'force majeure' clause and it is the prime example of what Macaulay describes as planning for contingencies. (See Chapter 2 and clause 12 of the Ruritanian Bus Contract in Chapter 3.)

'Force majeure' events are events which are beyond the control of the parties and the expression has been judicially defined to cover 'all circumstances beyond the will of man, and which it is not in his power to control, and such "force majeure" is sufficient to justify the non-execution of a contract. Thus war, inundations and epidemics are cases of "force majeure" and also the strikes of workmen.' Thus, in general terms, the occurrence of a 'force majeure' event brings the clause into operation and, in accordance with its terms, the contract is suspended or discharged by agreement. A party who has no 'force majeure' protection can find himself in the position of not being able to fulfil his contract, and in an action against him for breach can find that the court rejects his plea of frustration. He will then have to pay damages to the plaintiff.

Although the wording of these clauses varies according to the nature of the contract, as regards contracts for the international sale of goods they usually take the following form:

(1) A list of possible 'force majeure' events capable of impeding or preventing performance, together with a 'sweeping up' phrase designed to ensure that there are no gaps in the formula. For example:

> Strikes, lockouts, labour disturbances, anomalous working conditions, accident to machinery, delays en route, policies or restrictions of governments, including restrictions of export and other licences, or any other contingency whatsoever beyond seller's control, including war, to be sufficient excuse for any delay or non-fulfillment traceable to any of these causes.

(2) Provision on the occurrence of a 'force majeure' event for the parties to suspend or cancel the contract depending on the circumstances. The parties are usually under a duty to keep each other notified as regards their respective positions. (See clause 12 of the Ruritanian Bus Contract and *Toepfer v Cremer*, below.)

A clause should also provide an agreed basis for risk – and expense – allocation following delay or cancellation. Several examples have already been given, eg the post -1956 'Cape Surcharge'. Alternatively, the question of risk and additional expense or loss may be covered by an appropriate clause relating to insurance coverage.

Under the JCT standard form of building contract (1980 edn), clause 25 covers 'Extension of Time'. Notice of the cause of a delay to the works must be given by the contractor to the architect, who may grant an extension of time beyond the date for completion (see the *Waltham Holy Cross* case on p 126 above) for a variety of reasons, including (a) 'force majeure'; (b) exceptionally inclement weather; (c) loss or damage occasioned by one or more of the contingencies (eg fire, flood, damage by aircraft, etc) referred to as clause 22 perils – that clause governing insurance cover.

Cases involving 'force majeure' clauses include the following (illustrating the fact that even careful planning does not necessarily keep you out of court):

In *Czarnikow Ltd v Rolimpex* (1978), R, a Polish foreign trading organisation, agreed to sell 200,000 tons of sugar to C as part of the annual export quota. In Polish law R had a separate legal entity, distinct from the government, although it was subject to ministerial directions. The rules of the Refined Sugar Association were incorporated into the contract and rule 18(a) provided that if delivery was prevented by, *inter alia*, 'government intervention beyond the seller's control' the contract would be void without penalty. The seller was made responsible for obtaining the requisite export licence under rule 21; failure to obtain such not being 'sufficient grounds for a claim of "force majeure" if the regulations in force ... when the contract was made, called for such licences to be obtained'. The 1974 crop was poor and was needed for domestic consumption. A ministerial resolution imposed an immediate ban on all sugar exports. On the same date a formal decree was issued giving legal effect to the ban though it did not in terms revoke the export licences already ordered in compliance with rule 21. In reliance on the 'force majeure' clause, R informed C that the contract could not be fulfilled and the dispute was referred to arbitrators in London, who, relying on rule 18(a), found in R's favour.

Dismissing this appeal, it was held that (1) the arbitrators had established that R was not an organ of the Polish Government but an independent state organisation. The contract was therefore frustrated by 'government intervention' within rule 18(a) and was *not* self-induced, and R was accordingly relieved of liability under the contract; (2) the obligation under rule 21 to 'obtain' the requisite export licence implied no obligation to maintain it in force; R was not thereby precluded from relying on Rule 18(a).

In *Toepfer v Cremer* (1975), S sold B 5000 tons of soya bean meal cif Rotterdam. The contract was in the Grain and Feed Trade Association Ltd Form No 100, which contained a 'force majeure' clause entitling S to an extension of time for shipment and a clause which stated that, in the event of default by S, the damages were to be based upon the actual or estimated value of the goods 'on date of default'. The goods were to be shipped by 30 April 1973 but the worst floods on the Mississippi for over 20 years caused great delays to shipping. On 16 May S invoked the 'force majeure' clause, and by an extension notice informed B that he intended to ship the goods from 'Mississippi port(s)'. The date of shipment was thereby extended to 31 May, with a further extension (at B's option) to 30 June, which was the latest date for shipment. If goods of the contract description had been shipped by 30 June, S could have fulfilled his contract, provided B had been so notified by 10 July. S did not ship the goods. B claimed damages for non-delivery and, the market price having risen, contended that the date of default was 10 July. S maintained that the date of default was another, earlier time and that his extension notice was bad because it did not state any definite port.

The Court of Appeal held that damages would be assessed on the basis that the date of default was 10 July, for that was the last day for the performance of the contract. The extension notice was valid, for it was perfectly possible for S to intend to ship at one of the ports on the Mississippi. Further, since S had himself invoked the 'force majeure' clause and had given the extension notice, he could not be permitted to say that the notice was bad.

References and further reading

Brownsword, 'Henry's lost spectacle and Hutton's lost speculation: a classic riddle solved?' (1985) 129 *Solicitors' Journal* 860.

Brownsword, 'Rules and principles at the warehouse' (1977) 40 MLR 467, case note on *Amalgamated Investment v John Walker* (1977).

Cartoon, 'Drafting an acceptable force majeure clause' (1978) JBL 230.

Colinvaux, 'Suez survey' (1964) JBL 176 (and see also the detailed analysis of the *Suez Canal* cases by Mocatta J: [1970] 2 Lloyd's Rep 21).

Cornwell-Kelly, 'The Community concept of force majeure' (1979) NLJ 8 March at 245.

Hedley, 'Carriage by sea: frustration and force majeure' (1990) CLJ 209, case note on *The Super Servant Two*.

Lasok, 'Government intervention and State trading' (1981) 44 MLR 249.

Schmitthoff (1990), *The Export Trade*, 9th edn, ch 12 and ch 34 on hardship clauses.

Schmitthoff, 'Hardship and intervener clauses' (1980) JBL 82.

Stannard, 'Frustrating delays' (1983) 46 MLR 738.

Trakman, 'Frustrated contracts and legal fictions' (1983) 46 MLR 39.

Treitel (1994), *Frustration and Force Majeure*.

Questions

(1) P, a British exporter, has contracted to supply a quantity of sewing machines to Q, a Ruritanian importer, who is in business in Utopaville, the Ruritanian capital, at an agreed cif price. The goods were to be despatched by 1 May 1995. Ruritania, a mountainous country, has one port, Ruraport, and normally the goods would be sent to Utopaville via Ruraport. After an earthquake in April 1995, the port is out of action and P has to decide whether to have the goods taken overland, which will treble the cost of carriage, or whether to argue that the contract has become frustrated. Advise P.

(2)   A agreed to allow B and his family the use of A's holiday chalet for a week for £80. B paid a deposit of £8, the balance payable the day before the holiday was to commence. Two days before the holiday was due, B's children were taken ill with measles and B sent a doctor's certificate to this effect to A, saying that the holiday would have to be cancelled. A expressed regret, but demanded the balance of the agreed sum. Advise B.

What difference would it make if:

(a)   The chalet was washed away the day before the holiday was to start.

(b)   The previous occupiers of the chalet had left the place filthy and B refused to stay and booked hotel accommodation which cost £120 for the week.

(c)   A was paying for the chalet by means of a hire purchase agreement and because of non-payment of the instalments the owner of the chalet had retaken possession and refused admittance to B when he arrived.

(d)   The children had contracted smallpox instead of measles.

(3)   (a)   Explain by reference to decided cases what is meant by 'self-induced frustration'.

(b)   On 1 January S agreed to supply B with electronic equipment worth £25,000 within 30 days. On 28 January in response to S's telephone message that the equipment was ready, B sent a lorry to collect it from S's factory. On arrival the same day, B's driver was informed that the equipment would not be delivered to B after all. The driver was told by B to wait for further instructions and stay in the vicinity of the factory. Next day a government order was issued banning all sales of the equipment in question, with immediate effect. Advise B.

(4)   Explain how application of the Law Reform (Frustrated Contracts) Act 1943 would have altered the result in:

(a)   *Appleby v Myers* (1867);

(b)   *Fibrosa Spolka v Fairbairn* (1943).

(5)   'Exceptionally a 'force majeure' clause may be defeated by events.'

Discuss, with particular reference to *Metropolitan Water Board v Dick, Kerr & Co* (1918), *Wong Lai Ying v Chinachem Investment Co Ltd* (1979) and *Intertradex SA v Lesieur-Tourteaux SARL* (1978).

(6) 'The subject of frustration of contract has been associated, or confused, with various subjects, such as mistake, impossibility of performance, breach of contract, failure of consideration, illegality, failure of what is referred to as the common venture, and general considerations said to depend on reason and justice': Latham CJ in the Australian case of *Scanlan's New Neon Ltd v Toohey's Ltd* (1943). Discuss.

(7) In *Williams v Roffey Bros*, see Chapter 6, could the sub-contractor have successfully pleaded frustration?

13 Arbitration and litigation

Introduction

In the mid-19th century contract litigation occupied a significant amount of the time of the civil courts although there is evidence that even then businessmen were lobbying for High Court justice that was not only cheaper and quicker, but was also less dependent on the verdicts of juries unfamiliar with business matters and more in harmony with the commercial practices upon which trading expectations were founded. A century later, a survey of reported cases for 1957-66 revealed only 56 cases which were determined on the basis of points of contract law In the United States, Macaulay has similarly reported that 'law-suits for breach of contract appear to be rare'. What are the reasons for this decline in contract litigation during a period which has witnessed an enormous expansion in business activity?

The single most important reason must be the ever-increasing cost of litigation. Ignoring 'small claims', for which special facilities are now provided, the cost of using the judicial process, especially if an appeal is made, is so high at the present time that it operates as a significant barrier to claims that are not measured in many thousands of pounds. A 1984 newspaper headline read: 'Marathon Case May Cost Over £1 Million – a High Court contract action estimated to last 10 weeks and involving 12 barristers and 10,000 documents.' Even for a successful litigant, the damages and costs awarded may not cover all the expense that has been incurred.

Litigation is expensive in more than money spent on solicitors, counsel, witnesses and court fees. Protracted preparations and hearings can tie up highly paid personnel who could be more effectively occupied. A firm's goodwill and business reputation can be lost or damaged by litigation and the legal process is not conducive to continuing good business relationships. The cost of losing a regular customer may far outweigh the damages awarded in a successful action against him (and recall the *Atlas Express* case on p 167).

Another, quite different, reason must be *the diminished scope and applicability to transactional disputes of the general principles of contract law*. As we have seen, issues concerning contracts of employment and fair trading have moved almost entirely out of the province of contract law and into special courts or tribunals administering statutory provisions. Other, 'mixed' cases – relating, for example, to the sale or carriage of goods, consumer protection or consumer credit – are predominantly determined by statutory rules rather than the general principles of contract law.

The role of the mid-19th century appellate courts as (at least in theory) formulators of generalised, market-orientated rules has long disappeared. The concept of the market has been replaced by the realisation that there are many markets, all penetrated to a greater or lesser degree by statutory regulation. In an article on the commodity trades, the author complained that: 'There has been a deplorable tendency for national governments of exporters of agricultural commodities to take legislative action which has interfered with parties' ability to carry out their contractual obligations ... It affects the whole sanctity of contracts and, therefore, the whole basis of the contract system of trading.'

It is also important to point out that, as 'big business' has increasingly eliminated the individual entrepreneur – 'as groups of companies are gathered under one holding company by mergers and take-overs – the result is to *eliminate a significant source of contract-making'*, contract-breaking and potential litigation. As Atiyah continues: 'The role of the individual as the centre of a network of relationships has largely disappeared. And this is the sense in which it is correct to speak of an enormous decline in the role played by contract in modern society.'

A report published in 1962 pointed out that trading organisations had become larger in size but fewer in number, with the result that 'not only are there fewer potential litigants but that there is a greater inclination to compromise disputes. Large organisations will only litigate a dispute if the amount at stake is much larger or the principle involved is much more important than the trading concerns of the past would have tolerated without a contest'. The shifting of the risk of loss to insurance companies may also be a factor here, bearing in mind that such risk-bearers may pursue their subrogated rights through the courts, see eg *Harbutt's 'Plasticine'* (p 178) and its sequel *Wayne Tank and Pump Co Ltd v Employer's Liability Assurance Corpn Ltd* (1974).

The costs and the 'win or lose' nature of litigation have also clearly led the business community, from the late-19th century onwards, more and more towards *increased self-regulation* as regards contractual disputes. This can take a wide variety of forms. For example, the final clause of the Ruritanian Bus Contract in Chapter 3 provided that differences between the parties were to be settled by means of amicable negotiation. Only if it were not possible to reach 'an understanding' were the parties to submit their dispute to arbitration. Other clauses, the vendor's warranty (clause 11) and the 'force majeure' clause (clause 12), sought to make the contract 'judge-proof' regarding claims of defective performance and frustration.

Similarly, the high degree of planning, the 'everything within' nature of mechanical and electrical engineering contracts, has, as seen in Chapter 8, led to the claim that in this field arbitration and litigation have been 'abolished'. In this respect it is also important to notice the incidence of liquidated damages clauses, which, as seen in the *Waltham Holy Cross* case, regulate the amount of compensation to be paid on the occurrence of some possible future, specified breach such as delay in completion. Research by Beale and *Dugdale* (see p 30 above) indicates that, at least as regards the UK engineering industry, late delivery is regarded as a 'commercial problem' rather than 'a legal problem susceptible to solution by use of planning. Not surprisingly most buyers and sellers seemed to regard delivery dates as targets rather than firm promises'.

In general terms, mass-production methods and the rationalisation of patterns of business through, among other things, the development of *standard forms* have tended to reduce the scope for honest misunderstandings and *have encouraged or compelled the use of extra-legal dispute-solving techniques*, that may or may not be based on the contract documents. Losses suffered on one contract can be taken into account when negotiating the next; a credit can be issued; appropriate insurance can be taken out; or cancellation can be allowed for the sake of future orders. In cases where the government is a contracting party, the courts are rarely if ever used for settling differences, and we have noted in Chapter 8 departmental use of *'administrative' remedies* such as 'profit disallowance' or the removal of a company's name from lists of 'approved' contractors.

All in all, it appears reasonable to conclude that if contractual differences arise, the most favoured procedure is negotiate or arbitrate, and only as a last resort litigate. It is said that many years ago a sandwich-board man paraded outside the Royal Courts of Justice in the Strand displaying the slogan: *'Arbitrate, Don't Litigate.'* It is not uncommon today to find written into contractual arbitration clauses: 'and the arbitrator is not to be a lawyer'. *Arbitration is indeed now generally preferred to litigation*, and for this reason alone it is necessary to examine the general features of this quasi-judicial process which may be invoked not only, for example, by the parties to an international transaction but also, at the other end of the scale, by the consumer who takes his complaint against a supplier of goods or services to a small claims hearing or to arbitration established under a trade association's voluntary code of practice (see p 174 above, and below).

Commercial arbitration

The parties to a contract may decide to settle their differences by arbitration either before or after the dispute has arisen. Clauses providing for arbitration are very common in commercial contracts and the use of a standard form prepared, for example, by a trade association or an insurance company may make its use compulsory.

International trade transactions are often submitted to arbitration in London, where the required facilities enjoy the highest reputation for fairness and impartiality and an estimated total of 10,000 disputes per year are handled. It is not uncommon to find disputes settled in this way which arise out of contracts which have no connection with this country other than the use of an English standard form contract, eg *Tsakiroglou & Co Ltd v Noblee Thorl GmbH* (see Chapter 12), although the subsequent appearance of these parties in the House of Lords indicates that there are dangers attached to arbitration in England (see below). A typical clause from within this international context might read as follows:

> If any dispute, difference or question shall at any time hereafter arise between the parties in respect of or in connection with the present contract, the same shall be referred to the arbitration of a person to be agreed upon by the parties or, failing agreement, to be nominated by ... in accordance with and subject to the provisions of the Arbitration Acts 1950 to 1979 or any statutory modification thereof for the time being in force.

As Schmitthoff points out, so far as arbitration is concerned, contractual disputes can be roughly divided into:

(a) those concerning only questions of fact – for which it is preferable to use an arbitrator who has technical qualifications and an intimate knowledge of the trade: *quality arbitrations;*

(b) those where there is no argument about the facts, but where the problem rests on the construction of a document or application of rules of contract or commercial law: *technical arbitrations* – which should perhaps best be referred to an arbitrator who is a barrister with a commercial practice or to the commercial court (a specialist QBD judge); and lastly, and most probably:

(c) those disputes involving both questions of fact and law. In such *'mixed'* *arbitrations*, the arbitrator needs to possess technical skills, knowledge of the trade and expertise in the law. He must find the facts and apply the relevant law to them. It is his decision on legal matters which, as will be discussed shortly, is subject to the supervisory jurisdiction of the courts. Where, in such cases, a dispute moves out of the arbitration and into the court structure, the advantages of arbitration will be lost and this has been the cause of much concern to the business community.

On the question of businessmen's overall preference for arbitration, a report published in 1962 on declining use of the commercial court stressed that they inherently disliked the publicity involved in going to court and the system of oral examination and cross-examination ('feeling like a criminal'); they were – and this was 'a very potent factor' – discouraged by the increasing cost and delays of litigation; and foreign parties were less inclined to submit disputes to the courts than to arbitration in London. (The report did, however, point out that 'it may not be generally appreciated how continually businessmen are assisted in the settlement of problems which might have led to contested disputes' by the 'wealth of case law ... clearly enunciated' in decisions of the commercial court.) The commercial court's case load has since increased and it now hears over 100 actions per year.

While it is argued, and generally true, that arbitrations are cheaper, quicker and more convenient, more informal, inspire greater confidence (because arbitrators are chosen for their personal knowledge and experience of the trade), and, perhaps above all, they are private, it is not true to say that all these advantages are always present. For example, the advantages of expeditious proceedings and economy can be thwarted by a tardy defendant and, at least until recently, the finality of an arbitration award could be placed in jeopardy by a party – on the verge of losing his case – using, or misusing, the 'case stated' procedure so as to challenge the award in the courts. When this happens the advantages of arbitration are expunged because the proceedings may well finish up in the House of Lords.

Miller (James) & Partners Ltd v Whitworth Street Estates (Manchester) Ltd (1970) is a case which amply illustrates some of the pitfalls of arbitration:

> M, a Scottish firm of building contractors, agreed to convert premises in Scotland belonging to W, an English company. Negotiations proceeded in London and the RIBA form of contract, while making no reference to the law governing the contract, provided for arbitration of disputes and the appointment, in default of agreement between the parties, of an arbitrator by the President of the RIBA. The contract made no provision as to the place of arbitration or as to the law to govern its procedure.

> A dispute arose and the President appointed a Scottish architect as arbitrator. The arbitration was held in Scotland and followed Scottish procedure. When points of law arose, W asked the arbitrator to state his award in the form of a special case for the decision of the English High Court. The arbitrator refused, on the basis that he had no jurisdiction under Scots law (at that time) to do so. W, who conceded that the power to state a case was governed by the procedural law and that the procedural law might be different from the proper law of the contract, applied to the English courts to order the arbitrator to state a case. In the House of Lords, Lord Reid stated the crucial issue:

> 'The question in this appeal is whether this was a Scottish or an English arbitration. If it was governed by the law of Scotland the arbiter acted correctly. Under Scots law an arbiter is the final judge both of fact and law, and Mr Underwood was entitled and indeed bound to issue his final award. But if the arbitration was governed by the law of England he was bound to state a case in order that questions of law which had arisen might be decided by the English court.'

> The majority held that the proper law of the contract was English law, but that the procedure was governed by Scots law. They therefore reversed the decision of the Court of Appeal who had ordered the arbitrator to state a case – a proceeding unknown to Scots law at that time.

The 'case stated' procedure, by which points of law are taken at the request of a party from the arbitration tribunal to the court, rests on the doctrine of ouster: the jurisdiction of the courts cannot be ousted in questions of law. The origins of the procedure go back to an Act passed in 1854, which enabled a judge to stay proceedings brought before him if the party bringing the action had previously agreed to arbitrate in the event of a dispute. In *Scott v Avery* (1856), the House of Lords upheld an arbitration clause which stipulated that no court proceedings were to be brought *until* arbitration was over. While '*Scott v Avery* clauses' (which do not seek to oust the jurisdiction of the courts) came regularly to be found in commercial contracts, and questions of fact are within the arbitrator's sole domain, the right to appeal against an arbitrator's decision on a point of law was closely guarded by the courts. In a case in 1922, the rules of the Refined Sugar Association purported to oust the courts' power of review: *Czarnikow v Roth, Schmidt & Co Ltd*. This proposition was firmly rejected.

However, the 'case stated' procedure, at least as it operated before 1979, could lead to the situation described by Lord Wilberforce:

> It is surely regrettable that, after a choice of English arbitrators, these foreign parties should have been subjected to litigation in three courts on top of the arbitration and that on a preliminary point. I venture to think that a question of the proper law of a commercial contract ought to be regarded as primarily a matter to be found by arbitrators; for, after all, the question is one of estimating competing factors in the light of commercial intention. As was said long ago, 'the only certain guide is to be found in applying sound ideas of business, convenience, and sense to the language of the contract'. The expertise of City of London arbitrators (which motivates the use of London arbitration clauses) suggests that these considerations are best left to them ... If, for uniformity or otherwise, supervision of the courts is sometimes required, I cannot but think that, otherwise than in exceptional cases by leave, decision by the commercial judge should end the matter.

Thus, on the one hand, the 'case stated' procedure deterred some, particularly foreign, parties from using London arbitration because it entailed the possibility of submission to lengthy and costly judicial review right up to the House of Lords. On the other hand, some parties were also abusing the system of review in order to postpone payment of a substantial award against them. This could be a paying proposition for some firms in times of high inflation and borrowing rates. The Arbitration Act 1979 sought to meet these problems by abolishing the special 'case stated' procedure and substituting a strictly limited right of appeal from reasoned awards. The law was amended to the effect that, among other things, an appeal to the High Court against an award requires either (i) the consent of all parties, or (ii) the leave of the court, which will not be granted unless the legal point at issue could substantially affect the rights of one or more parties, and which may be conditional on the applicant paying the whole of the claim into court. Any further appeal has also been restricted to questions of law of general public importance.

In addition, limited rights have been granted to parties to contract out of the judicial review procedure. This derogation from the doctrine of ouster is intended as an encouragement particularly to foreign parties to use London arbitration without the risk of judicial supervisory jurisdiction. Such arbitration is a valuable invisible export.

The first case to be heard under the provisions of the 1979 Act, *The Nema* (1982), involved the question of whether a voyage charterparty had been frustrated by a lengthy strike at the port of loading. A shipping arbitrator held that it was frustrated and following appeals to the High Court and Court of Appeal, the House of Lords affirmed the arbitrator's decision; for a similar story, see Colinvaux, 'Suez Survey' on p 232. Bearing in mind the 'radical change in performance' basis to the doctrine of frustration, it is of interest that in this case Lord Diplock considered that a decision may follow closely;

> ... from a commercial arbitrator's findings as to mercantile usage and the understanding of mercantile men about the significance of the commercial differences between what was promised and what in the changed circumstances would now fall to be performed.

In *The Nema*, the House of Lords laid down guidelines to be observed by the courts when considering applications for leave to appeal from the arbitrator's award. The basic question is: would the decision of the court add significantly to the clarity and certainty of English commercial law?

Small claims

Other changes in both the law and business practice have occurred in the field of *small claims*. The Fair Trading Act 1973 puts the Director General of Fair Trading under a duty to encourage trade associations 'to prepare, and to disseminate to their members, *codes of practice* for guidance in safeguarding and promoting the interests of consumers'. Around 30 codes have been approved covering cars, travel agents, laundries and cleaners (see Chapter 9) and other sectors.

Such codes, apart from influencing the re-writing of trade association standard form contracts (eg the removal of exemption clauses from tour operators' booking conditions) also contain arbitration procedures for *consumer* complaints. The Code of Practice for the Motor Industry, negotiated by the Office of Fair Trading, the Retail Motor Industry Federation Ltd, the Society of Motor Manufacturers and Traders and the Scottish Motor Trade Association, was drawn up to govern the conduct of manufacturers and dealers in relation to the manufacture and supply of new and used cars and related products and services. The Code contains the following complaints procedure for the consumer:

(a) refer the complaint to the dealer;

(b) if it relates to a new car warranty and the dealer does not resolve the question, refer it to the manufacturer direct;

(c) if satisfaction is not achieved, write to the relevant trade association, provided the dealer is a member;

(d) the trade association will try to effect a settlement between the consumer and its member;

(e) if conciliation fails, the trade association will normally provide for a 'documents only' arbitration before an arbitrator appointed by the Chartered Institute of Arbitrators. A small fee is payable;

(f) a written award is made which is enforceable in the courts;

(g) such a procedure is available instead of, and not to the exclusion of, legal action.

(The Consumer Arbitration Agreements Act 1988 prevents *compulsory* arbitrations where a person is 'contracting as consumer' if the dispute is within county court jurisdiction limits.)

There are disadvantages in self-regulation: firms may not be members of the relevant association or, even though members, they may not honour the code. However, such arbitrations are inexpensive where, as is normal, they are conducted on a 'documents only' basis and are subsidised by the association. Independent arbitrators are found by the Chartered Institute of Arbitrators. The settlement of consumer complaints under the codes of practice is on the increase and this is mainly the result of energetic advertising campaigns and, therefore, increased consumer awareness.

New forms of arbitration under the Manchester and Westminster (London) schemes and small claims proceedings in the county court were all introduced in the early 1970s. In each case the aim is – or was – to provide easy and cheap procedures for the enforcement of small claims (eg under the Sale of Goods Act) which would lapse if, the supplier being unwilling to meet his obligations, the consumer was not prepared to mount a full-scale legal action with its attendant expense, formality and delay. However, cuts in government expenditure and an inability to raise funds from other sources led to the closure of the London and Manchester schemes.

Until June 1980, Manchester-based claims were accepted up to an eventual limit of £1,000 and generally restricted, in contract matters, to consumers. Fees were minimal and, unlike county court proceedings, legal representation was not allowed. However, like arbitration under a code of practice, the scheme was voluntary, and research established that a third of the business parties against whom claims were started failed to co-operate. The claimant undertook to abide by the arbitrator's award which was final; no right of appeal on a point of law was provided. The Westminster (later London) Small Claims Court, which closed in late 1979, operated on a similar basis and could, in theory, hear claims originating from anywhere in England and Wales. The collapse of these schemes means an end to 'the germ of what may be a great and crucial development in the field of access to justice' unless they can be revived in the future.

Small claims proceedings are therefore at present confined to those brought before the district judge of the county court. This is an informal arbitration system for claims which generally do not exceed £1,000. (This figure may soon be raised to £3,000.) Such arbitrations are on the increase but there is evidence that the service is being monopolised by retail shops and stores using it for debt collection. An explanatory guide, *Small Claims in the County Court – How to Sue and Defend Actions without a Solicitor*, states that:

> The purpose of arbitration is to enable people to have small disputes resolved in an informal atmosphere, avoiding so far as possible the strict rules of procedure usually associated with court proceedings. This does not mean that rules are not observed because the object of all court procedure is to protect the interests of each party to an action and to ensure that the case is tried fairly. Nevertheless the formalities are kept to a minimum and you should have no difficulty in handling your own case.

An award may be enforced as a judgment of the court and the possibility of appeal is strictly limited.

By coincidence, the very day (13 June 1995) of reviewing this brief outline of the county court small claims jurisdiction, two articles on the subject appeared in *The Times*. 'Do-it-yourself justice' indicates that the procedure is not necessarily 'user-friendly'; eg 'some judges are wonderful but some are patronising and not easy to understand'. 'A litigant's story' is a 'horror' story of a case filed against an insurance company in August 1993 and lost in June 1995 when the company, as is allowed, was represented by a barrister.

Breach and the recovery of damages in the courts

A breach of contract is a civil wrong for which the most commonly sought remedy is an award of damages. (The injured party's right to terminate the contract has been discussed in Chapters 7 and 9.) The basic purpose of damages is to compensate the injured party for the loss he has suffered as a result of the breach.

By the mid-19th century, when the basis of the modern law was established, damages came to be regarded as the acceptable form of 'insurance' against the risk of default by a contracting party. Operating within the context of a market economy, the basic aim of the law was to ensure that a party was compensated for loss for which a market value could be found. However, it was also concerned to see that the 'engines of industry' were slowed as little as possible by breach situations. The injured party could only terminate the contract following a serious breach and if he did so he had a duty to mitigate his loss.

This is shown in an early illustration of the market price rule in contracts for the sale of goods. In *Gainsford v Carroll* (1824), the seller having failed to deliver a quantity of bacon, it was held that the buyer, having terminated the contract, ought to have gone into the market at once for a replacement supply. As he had failed to do this, he could not recover damages in respect of the increase in the market price after that time. He could only recover damages equal to the difference between the contract price and the market price at the date of the breach.

As the law developed, freedom and sanctity of contract demanded that contracts be enforced not so much by the law compelling adherence to contracts but by placing before a party the choice of either performing his obligations or compensating the other party for the loss which arose as a result of his breach. By way of contrast, Soviet law, operating against a background of central economic planning and output quotas, was very much more concerned with ensuring that contracts were actually performed: 'the contract becomes an exercise in managerial initiative' and 'the purpose of the law is thus to ensure performance by the stick of legal sanction'.

In English law the remedy of *specific performance* is rarely granted. It is generally unrealistic to speak of compelling performance in cases where a party is refusing to perform, has so managed his affairs as to put performance beyond his capabilities, or has broken his contract in a serious way. Hence specific performance tends to be granted only where it is economically realistic to do so and damages are considered to be an inadequate remedy. Thus the remedy will not be granted for contracts for the sale of goods which are readily available in the market, but it will be granted where the contractual subject matter is land, property, or other things which fall within the concept of 'commercial uniqueness'.

An award of damages is not normally the remedy that immediately springs to the mind of the average consumer whose goods turn out to be faulty. He will probably be more interested in getting his goods replaced or repaired at little or no additional cost. Here he will have to rely on the goodwill of the supplier or manufacturer or alternatively proceed under the terms of a guarantee. If he fails to gain satisfaction, the conciliation and arbitration facilities discussed above are available – as are the courts.

The question of loss or damage

The statement that the injured party may recover damages for the loss sustained as a result of the breach obscures as much as it reveals. In fact we have it on judicial authority that the law relating to damages is 'a branch of the law in which one is less guided by authority laying down definite principles than in almost any other matter one can consider'. Since 1925 when this statement was made, the law of damages has moved no nearer to 'definite principles'. One question that lawyers have concentrated upon is: For what *kind* of damage or loss is the injured party entitled to recover compensation?

The traditional approach to this question is to say that the law protects the *expectations created by the contract*. Damages are therefore awarded to put the injured party, so far as money can do it, in the same position as if the contract had been properly performed. He is entitled to damages for the loss of his bargain so that his expectations arising from the contract are protected. (Contrast the assessment of damages in *Doyle v Olby (Ironmongers) Ltd* and damages for misrepresentation generally in Chapter 10.) An award of damages to compensate the injured party for loss of the benefit he would have secured had the contract been properly performed may require, for example, recovery for loss of profits. Thus: P's only coach breaks down and he engages D to repair it. It is agreed that the repairs will be completed by 1 April because, as P tells D, on 2 April P has to commence performance of a lucrative contract taking a party of law students to Brussels. If D fails to complete the repairs and P loses his contract, P will probably be able to claim his lost profit from D, see *Hadley v Baxendale* and similar cases below.

An alternative view, which is being increasingly applied, is that some situations require that for the injured party to obtain adequate compensation it is necessary to put him back in the position in which he would have been had the contract *never been made*. This is to be done by compensating him for expenses incurred and other loss suffered *in reliance on the contract*. In 1973 Ogus wrote that this was 'a murky area where ... much remains unchartered' and the cases have not met with general approval. Nevertheless, it is clear that if an expectation interest (economic value of the bargain) award is pursued, the plaintiff must give satisfactory evidence of the value of his expectations. If this is not possible, a reliance interest claim may be appropriate:

> In *Anglia Television Ltd v Reed* (1972), A did not claim their profit from a film which had to be abandoned following R's breach. They could not say what that profit (if any) would have been had R come from America as agreed to take the leading role. A therefore claimed a reliance interest award, based on £2,750 expenses incurred and wasted. The court upheld their claim. It was stated that loss caused by such wasted expenditure was recoverable provided that 'it was such as would reasonably be in the contemplation of the parties as likely to be wasted if the contract was broken': for a review of the cases on reliance loss, see *CCC Films (London) Ltd v Impact Quadrant Films Ltd* (1985).

A third type of claim, for *restitution*, can also arise where, for example, the party in breach has wholly failed to perform his part of the contract. If S agrees to deliver goods to B and, B having paid in advance, S fails to deliver, then S must restore the price to B. The question of the relationship between claims for loss of bargain, reliance loss and restitution has raised many problems in the cases. However, in appropriate circumstances, there is no doubt that such claims can be combined so long as the plaintiff does not try to recover more than once for the same loss.

For example, where the expectation interest is calculated on the basis of gross profits (without deduction for expenses), the plaintiff is not entitled to both gross profits and the wasted expenditure because in order to earn the profits those expenses would have to be incurred. In *Millar's Machinery Co Ltd v David Way & Son* (1935), machinery was purchased, paid for and installed. The buyer nevertheless rejected the machinery as not being in accordance with the contract. He recovered the price (restitution), installation expenses (reliance loss) and net loss of profits resulting from the breach (loss of bargain).

In *Banco de Portugal v Waterlow & Sons Ltd* (1932), W contracted to print notes for the Portuguese central bank. They wrongly allowed a large number of notes to be delivered to X who put them into circulation in Portugal. B withdrew the whole issue and exchanged the notes. A majority of the House of Lords awarded damages on the basis of the face value of the notes in question (£600,000); the minority were in favour of an award equivalent to the cost of printing the notes (£9,000).

Remoteness of loss

A further question which may arise as regards the loss for which the injured party may recover is governed by the rules relating to remoteness of damage. A breach of contract may initiate a course of events which results in loss to the plaintiff. However, the law will not necessarily hold the defendant liable for all such loss. It may regard part of the loss as being too remote: 'In the varied web of affairs the law must abstract some consequences as relevant, not perhaps on grounds of pure logic, but simply for practical reasons.'

The main 'practical reason' is that if the plaintiff in all cases were to recover all his loss (contrast the position as regards fraudulent misrepresentation), parties would not enter into contracts at all or only at a high price. The remoteness rule places a limit on damages, as do the rules on mitigation as we will see.

The basic test of remoteness, laid down in *Hadley v Baxendale* (1854), is whether the loss was within the reasonable contemplation of the parties. It was laid down by Baron Alderson that:

> Where two parties have made a contract which one of them has broken, the damages ... should be such as may fairly and reasonably be considered either arising naturally, ie according to the usual course of things, from such breach of contract itself, or such as may reasonably be supposed to have been in the contemplation of both parties, at the time they made the contract, as the probable result of the breach.

> H's flour mill at Gloucester, which was driven by a steam engine, came to a standstill owing to a broken crankshaft. It was necessary to send the shaft to the makers as a pattern for a new one. B agreed to carry it to Greenwich but in breach of contract delayed its delivery and H did not receive the new crankshaft for some five days after he would otherwise have done. The mill being idle during this period, H sued for £300 loss of profits occasioned by the delay.

> It was held that the stoppage did not arise in 'the usual course of things' but was the result of special circumstances (H had only one crankshaft) which were not within the reasonable contemplation of the carrier at the time the contract was made. B was therefore not liable for the loss of profits; he was only liable for nominal damages.

Everyone is *taken to know* the usual course of things (this is presumed or imputed knowledge) and to know the consequences of breach in such circumstances; but knowledge of special circumstances must be actual in order to attract liability for special loss.

In *Hadley*, the miller's special circumstances militated against the application of the first leg of the remoteness rule, and his failure to communicate his lack of a spare crankshaft to the carrier meant that he was not covered by the second leg either. It has been said of this case that the court implied that 'the optimal mill owner would not allow himself to be caught without a spare. Avoidable consequences must be avoided by those with power to avoid them; it would distort the market system to allow an offender against this principle to cast his losses upon another party, since a market system required the penalties for bad planning of enterprise to fall upon those who planned badly' (Friedman, *Contract Law in the USA*). Alternatively, it may be said that the court considered it to be unfair to impose such a wide liability for damages upon a carrier unless he was aware of the circumstances and had the opportunity to settle special terms.

Words such as 'loss', 'reasonable contemplation' and 'communication' are capable of manipulation, and in the modern business world it may more readily be assumed (than was the case in 1854) that a party has a fair knowledge of another's operations and techniques. This must be the case for members of the same trade association or for the parties to a well-established standard form of contract (see *British Crane Hire Corpn Ltd v Ipswich Plant Hire Ltd* on p 104 above). It has been said that each party 'must be taken to understand the ordinary practices and exigencies of the other's trade but it must be remembered when dealing with the case of a carrier of goods ... he is not carrying on the same trade as the consignor of goods and his knowledge of the practices and exigencies of the other's trade may be limited and less than between buyer and seller who probably know far more about one another's business'. Nevertheless:

> In *The Heron II (Koufos v Czarnikow Ltd)* (1969), sugar merchants chartered K's vessel to carry 3000 tons of sugar from Constanza to the market at Basrah. The vessel unjustifiably deviated from the agreed route and arrived nine days late. Owing to a fall in the market (which was not unusual or unpredictable), C, who intended to sell the sugar on arrival, lost £4,000. The House of Lords found that although K knew there was a market for sugar at Basrah he did not know C's precise intentions. Nevertheless, the loss was not too remote a consequence of the breach and K was liable.
>
> Lord Reid was of the opinion that K knew enough in the sense that, as a reasonable man, he should have realised that the loss resulting from the ship's delay was 'not unlikely', and this degree of probability was sufficient to make him liable.
>
> The cargo owner had lost the chance of selling at a particular time; that chance was something the shipowner could have contemplated.

The more information a party possesses regarding the risks attached to contract performance, the more he is able to modify his terms. Actual knowledge of 'special circumstances' would induce a party to increase his price, exclude the risk or insure against its occurrence.

Difficult questions of remoteness or 'reasonable contemplation' arose in *Parsons (Livestock) Ltd v Uttley Ingham & Co Ltd* (1978), where a decision for the plaintiffs rested on the view that the remoteness test was satisfied as the defendants could have contemplated a 'serious possibility of injury' of the type which had occurred:

> UI supplied P with an animal feed hopper to be used for storing pig food. The hopper was not properly ventilated and the food became mouldy. P's pigs became ill as a result and many of them died from E coli, a rare intestinal disease.
>
> UI were held to be liable for the loss. Some harm to the pigs was in the reasonable contemplation of the parties as a result of the breach, although the *particular disease* and its consequences would have been considered an unlikely result of the breach at the time the contract was made.
>
> P recovered damages taking into account the value of the pigs which had died, the expenses involved in dealing with the infection and the loss of profits they would have made from the pigs which had died.

Mitigation

The injured party's so-called 'duty' to mitigate the loss means that he will not be compensated for loss which he could have avoided by taking reasonable steps: see Viscount Haldane LC in *British Westinghouse Electric and Manufacturing Co Ltd v Underground Electric Railways Co of London Ltd* (1912).

As seen earlier, where a seller fails to deliver goods, the buyer must immediately or within a reasonable time go into the market and secure substitute equivalent goods. His damages will then be assessed on the basis of the difference (if any) between the contract price and the market price. The buyer cannot delay at a time of a rising market.

Non-pecuniary loss: disappointment and distress

Other factors have operated in recent years to widen the scope of loss in the context of damages for breach of contract. Apart from the general run of economic loss cases, it has for many years been clear that where a breach causes personal injury, an award of damages can take account of pain and suffering: eg *Godley v Perry* (1960), in which G bought a catapult which broke and as a result lost an eye (see p 118 below).

More significantly, in recent years, parallel to similar developments in negligence cases and perhaps as a result of the growth of consumer protection, inroads have been made into the old rule that contract damages could not be awarded for injured feelings:

In *Jarvis v Swan's Tours Ltd* (1973), J booked a winter holiday in the Alps with S, whose brochure listed many attractions. The holiday fell far short of J's expectations and in the second week he was the sole visitor. On appeal on the issue of damages, the award was increased from £32 to £125: 'damages can be given for the disappointment, the distress, the upset and frustration caused by the breach.'

In *Cox v Phillips Industries Ltd* (1976), C, an experienced metallurgical engineer, having been promoted under a new contract with P, was later wrongfully removed to a position of lesser managerial responsibility. His salary was not affected but he became 'depressed, anxious, frustrated and ill'. It was held that C could recover £500 damages for the emotional distress caused by breach of the promise of promotion.

However, *Cox* was overruled by the Court of Appeal in *Bliss v SE Thames Regional Health Authority* (1987), a similar case involving a consultant orthopaedic surgeon. The court was not willing to extend the *Jarvis* decision, relating to 'a contract to provide peace of mind or freedom from distress', to a commercial wrongful dismissal context. The court laid stress on the House of Lords decision in *Addis v Gramophone Co Ltd* (1909) where it was held that a plaintiff wrongfully dismissed in an abrupt manner could not recover damages for injury to his reputation.

Contributory negligence

Loss may be caused partly by the defendant's breach and partly by the plaintiff's contributory negligence. *In tort*, the Law Reform (Contributory Negligence) Act 1945 allows for apportionment of fault liability and a reduction of the injured party's damages to the extent that he was himself responsible for the loss. Does the 1945 Act apply to breach of contract cases? There are three possible situations:

(1)   The defendant was in breach of a contractual duty of care and a duty of care in tort (see, for example, *Esso Petroleum Co Ltd v Mardon* on p 189). The plaintiff is also careless. Here the Act can apply, as in *Forsik Vesta v Butcher* (1989) where the loss arose partly as a result of the professional negligence of the defendant, which amounted to both a breach of contract and to a tort against his client, and partly as a result of the plaintiff's own carelessness; see also *Sayers v Harlow UDC* (1958).

(2)   The defendant was in breach of a contractual duty of care but his conduct is not tortious; the parties' relations being governed solely by the contract. The plaintiff is also careless. At present there is no clear authority on this point.

(3)   The defendant was (without negligence) in breach of a strict contractual duty. The plaintiff is careless. Because the defendant's conduct does not amount to 'fault' under the 1945 Act ('negligence, breach of statutory

duty'), the Act does not apply and no apportionment of loss is to be made: *Barclays Bank plc v Fairclough Building Ltd* (1995). In this case, the defendant builders were in breach of a contractual provision which did not depend on a failure to take reasonable care. In the Court of Appeal, Nourse LJ was of the opinion that it ought to be a cause of general concern that the law should have got into such a state that a contractor who was in breach of obligations expressly undertaken by him was able to persuade the judge that the building owner's damages should be reduced because of his own negligence in not preventing the contractor from committing the breaches.

Liquidated damages clauses

The parties to a contract may validly include in their agreement a clause providing for a fixed or calculable sum to be paid on the occurrence of an anticipated possible breach, eg 'The contractor shall pay the building owner £50 per week or part thereof for delay in completion of the works.' Such a clause usually indicates the parties' willingness to avoid litigation over questions such as remoteness of loss and assessment of damages – the breach itself not being in dispute. However, the party in default may resist the operation of the clause and plead that it is an unenforceable *penalty*. If the court decides that the sum fixed is a 'genuine pre-estimate' of the actual loss likely to be suffered by the injured party in the event of the specified breach, then it is recoverable, whatever the actual loss, and is known as 'liquidated damages'. Such damages have been 'made certain' by the parties before the breach (which may in fact never occur), as opposed to 'unliquidated damages' which can only be quantified by the court after a breach has occurred.

A liquidated damages clause must be distinguished from both a limitation of liability clause (see Chapter 9) and a penalty, neither of which are genuine pre-estimates of loss. A limitation of liability clause merely attempts to put a maximum limit on the amount of damages recoverable and the figure being fixed by one party only, at a sum usually well below that which is likely to result from the breach, it operates only to the benefit of that party – to the extent, however, that the clause itself is now allowable under the Unfair Contract Terms Act 1977. This is not to deny that a liquidated damages clause may in practice limit liability (where actual loss exceeds the agreed figure), but its object is to benefit both parties by avoiding litigation on the matter. The essence of such a clause is that the stipulated figure can be seen as a genuine pre-estimate of loss: 'It is essential that the sum assessed should be reasonable in relation to the damage anticipated and to all known facts, even though precise calculation is not possible.'

If the sum fixed is obviously 'extravagant and unconscionable in amount in comparison with the greatest loss which the injured party could suffer as a result of the breach' (and is probably inserted by one party, this time so as to operate as a threat against the other who in the nature of things is more likely to default, eg a building contractor or the manufacturer and installer of machinery), then it is viewed by the courts as a penalty. Such a sum is not recoverable but the injured party can nevertheless recover on the basis of unliquidated damages for actual loss. When distinguishing between a penalty and a liquidated damages clause, the vital factor is the reasonableness of the amount; the use of either term by the parties in the contract is *not* in itself conclusive.

The basis of the law relating to liquidated damages was laid down by Lord Dunedin in *Dunlop Pneumatic Tyre Co Ltd v New Garage and Motor Co Ltd* (1905). More recently:

> In *Robophone Facilities Ltd v Blank* (1966), B agreed to rent one of R's telephone answering machines for seven years at £17 11s per quarter. A clause in the agreement stated that if it was terminated for any reason, B was to pay R 'all rentals accrued due and also by way of liquidated or agreed damages a sum equal to 50% of the total of the rentals which would thereafter have become payable.' B cancelled the agreement before the machine was installed. It was held that R could recover agreed damages of £245 11s. Since R's facilities for supplying the machines exceeded and were likely to continue to exceed the demand, they were entitled to recover their loss of profit.

As regards building contracts, there are a number of defences available to the contractor against the enforcement of a liquidated damages clause by the employer. They include (i) the sum is really a penalty; (ii) there is no agreed date from which damages for non-completion will accrue; (iii) an extension of time has been granted (on the last two points see the *Waltham Holy Cross* case on p 126 above; (iv) the employer has waived the completion date; and (v) the employer has impeded the contractor.

Specific performance

By an order for specific performance, the court directs one of the parties to perform his obligations under the contract in accordance with its terms. We have encountered this equitable and discretionary remedy in various cases eg *Redgrave v Hurd* on p 185 and, earlier in this chapter, attention was drawn to its limited availability. While traditionally specific performance will not be granted if damages are an 'adequate' remedy, there are recent indications of a more liberal judicial attitude as regards the scope of this remedy. Thus: 'the standard question "Are damages an adequate remedy?" might perhaps be rewritten: "Is it just, in all the circumstances, that a plaintiff should be confined to his remedy in damages?".'

Although still taking the view that damages cannot adequately compensate for breach of a contract for the sale of a particular piece of land or property, damages have generally been considered an 'adequate remedy' in sale of goods cases unless the goods are 'commercially unique'. However, in *Perry & Co v British Railways Board* (1980), during the steel strike of 1980, P obtained an order for specific delivery of a quantity of steel owned by him against BRB who, in fear of strike action, had refused to allow it to be moved. In this case it was said that damages might be an inadequate remedy because they 'would be a poor consolation if the failure of supplies forces a trader to lay off staff and disappoint his customers.' At the time of *Perry*, steel was very difficult to obtain, as was petrol during the 1973 shortage. Thus, in *Sky Petroleum Ltd v VIP Petroleum Ltd* (1974), S, who were contracted to take all their petrol from VIP, were granted an interim injunction to stop VIP withholding supplies. This amounted to temporary specific performance of a contract for the sale of goods for which – although there were normally alternative sources of supply – the market had failed.

The general rule that a *contract of employment* will not be specifically enforced on the ground that it would be contrary to policy to make one person work for or employ another is now subject to various statutory and other exceptions. For example, a person who is dismissed from a public office in breach of his terms of appointment may be entitled to re-instatement: *Ridge v Baldwin* (1964). The employment relationship is much less personal than in former days.

Traditionally, the courts have also refused to specifically enforce a contract under which one party is bound by *continuous duties*, the due performance of which might require constant supervision by the court. However, in some such cases specific performance has been ordered and it has been suggested that the difficulty of supervision is sometimes exaggerated. There are various devices that the court could adopt to overcome such difficulty, such as appointing a receiver and manager, and there are several judicial statements in recent cases to suggest that 'constant supervision' is no longer a bar to specific performance but merely a factor to be taken into account. Bearing in mind that, according to the circumstances, damages may be awarded in lieu of, or in addition to, specific performance, the latter remedy may become of increasing significance in the future.

References and further reading

Commercial arbitration

Ferguson, 'The adjudication of commercial disputes and the legal system in modern England'(1980) 7 *British Journal of Law and Society* 141.

Ferguson, 'The legal status of non-statutory codes of practice' (1988) JBL 12.

Flood and Caiger, 'Lawyers and arbitrations: the juridification of construction disputes' (1993) 56 MLR 412.

Marshall, 'The Arbitration Act 1979' (1979) JBL 241; see also (1980) JBL 348 and (1981) JBL 362.

Parris (1985), *Arbitration: Principles and Practice,* Collins.

Harvey and Parry (1992), *The Law of Consumer Protection and Fair Trading,* particularly ch 8.1 and ch 13.2.

Polonsky, 'Arbitration of international contracts' (1971) JBL 1.

Schmitthoff (1990), *The Export Trade,* 9th edn, ch 31 'International Commercial Arbitration'.

Schmitthoff, 'Defective arbitration clauses' (1975) JBL 9.

Thomas, '*The Antaios: The Nema:* guidelines reconsidered' (1985) JBL 200.

Recovery of damages

Barton, 'The economic basis of damages for breach of contract' (1972) 1 *Journal of Legal Studies* 277.

Burrows, 'Mental distress damages in contract – a decade of change' (1984) LMCLQ 119.

Burrows, 'Specific performance at the crossroads' (1984) 4 *Legal Studies* 102.

Burrows (1994), *Remedies for Torts and Breach of Contract.*

Danzig, '*Hadley v Baxendale*: a study in the industrialization of the law (1975) 4 *Journal of Legal Studies* 249.

Farnsworth, 'Legal remedies for breach of contract' (1970) 70 *Columbia Law Review* 1145.

Ogus (1973), *The Law of Damages,* particularly chs 3, 8 and 9.

Owen, 'Some aspects of the recovery of reliance damages in the law of contract' (1984) 4 OJLS 393.

Tillotson, 'The Portuguese bank note case: legal, economic and financial approaches to the measure of damages in contract' (1994) 68 *Australian Law Journal* 93.

Treitel, 'Damages on rescission for breach of contract (1987) LMCLQ 143.

Waddams, 'The Date for the Assessment of Damages' (1981) 97 LQR 445.

Questions

(1) Consider:

    (a) the practice of commercial arbitration in relation to Macaulay's view of the planning function of contract;

    (b) the statement that: 'In view of the expense and delays often arising in arbitration, it is probable that its popularity as an institution for the settlement of commercial disputes must rest on other factors': Kay, *Arbitration.*

(2) How has the Arbitration Act 1979 sought to 'restore London to pre-eminence' as regards arbitration of international contracts? Has it succeeded?

(3) Examine and comment upon the arbitration facilities provided in ABTA (Association of British Travel Agents) Codes of Practice since the mid-1970s. See, for example, Harvey and Parry, *The Law of Consumer Protection and Fair Trading* (and references therein), Kay and Sewell, *A Practical Approach to Contract and Consumer Law* and current holiday brochures.

(4) Compare and contrast the following decisions dealing with the assessment of damages following a buyer's breach of a contract to purchase a motor car: *Thompson Ltd v Robinson (Gunmakers) Ltd* (1955), *Charter v Sullivan* (1957) and *Lazenby Garages Ltd v Wright* (1976).

(5) In *Wroth v Tyler* (1974) damages were assessed on the basis of the difference between the contract price and market price, not at the time of breach, but at the date of judgment:

    (a) Why was this so?

    (b) Explain the relationship between the above decision and those in *Grant v Dawkins* (1973) and *Johnson v Agnew* (1980).

(6) (a) 'The decisions in *Hadley v Baxendale* and *Victoria Laundry (Windsor) Ltd v Newman Industries Ltd* can be explained and reconciled by reference to the defendants' occupations and the plaintiffs' resources.' Explain this statement.

    (b) B ordered from S, a firm of aircraft dealers in England, an American executive jet aircraft costing £500,000. On being informed that the aircraft was ready for collection, B cancelled the order. At that time S could not have obtained more than £450,000 for the aircraft on the open market but, before reselling, import duty on aircraft was increased and in consequence S were able to resell the aircraft for £550,000. Advise S what measure of damages, if any, they can recover from B for breach of contract.

(7) (a) What is meant by the 'reasonable contemplation' test in relation to contract damages?

(b) Under the relevant clause in their building contract, property owners X Ltd are seeking to enforce a liquidated damages clause against Y Ltd, the builders, for non-completion of the work. However, Y Ltd claim that an extension of time has been granted by the architect and that the sum stipulated is in any case a penalty. Discuss the legal position.

(c) B, a builder, agreed to build an extension to H's seaside hotel, the extension to be ready in time for the start of the summer season on 1 June. B further agreed to pay H 'by way of penalty' £200 per week for every week or part of a week for which completion of the contract was delayed beyond 1 June. This sum of £200 represents the approximate weekly profit that H would make if the hotel extension was fully booked up.

The building work is not completed until 17 June and H claims £600 from B. In fact, because of poor weather, the bookings in the hotel were so bad that H was able to accommodate all his visitors in the existing hotel buildings. State, with reasons, whether H will be entitled to the £600.

(8) Ian books a holiday with Kontihols Ltd for himself, his wife Julie, and their two children aged five and two. When they arrive in Spain their hotel is overbooked so they are given a villa which is nearly 30 minutes walk from the hotel where they have to go for meals. They have to buy a push-chair for the younger child because the trip between the villa and the hotel has to be made several times a day. On one occasion the heel of Julie's shoe breaks off while she is walking to the hotel. Ian gets sunstroke and has to stay in bed. During this period Ian eats only cold food because of the time it takes Julie to bring the food from the hotel. They cannot go out at night because there is no one to babysit. Advise Ian and Julie who wish to claim damages for themselves and their children for loss of enjoyment and for the extra expense they incurred owing to the hotel being overbooked.

(9) Following a breach of contract, the plaintiff's right of action may become 'statute-barred' under the Limitation Act 1980. Explain this statement and the relevance of *King v Victor Parsons & Co Ltd* (1973).

14   Answering problem questions in law

Introduction

The aim of the following advice is to help you to produce good written answers to problem questions. The advice is essentially about TECHNIQUE. It assumes you have a reasonable (or better) knowledge of the law in question – no one can produce a good answer without it – but sound technique is half the battle.

What we are concerned with here is the marshalling and presentation of legal knowledge to best effect when answering the question set – *and that question alone*. Therefore it is very important to understand that the reader (tutor or examiner) will want to see not only the ability to set it down legibly and grammatically, correctly spelt and with an appreciation of correct sentence construction and style. (Most judges possess these attributes – read the cases!) A student's best answer will display the virtues of relevancy, succinctness and precision – and these qualities must be sought for and achieved.

Several academic writers have addressed the difficulties and pitfalls involved in answering legal questions (problems and essay questions) and you should read their findings. For example:

Phillip Kenny, *Studying Law*, Butterworths.

Glanville Williams, *Learning the Law*, Stevens.

Bradney *et al*, *How To Study Law*, Sweet & Maxwell.

Elements and approach

The problem questions of the type under consideration (there are many of them at the end of each chapter) are usually made up of a set of facts – a sequence of events – relating, for instance, to the negotiation of a business transaction or its alleged breach.

For example:

X writes to Y on 1 November offering to sell 500 bottles of 'Nouveau Beaujolais' at £2 per bottle and stating that the offer 'will remain open only until 5 pm on 5 November'. Y receives the letter at 9 am on 5 November and immediately tries to telephone X. X, however, is out and therefore Y leaves a message on X's answering machine asking X if he would agree to £1.85 per bottle.

Later the same morning, Y changes his mind and sends X a telemessage stating: 'Disregard earlier phone call. I accept your offer at £2 per bottle.' X returns to his office at 1 pm and, on hearing Y's telephone message, he immediately sells the wine to Z. At 2 pm X receives Y's telemessage.

Discuss the legal position.

In accordance with the instructions given ('Discuss ...', 'Advise ...', etc), relevant law is to be applied to the facts stated in order to resolve whatever problems or issues have arisen for the participant(s). It is not normally the case that the *facts* themselves are in dispute. They are *given* and are not to be changed. (Some *questions* are in several parts, the facts being changed slightly in each part.)

The approach to adopt for the type of question set out above is, broadly speaking, as follows:

Given that you recognise the area(s) of law involved (eg offer and acceptance and the correspondence and communication thereof, revocation, etc), it should become apparent that:

(A)   Certain points/matters/incidents are clearly covered by the rules found in the cases (or statutes); however:

(B)   The question inevitably throws up areas of doubt: contentious points/issues/'grey areas', which are *not* clearly covered by the legal rules.

Thus there are two main tasks, both necessary, but one more difficult than the other:

(A)   Establish a framework of rules (with authorities) to cover settled matters

Your statements of law should be expressed so far as possible in terms of the problems's participants. In that way you are applying the law to the facts. For example, 'and X's act of selling the wine to Z at 1 pm on 5 November is not of itself a revocation of his offer because such revocation must be communicated to the offeree, Y, as seen in the case of'.

Warning: Do not *unsettle* matters which are clearly, unequivocally, expressed. For example, 'X writes to Y on 1 November offering to sell 500 bottles.' This statement is to be taken as read: X makes an offer, a written offer, to Y. There is no 'grey area' here; no need to ask: 'Is X making an invitation to treat?' No need to discuss the different legal effects, nor to discuss intention to create legal relations, or consideration either.

ALSO: It is very often the case that facts which are necessary for the answer have been *deliberately omitted*. For example (from a different problem in the same area): 'B's letter of acceptance was posted on the evening of 4 April but owing to a misdirection it did not arrive at C's office until 14 April.' What is not stated is *why* the letter was misdirected. In contract law terms this is vital. Was the fault that of the offeree B or did the blame lie with the Post Office? Here one should draw a reasonable inference. The actual words used suggest that B was at fault. Gaps should be filled by reasonable inference, not by colourful speculation.

The point made above reminds us that the facts – and working *from* the facts – are paramount. Hence you must read and re-read the question noting every relevant detail. For example from the 'Nouveau Beaujolais' problem: 'tries to telephone X' and 'asking X *if* he would agree'.

(B) *Identify 'grey areas' (we have begun to do this immediately above) and, showing a capacity for legal method, reach a solution to the problem*

Or perhaps one should say that only through a grasp of legal method can the 'grey areas' and issues be *recognised* and *resolved*. What does this entail? At least it involves the ability to find and use the cases and other authorities, to analyse these sources – the principles and legal reasoning underlying the decisions, and, by an application of the law to the facts, to be able to deduce (draw as a logical conclusion) a good answer from the sources.

For example:

(1) The facts may fall somewhere between two cases, themselves having similar facts but different (distinguishable) decisions. Thus: 'Y leaves a message ... asking X if he would agree to £1.85 per bottle.'

Is this a counter-offer (and a lack of correspondence)? Or is it an enquiry or request for further information? Are we dealing with *Hyde v Wrench* or *Stevenson v McLean*? Which of the two do we follow?

(2) The facts may reflect those of a leading case(s) but a new element has been introduced. The facts may raise a complication that can only be met by reference to a very recently decided case. Are you up to date? Examiners are fond of testing your awareness of current legal issues.

Thus: 'Y ... tries to telephone X. X, however, is out and therefore Y leaves a message on X's answering machine ...'. What is the purpose behind Y's message (see 1 above)? Is this 'communication'? Cases? Conclusion to be drawn?

Or 'Y changes his mind and sends X a telemessage stating'. What is the purpose of this message? What is a telemessage? What are the rules (relating to communication) which will apply to it?

(3) The facts of the problem may be seen to go a step *beyond* the established rules. Should the law be extended? If so, in what way? Here one may require recourse to *obiter dicta* in a recent leading case, or a dissenting judgment of obvious weight, or the critical writings of leading legal academics.

Further guidance on technique

(1) In the contract problem we have already begun to deal with Y's message in which he asked if X would agree to £1.85 a bottle. We have already suggested that there are two different ways of categorising that message in contract law terms. Here we have what we might call a fork in the road through the problem. Although you will do better to take the correct route – explaining why – than to do otherwise, it will usually be the case that the choice of 'route' is arguable, so that all will not necessarily be lost if you take the 'route' less favoured by the questioner. What is important is that you have seen the issue and the choices involved.

In *Studying Law*, Phillip Kenny puts this point very well. Where, as is usual, there are *several* issues within the question (here, among others, 'correspondence' followed by 'communication'), he explains that 'it is important to remember that each problem raised must be dealt with' and 'they will commonly require answering in *a conditional sequence.*' This means that *the answer to one stage of the question will depend on your answer to the previous stage.*

It is worth repeating that you must (a) see that there is a legal issue, (b) know what the 'routes' or choices are, and (c) make the correct choice. If you go the wrong way you will still score marks depending on how arguable the debatable point is. Having made your choice, it may well be advisable to indicate briefly the legal consequences of the *other* route.

In this way you have indicated that a choice has been made. A common mistake lies in either *not* seeing that there is an issue and a choice, or in being over-dogmatic about the correct 'route'. *Later*, the issue is seen or second thoughts emerge. Towards the end of the answer, and wholly inappropriately, the alternative answer is provided – a 'volte-face', a contradiction, and a very muddled answer.

(2) It quickly becomes apparent when dealing with problem questions that there is 'more in them' – more issues – than a superficial reading reveals. They must all be 'seen' and dealt with, and in a logical order.

Problem-solving means clearing up the mess not shuffling it around. You should be aiming for a clear, well-ordered and comprehensive answer. The order your answer takes may be dictated by a time-sequence, the chronology or order of events as set out in the question or, somewhat differently, according to the possible legal actions that can be brought by various participants in the problem, one against the other.

(3)   This raises the question of PLANNING your answer. It is doubtful if even an experienced lawyer could pick up his or her pen and write a clear, well structured answer to a problem of the sort usually met without preliminary preparation. Issues should be noted, together with relevant cases, and put into the correct order. This is a process which will require close attention to, and rechecking of, the problem's facts. A point may well have been overlooked and will now be revealed. The answer develops, becomes better structured and more comprehensive.

This should and can be done in preparation for tutorials/seminars. Even, or particularly, in examinations a short time should be set aside for rapid planning of your final version.

(4)   The emphasis we have put on FACTS should not lead you to think the problem can be answered in purely factual, common-sense terms. As said earlier, you must draw out of the facts the legal issues involved and the legal answers they require. Get quickly to the issues that the parties face. (Do *not*, for example, start your supposed answer by summarising the question. Believe me, it is done.)

It is a good idea to start your answer with a *very brief* first paragraph in which you merely identify the legal points and issues posed by the problem.

As Glanville Williams puts it, this does not mean that you should 'preface your answer with a general disquisition on the department of law relating to the problem'. However, you can show, in a brief introductory paragraph that you appreciate which legal issues are involved.

Most lecturers rightly warn against lengthy introductions – some students never get any further – but certainly as a part of the planning process, this first point of technique is extremely useful in being able to 'see the wood from the trees'.

(5)   When writing your answers, try to develop what might be called the appropriate legal style. A guide to what this is will be found in the best examples of legal writing – in the reports, casebooks and textbooks. Its main features are clarity and balance while imparting a steady flow of relevant information specifically directed to the parties who figure in the problem question.

(6)   Be careful to follow the question's rubric ('Discuss the legal position' or 'Advise Roddy Ltd'). This must be done in relation to the stated facts (plus others which may be deduced). *No* problem question is an invitation to write all you know about the area into which the problem falls. RELEVANCE IS CRUCIAL. The 'scatter-gun' or 'carpet-bombing' approach will *never* gain a good mark.

(7) It is important to remember that the language of the law is (or should be) the language of tightly worked clarity with appropriate use of 'technical' words and expressions (eg consideration, promissory estoppel, rescission, etc). Refer to judges and courts by their correct titles (eg the Master of the Rolls or Lord Denning MR *not* Denning).

(8) In purporting to come to a conclusion, do not merely repeat what has gone before. This is called 'padding'.

(9) The ability to answer questions of this sort comes through PRACTICE which you can obtain in tutorials/seminars (so long as the proper PREPARATION has been done by a thorough reading of your textbook and the cases, etc). You should also tackle questions from previous examination papers.

Using authorities in your answer

An answer which does not draw on relevant cases and statutes is not really an answer at all, because it does not incorporate the authoritative statements of law – the legal reasons – which underlie your argument. These are the most important points to remember when citing authorities, particularly cases, in your answer:

(a) Only cite relevant cases. This basically means stating the legal principle which is the basis of the decision in question.

(b) As previously mentioned, the principle or rule should be stated clearly and succinctly and in such a way as to provide the reason why your argument *in relation to the facts of the problem* advances as it does.

(c) Usually one states the *rule*, then the *authority* (the name of the case with the briefest indication of its salient facts, and then its bearing on the problem. For example 'Where the post is the recognised medium of communication, the general rule is that acceptance is operative from the time of posting (not the time of receipt by the offeror): *Household Fire Insurance Co v Grant* (1879) in which the company's share allotment letter was lost but it was nevertheless held that the contract of shareholding was binding on G. On the other hand, an offeror's revocation (like his original offer) must actually be communicated to the offeree to be effective: see *Henthorn v Fraser* (1892) in which the letter of acceptance and revocation crossed in the post. In the problem, 'A posted his letter of acceptance on 4 April whereas O's revocation'.

In this example two issues have been disposed of in a brief but authoritative fashion, and they provide the legal platform on which to base a solution to this part of the problem: the cases furnish the basis on which the legal analysis of the facts of the problem rest.

(d) You should try to cite a case by name whenever possible. If in difficulty give the name of one party or your next best indication of the authority.

(e) A long recital of the facts of a case is *never* called for in a problem question and most probably in no question. What may well be important is to point out significant similarities or differences between the facts of cases which have a bearing on the problem – such that Case A is to be applied and Case B is distinguished.

(f) The incorporation of *statutory rules as authorities* usually follows along much the same lines as for cases and for the same reasons.

For example (from a different problem question): 'In the case of business liability under s 1(3) of the Unfair Contract Terms Act 1977 (and a local authority's business activities are caught by s 14) a person cannot exclude his liability for death or personal injury resulting from negligence: s 2(1). Therefore, D's claim in respect of his broken arm, caused by the attendant's leaving the brush on the floor, will succeed. However, as regards the question of D's own contributory negligence.'

Some final points

(1) Make sure you answer ALL the question. Some questions contain a *rider*, eg 'Would it make any difference if ...' Check that you have not missed anything.

(2) Similarly, some questions contain *several parts*, say (i) – (iv) or (a) – (d). These are invariably *alternative* situations to be dealt with *separately*.

(3) As we have said, continued practice enables you to identify the legal issues that the facts of the problems raise. In real life legal problems rarely fit solely into one area, say, offer and acceptance (or even contract) and it is the same with many problem questions. A problem may raise issues relating to contractual intention, consideration and promissory estoppel; or the relationship between terms, representations and remedies; or questions of negligence, contractual liability and the regulation of exclusion clauses by statute.

It is a great mistake to put your legal studies into separate compartments. The facts, of life and of problems, do not allow you to do so.

(4) In *Studying Law*, Phillip Kenny gives illustrations of a mediocre and a first-class answer to a particular problem question, together with commentaries on them. Make sure you read, absorb and put into practice the advice given.

(5) *How much do I write?* Kenny's example of a first-class answer approaches 1,000 words (five sides of A4). It has nine cases neatly built into the argument and seven references to the Unfair Contract Terms Act and its relevant sections. The essay is expressed in 'lawyerly language'.

This is certainly a model to aim at for coursework, and it would certainly constitute a first-class pass in an examination. If you are (and why not) a first-class student, you could produce such an answer in 45 minutes.

Check list

If you follow the advice given, you will have displayed:

- Knowledge of legal principles and rules.

- Ability to apply them.

- Capacity for legal method including analytical and critical ability and powers of reasoned argument.

- Ability to express yourself in a 'lawyerly way'.

Reminders

- Carefully read and *re-read* the question *set*.

- Do *not* waffle.

- *Plan* your answer.

- Give your answer *balance*, cover all relevant issues and *quickly* get to the heart of the problem from the given *facts*.

- Read through and *check* your answer: is it *consistent*, do you contradict yourself?

- *Write legibly*.

- *Practice* is the key to success. Use the questions in tutorial sheets, past examination papers and at the end of the chapters in this book.

Index

D

E

267

U

W